FISCAL SYSTEMS
AND ECONOMIC DEVELOPMENT:
CASE STUDIES OF SELECTED COUNTRIES

FISCAL SYSTEMS AND ECONOMIC DEVELOPMENT: CASE STUDIES OF SELECTED COUNTRIES

Edited by

Sohrab Abizadeh and Mahmood Yousefi

Nova Science Publishers, Inc.
Commack

Art Director: Maria Ester Hawrys
Assistant Director: Elenor Kallberg
Graphics: Denise Dieterich, Kerri Pfister,
          Erika Cassatti and Barbara Minerd
Manuscript Coordinator: Sharyn Beers Schweidel
Book Production: Tammy Sauter, Benjamin Fung,
          Christine Mathosian and Joanne Bennett
Circulation: Irene Kwartiroff and Annette Hellinger

Library of Congress Cataloging-in-Publication Data

Sohrab Abizadeh and Mahmood Yousefi
    Fiscal systems and economic development: case studies of selected
countries / Sohrab Abizadeh and Mahmood Yousefi
        p.   cm.
    Includes bibliographical references and index.
    ISBN 1-56072-294-0 (library binding : alk. paper)
    1. Finance, Public -- Cross-cultural studies. 2. Economic development.
    I. Abizadeh, Sohrab.and Mahmood Yousefi
HJ235.F57   1996
336 - - dc20   95-48997
                                                                      CIP

Copyright © 1996 by Nova Science Publishers, Inc.
          6080 Jericho Turnpike, Suite 207
          Commack, New York 11725
          Tele. 516-499-3103   Fax 516-499-3146
          E Mail Novascil@aol.com

Printed in the United States of America

CONTENTS

PREFACE

International interdependence requires a better understanding of global issues. The availability of sources in global fields of inquiry help this understanding. The present collection of essays focuses on the fiscal systems of several countries whose political, historical, and economic conditions vary.

The impetus for this volume is a dearth of available texts on fiscal systems of different regions of the world. In an attempt to mitigate this problem, the present collection provides readers with an understanding of fiscal systems of different countries. This book is intended to serve as a supplementary text for courses in Public Finance and Economic Development at the junior, senior, or MBA level. It could also serve as a source of reference for practitioners and policy analysts interested in global issues.

Almost all countries strive to improve the economic and social well-being of their citizens through the operation of their fiscal systems. The success of these policies hinges on the extent to which market forces are allowed to operate freely. Fiscal systems also need to be mindful of the aspirations of the citizenry. For these reasons, the objectives of fiscal systems vary among different countries.

The differing fiscal systems encompass a variety of tax instruments and expenditure measures which are circumscribed by each country's economic and political conditions. A country's tax structure is affected by its economic development, the nature and scope of existing tax machinery, and political acceptability of taxes. Government spending is also determined by the foregoing factors. Inherent in tax and expenditure policies of various countries is the extent to which authorities are concerned with social welfare issues.

This book contains the work of five economists with differing experiences. They examine the nature of tax structures, budget policies, and development objectives of six countries. The countries examined are at various stages of industrialization and development. The authors carefully present a mix of theoretical and practical issues which characterize the fiscal dilemma of these countries.

Chapter I, on government expenditure patterns, presents a brief summary of controversies surrounding Wagner's law. Drawing from a selective body of knowledge, it focuses on the relationship between the growth of public spending and economic development. This chapter attempts to provide a balanced review of theoretical and empirical studies of public sector growth.

Chapter II delineates the relationship between tax structure changes and industrialization. It summarizes a selective body of knowledge on the role and importance of tax changes during the course of development. The chapter concludes that the conflicting body of empirical evidence on tax structure change may stem from different concepts of economic development and the design of an ideal tax system in fostering economic growth.

Chapter III focuses on Japan's public sector economics. It traces the economic performance of Japan since WWII and highlights the main factors which have contributed to Japan's economic success. This chapter examines the growth of public sector, budgetary process and policies, and Japan's tax system. The author draws the readers' attention to the emergence of general account deficits as a new phenomenon in Japan. This phenomenon has become a current surce of preoccupation for the Japanese government and policy analysts.

Chapter IV focuses on public finances in Turkey. The author sets the stage for the discussion of economic changes that took place in 1980s by tracing the political and economic history of Turkey back to the early 1920s. This chapter discusses the role of etatism, the forerunner of state planning, in modern day Turkey. The focus of this chapter is on policies initiated by Turgut Özal, the architect of 1980s economic policies. After an examination of taxes and expenditures, the chapter focusses on the influence of wage policites, price supports, monetary policy, and State Economic Enterprises on inflation. An important conclusion of this chapter is that inflation partially stems from the incomplete autonomy of the central bank in Turkey.

Chapter V focuses on the government expenditures and taxation trends in Canada. After providing a brief history of fiscal federalism, the author provides a detailed explanation of the Canadian fiscal structure. This chapter makes specific references to the economic reforms of recent decades. Special attention is paid to the controversial goods and services tax (GST) which was introduced in 1991. The author speculates that despite frequent pronouncements by the current Liberal government to re-place the GST minimal changes are to be expected.

Chapter VI gives an analysis of the Korean fiscal system. In their analyses, the authors examine, the history of economic progress in Korea since the early 1960s. The authors argue that Korea's economic success is a model for many LDCs to emulate. They point out that this success was shaped by a combination of factors such as the Korean War, its Confucian heritage, an educated labor force, relative political stability, and pursuit of appropriate fiscal and monetary policies. An important feature of this chapter is the discussion of fiscal incentives which have contributed to Korea's economic success.

Finally, chapter VII presents a discussion of fiscal system during Ghana's economic recovery program(ERP). The author discusses how Ghana has been transformed from an economic basket case, one with deteriorating economic conditions until the early 1980s, to one with improving economic prospects. This chapter traces the routes of economic crisis in Ghana and emphasizes the role of international aid agencies in this country's economic turnaround. The author gives a comparative analysis of public finances before and after the ERP.

CONTRIBUTORS

Sohrab Abizadeh, Professor of Economics, University of Winnipeg, Winnipeg, Manitoba, Canada

John Kofi Baffoe, Assistant Professor of Economics, Nippising University, North Bay, Ontario, Canada

Donald Cummings, Assistant Professor of Economics, University of Northern Iowa, Cedar Falls, Iowa, U.S.A.

Bülent Uyar, Associate Professor of Economics, University of Northern Iowa, Cedar Falls, Iowa, U.S.A.

Mahmood Yousefi, Professor of Economics, University of Northern Iowa, Cedar Falls, Iowa, U.S.A.

ACKNOWLEDGMENTS

Each of the editors contributed equally to the development and completion of this book. The order of appearance of their names is merely an alphabetical arrangement. The idea was originally conceived three years ago. Subsequently, the editors arranged for two sessions of the Annual Meeting of the Missouri Valley Economic Association (St. Louis, March 1, 1992) for the presentation of the initial draft of almost all country chapters.

We have benefited from the help of many colleagues and institutions in the preparation of this book. We would like to acknowledge the support of several participants of the March 1, 1992 sessions of the Missouri Valley Economic Association Conference as well as the officers of the Organization.

We would like to thank our institutions, the University of Northern Iowa and the University of Winnipeg, for partial financial support. We extend our thanks to our friends and colleagues, Professors Fred Abraham and Alexander Basilevsky, for their encouragement and comments. We would also like to thank our able Research Assistant, Cassaundra Iwankow. Our thanks go to Sally Wetherell for being cheery and helpful. Our special thanks go to Judy Hanson whose secretarial help and patience were crucial to the completion of this work.

Sohrab Abizadeh
September 1994

Mahmood Yousefi
September 1994

CHAPTER ONE

GOVERNMENT EXPENDITURE PATTERNS AND ECONOMIC DEVELOPMENT

Mahmood Yousefi and Sohrab Abizadeh

I. INTRODUCTION

The public finance literature abounds with studies that deal, directly or indirectly, with Wagner's "Law". The empirical studies of Wagner's hypothesis are inconclusive; some vindicate it while others refute it. For instance, Wagner's hypotheses is confirmed for a few countries for which time-series are available. The country studies for Canada, Sweden, the United Kingdom, and Norway respectively by Bird (1971), Hook (1962), Peacock and Wiseman (1967), and Johansen (1968) point in this direction. Studies by Musgrave (1969), Wagner & Weber (1978), Lall (1969), Mann (1980), and Lotz and Morss (1970) do not find a systematic relationship between the government share of expenditures and per capita income. On the other hand, studies by Thorn (1967), Williamson (1961), Beck (1979), and Martin and Lewis (1956) find a significantly positive relationship between the government share and per capita income. A plausible explanation for this contradictory evidence is suggested by Musgrave (1969) and Gandi(1971). These authors contend that Wagner's hypothesis does not hold over all ranges of income. Instead, they believe that the strong influences of economic development on government share is to be found in countries in the middle range of development.[1] This explanation is well articulated by Herber (1983).

The purpose of this chapter is to briefly explain Wagner's law and its various interpretations. In the second section, we concentrate on a brief examination of selected empirical studies of Wagner's hypotheses. In the final section, we discuss some of the shortcomings of the empirical tests of Wagner's Law and provide some suggestions.

II. THE STATEMENT OF WAGNER'S LAW

Around the turn of the century, Adolph Wagner formulated his famous law of increased state activity for industrializing nations. By linking the growth of public expenditures to economic development, Wagner maintained that the share of public sector grows more rapidly than community output.[2] As Peacock and Wiseman (1967, p. XXXII) point out, the law "was not necessarily to be valid for all time." The essence of Wagner's hypothesis is that:

> The law [of increasing state activity] is the result of empirical observation in progressive countries, at least in Western European Civilization; its explanation, justification and cause is the pressure of social progress and the resulting changes in the relative spheres of private and public economy, especially compulsory public economy. Financial stringency may hamper the expansion of state activities, causing their extent to be conditioned by revenue rather than the other way round, as is more useful. But in the long run the desire for development of progressive people will always overcome these financial difficulties (p. 16).

As Peacock and Wiseman suggest the foregoing statement has several implications. First, to the extent that increased state activity is an accompaniment of social progress, increased spending is a must. Second, Wagner's hypothesis is not concerned with short run change or the actual process of change. Instead, it is concerned with the secular growth of public expenditures. Third, "Wagner, does not suggest that the actual extent of state activity can be fixed a priori." Instead, he cites a number of empirically verifiable instances for which "as output per head increased ...state...expenditure grew more proportionately" (p. 18).

Bird (1971, p.3) makes the following observations about the law. First, Wagner's ideas were formulated in accordance with the conditions of Germany in the late nineteenth century. The law was, obviously, "framed to refer only to states in which income was rising **as a result of industrialization**" (emphasis in the original). Consequently, the necessary conditions for the operation of the law are: "(1) rising per capita incomes, (2) technological and institutional change ..., and (3) ...democratization ... of the polity."

Second, Wagner himself thought that his hypothesis was "a proposition in the positive theory of public expenditure ... however, his exposition of the law was inextricably entangled with his own normative assumptions as to the nature of the state and state activity" (p. 3). This problem coupled with Wagner's organic concept of stat--state having general will and preferences of its own--explains why the `law' does not stand up to critical analysis. Finally, Wagner did not allow for the impact of wars on public expenditures. His optimistic view of the world led him to expect fewer wars and wars of shorter duration.

The underlying reasons behind the law of increasing state activity are three broad categories of expenditures. Those pertain to expenditures: (1) for expanding administrative and protective functions (internal and external) functions of the state, (2) necessary for the smooth operation of markets, and (3) for social and cultural considerations. Increased state activity arises from the need to maintain and improve the quality of services it provides. It also arises from the need to minimize frictions, within society, stemming from increased division of labor and complexities of life. The second group of expenditures deal with the adoption of corrective measures in offsetting the onset (or expansion) or large private monopolies (in the interest of economic efficiency). The third group of activities are to be undertaken in areas of education and redistribution of income. Wagner was not explicit as to "why he thought these activities would expand ... he appears to have assumed, in essence that they constituted `superior good' or `luxuries'" (p. 2).

In their criticism of Wagner's hypotheses, Peacock and Wiseman maintained that Wagner's assertion about the quantitative and qualitative rise of public service in response to output increases "stem not only from technical considerations, but also from Wagner's view that it is the duty of the state to behave in that way." Further, the authors suggest that Wagner did not succeed in demonstrating the secular growth of the community output. "His `proof' of the existence of such a law, therefore, depends upon the validity of the organic theory of the state upon which he relies" (Peacock and Wiseman, 1967, p. 19). The authors also criticized Wagner for his neglect of war and the fact that the possible increase in expenditures is limited by the "tolerable tax burdens."

This kind of criticism has led to the development of what may be considered amended versions of Wagner's law. Three such versions are the "Displacement Effect" hypothesis, the productivity gap approach, and "Stages of Industrialization" hypothesis.[3]

A. THE "DISPLACEMENT EFFECT" HYPOTHESES

The essence of this hypothesis may be summarized as follows. During "normal" times, when societies are not subject to violent external threat or social upheaval, "people's ideas about the `tolerable' burdens of government taxation tend to be fairly stable" (Peacock and Wiseman, p. 26). The extent to which government expenditures may rise depends on the desirability of such expenditures and the political feasibility of higher level of taxes. However, the rate of increase of these expenditures is unspectacular. Factors such as the disincentive effects of high marginal tax rates and popular notions of tolerable tax burdens curb the size of expenditures. The citizen and the government, however, may hold divergent views about the size of public expenditures and the level of taxes.

The emergence of social disturbances narrows the gap between these divergent views. Social upheavals

> destroy established conceptions and produce a displacement effect. People will accept, in a period of crisis, tax levels ... that in quieter times they would have thought intolerable, and this acceptance remains when the disturbance itself has disappeared. As a result, the revenue and expenditure statistics of the government show a displacement after periods of social disturbance (p. 27).

Peacock and Wiseman pointed out that the displacement effect need not always be upward; although it has been so in contemporary Britain.

An associated characteristic of the displacement effect is the corresponding changes in "the size of the governmental unit upon which responsibility for public economic activities rests" (p. 29). This phenomenon is referred to as the "Concentration Process." Economic development is accompanied and is affected by improvements in the means of transportation and communication. Thus, the process of development may generate two types of pressure for larger organs of government. First, the very nature of improved communication and transportation spread the knowledge about the standard of public service elsewhere in the community. This increases the likelihood for improved and uniform service and hence the centralization of control over public expenditures. Second, improved communication and transportation "may not only make such larger areas of control possible, but may also make them economically efficient" (p. 29). Since the smaller political units have a history and tradition of themselves counter social pressures are to be expected. A caveat is in order at this juncture. That is, the concentration process need not accompany the displacement effect and can occur independently. We should, however, expect some relationship between the two.

B. "THE PRODUCTIVITY GAP" APPROACH

Peacock and Wiseman (1979) found a modern counterpart of Wagner's law of increasing state activity in Baumol (1967) and Baumol and Oates (1975). The basic idea is as follows: Let the "output" of government at any time be a constant fraction of labor productivity. Allow productivity (and output) to grow exponentially in the private sector. Assume that both public and private expenditures on goods and services are equal to their respective labor costs. Further, assume that the wage rate $(\bar{w})$ is the same in both sectors. Then, the ratio of government expenditures (G_{et}) to total expenditures (N_{et}) is identical to the ratio of labor productivity in the public sector (L_{gt}) to total productivity $(L_{gt} + L_{pt})$. That is,

$$(1) \quad \frac{G_{et}}{N_{et}} = \frac{L_{gt}}{L_{gt} + L_{pt}}$$

Given the supply of labor, as $t \to \infty$, the only way (1) is maintained is by transferring labor from the private sector to the public sector. Since the government sector is less productive than the private sector, and given $\bar{w}$, $\frac{G_{et}}{N_{et}}$ must rise.

In other words, if government goods and services in real terms are to remain as even a fixed proportion of total goods and services as in real terms, government expenditure as a proportion of total expenditure must rise through time. Intellectual history repeats itself; Baumol's Theory of unbalanced growth is the modern counterpart of Wagner's famous Law of Increasing State Activity (Peacock and Wiseman, 1979, p. 11).

If the public sector experiences fewer productivity gains than the private sector, we may believe "that the cause of unbalanced growth lies in the inherently greater labour intensity in the public sector compared with the private sector" (p. 12).

Peacock and Wiseman recognized the difficulty of measuring the productivity of government services. They also acknowledged the lack of evidence suggesting technical barriers (opposing innovations) in the public sector are higher than in the private sector.[4] The authors, however, suspected the existence of greater institutional barriers in the public sector. The suspicion stems from the economic theory of bureaucracy; that those "in charge of productive operation ... have a monopoly of supply and a monopoly of information about the way in which supply is produced" (Peacock and Wiseman, p. 12). Another difficulty arises from the nature of the bureaucrat's "products." They are not priced and the bureaucrats are not constrained by the objective of maximizing profit or output.

C. "STAGES OF INDUSTRIALIZATION" HYPOTHESIS

This hypothesis is attributed to Herber (1983, pp. 326-28). Herber began by noting that Wagner's law was couched in the context of industrializing nations. So a meaningful discussion of the hypothesis "should delimit the industrialization era in a nation's history" from both the pre- and post-industrial stages. In the latter stage, the nation is not only affluent in terms of living standards, "but on a distributional basis as well" (p. 326). The stages approach presumes that countries undergo three stages in their industrialization process (Shown graphically in figure 1).

Measure real per capita income (Y), in dollars, along the horizontal axis and real per capita output of public goods (PG), in dollars, along the vertical axis. Lines PG_1 and PG_2 respectively reflect situations where the share of the public sector in total output is constant and changing. According to the stages hypothesis, $\frac{PG}{Y}$ would decline in the pre-industrialization and post-industrialization period. Herber offers the following reasons for this conjecture. First, in the pre-industrialization stage, "most subsistence wants and goods have traditionally been provided by the private sector through market-type arrangements ..." (p. 327). As economic development takes place, the private share of total output increases and $\frac{PG}{Y}$ continues to fall. Second, as Y increases, the reallocative impor-

tance of each sector may change. For instance, investment in social over-
head (education, communication, transportation) may assume a larger
role. Due to the inherent nature of these products (heavy fixed costs and
consumption externalities) the government assumes a larger role than the
market in their provision. Once the country has reached the industrialization stage, say at per capita income levels above $3,000, Wagner's hy-
pothesis holds. The $\frac{PG}{Y}$ rise continues until the onset of post-industrial

maturity. Finally, once the society has entered post-industrial maturity,
say at per capita income levels exceeding $10,500, "government may al-
ready be providing adequate quantities of [public goods],...so society will-
increasingly turn to additional private sector output" (p. 327). Further, the
public may become resistant to a "too large" public sector in response to a
cultural preference for market activity and its commensurate relaxation of

compulsory taxation.[5] The outcome of this process is a decline in the $\dfrac{PG}{Y}$

ratio.

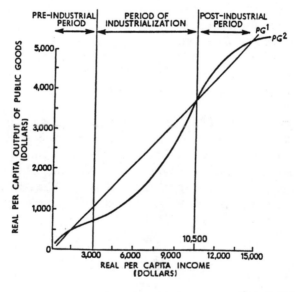

Source: Herber 1983, p.326

Figure 1. Relative Changes in Public Sector Economic Activity
During Industrialization Process

III. EMPIRICAL STUDIES OF WAGNER'S LAW

Empirical studies of Wagner's law have produced mixed results. Some vindicate the law while others refute it. The inconsistency of relevant empirical evidence emanates from two sets of considerations. One set of factors has to do with the imprecise nature and formulation of the law itself. Musgrave (1969), for instance, argues that Wagner was not clear as to whether the rise in public spending is in absolute or relative terms. Musgrave (p. 74), however, proceeds to state that "the proposition of expanding scale, ... must be interpreted as postulating a rising **share** of the public sector in the economy." Logically, a rise in absolute spending does not fail to materialize in an expanding economy.

A second set of factors is technical in nature. Goffman (1968), for instance, while in agreement with earlier studies which questioned the validity of Wagner's law, raises some serious questions about the measurement techniques of these studies. He points out that the direct ratio of government expenditure to GNP, used in some studies, tends to overstate the extent of government spending. Instead, Goffman offers the income elasticity of demand for government services as a more accurate measure. Michas (1975) put forth another technical reason for the apparent inconsistent empirical tests of Wagner's law. That stems from the discrepancy between the verbal and quantitative formulation of the law. He suggests that the issue of mixed results "can only be resolved when researchers utilize an appropriate and **uniform formulation** (emphasis added) of Wagner's Law" (p. 77).

Generally, two types of empirical tests of Wagner's law (or its variations) have been carried out: time-series tests and cross-sectional analyses. By and large, time-series studies, particularly those pertaining to the developed countries, support Wagner's law. On the other hand, cross-sectional studies seem to refute it. The majority of time-series use bivariate regression techniques; although the use of multiple regression techniques is not too uncommon.

A. TIME-SERIES STUDIES

These studies, basically, have related government expenditures (or its share in national output) to national income (or per capita income). We discuss five representative studies by Gupta (1967), Enweze (1973), Ganti and Kolluri (1979), Mann (1980) and Ram (1987). We also discuss a study by Yousefi and Abizadeh (1992) which is not necessarily a representative of this genre.

Gupta's study is not really a test of Wagner's law. Instead, it is designed to examine the "displacement effect" for several Western industrialized countries (Canada, Germany, Sweden, the U.K., and the U.S.) Gupta tries to examine the displacement effect "not only with regard to World Wars but also with regard to the Great Depression" (p. 425).

In his statistical technique, Gupta adopts a double logarithmic function of the form

$$(A1) \qquad \text{Log } G_c = \text{Log } a + b \text{ Log } Y_c$$

In equation $(A1)$ G_c and Y_c respectively denote per capita total government expenditure (excluding war-related spending) and per capita income (at constant prices). The coefficient b is a measure of the "income elasticity" of G_c. This coefficient also helps "to provide some measure of the shift in the level and change in the `income elasticity' of G_c associated with a social upheaval" (p. 431).

The time span of study is different for each country, e.g., 73 years for the U.K. and 37 years for the U.S. Time periods are divided into subperiods to isolate the influence of social upheavals. The results of regressions, presumably, corroborate the displacement effect. For instance, for the United Kingdom, the displacement effect took place "after both World Wars ..." (p. 434). Also, the shift which is of greater importance for the time-pattern of American public expenditure "is associated with the Great Depression, which accounts for about 136 percent to 70 percent increase in G_c with relation to Y_c " (p. 439).

The statistical results of Gupta are subject to many criticisms.[7] First, it is difficult to infer any displacement effect from a bivariate analysis. We need to isolate the influence of factors such as urbanization, demographic changes, the ability to pay taxes as well as attitude toward taxes, and changes in the structure of the economy, before we can make such inferences. Second, the statistical results may suffer from a simultaneity bias in a sense that the G_c affects Y_c and is in turn affected by it. Finally, some of the sub-period regressions use as few as seven observations. Thus, reliability of such regression results are questionable.

Ganti and Kolluri (1979) tried to provide new evidence on Wagner's law by estimating the income elasticity of demand for non-defense government expenditures in the U.S. In pursuit of more efficient estimates, they employed "a simple but fairly meaningful model of public expenditure in the context of Zellner's reformulated errors-in-variables approach..." Ganti and Kolluri concluded that their findings strongly support "Wagner's Hypothesis. Depressing effect of defense expenditures on nondefense government expenditures does appear to be confirmed especially over long periods of time" (p. 231).

A somewhat different bivariate analysis was undertaken by Enweze (1973). He concentrated on the analysis of Wagner's hypothesis for 14 selected developing countries. Enweze examined: (a) trend factors, (b) income factors (elasticities), and (c) temporal changes (allocation of revenues to various expenditure categories). Time trends of expenditures indicated that general services expenditure (inclusive of defense and administrative expenditures) ratio rose "in 10 countries in the sample, and remained fairly constant in the remaining 4 countries" (p. 443). Social Services expenditures and the economic services expenditure depicted roughly a similar picture.

The elasticity measures were derived from:

$$(A2) \qquad \text{Log } E = a + b \text{ Log } Y + \mu,$$

where E, Y, and μ respectively denote the government expenditure category, GNP, and the error term.[8]

The results of 98 regression equations (seven for each of 14 countries) revealed that elasticities, on the average, were greater than unity. That is "a 1 percent increase in GNP will lead to more than 1 percent increase in expenditure on each functional category" (p. 446). The results also indicated that changes in economic services and defense expenditures are not necessarily related to tax and nontax revenues. Further, it was observed "that health and welfare expenditures tend to be undertaken more on the basis of need than revenue availability" (p. 453). These results seem to contradict the notion of tolerable tax burden, at least in the context of developing economies.[9]

Mann (1980) concentrated on a time-series test of Wagner's law for Mexico. Since the empirical testing of Wagner's Hypotheses was difficult and several versions of the principle had been posited, Mann tested six versions for Mexico. Basically, the regression equations were bivariate and of double logarithmic form. The independent variable was per capita GDP (in constant pesos) and the dependent variable was public expenditure in constant pesos (or the share of public expenditure in GDP, or expenditure per capita, depending on the version used). Altogether Mann reported the results of 22 equations. Almost half of the equations covered 1925-76 and the other half cover 1941-76. Generally, the income elasticities of government expenditure "for the 1941-76 period are higher than those for the longer 1925-76, for the late 1920s and 1930s represented an era of essentially passive, laissez-faire public policy." It was after the 1930s "that the public sector began to adopt more active interventionist policies and programs" (Mann, 1980, p. 193). As a whole the results of Mann's regression equations "tend to disprove the usefulness (to Mexico) of Wagner's approach ..." (Mann, 1980, p. 193).

Mann also examined some "structural hypothesis" to link public expenditure evolution to the changing structure of the economy. These hypotheses dealt with the share of GDP produced in both manufacturing and primary sectors and the extent of urbanization. Even though "the explanatory power of many of the equations was not great, a direct and statistically significant association was found between the proportional levels of spending ... and the changing industrial and demographic structures of Mexico" (Mann, 1980, p. 197). Essentially, in Mann's view, the structural hypotheses tended to be of greater value, in the Mexican context, in explaining the Wagnerian hypothesis. Mann warned the reader in reaching this type of conclusion since "there exist a variety of institutional/ideological phenomena which are simultaneously operative on the dependent variable in there regressions" (Mann, 1980, p. 197). As a whole, Mann's results displayed high R^2 and t-values.[10] But, essentially the study is subject to the same criticisms alluded to earlier.

Ram (1987) reexamined the validity of Wagner's hypothesis for a large sample (115) of Developed and Less Developed Countries. He tested the relationship between government expenditure and GDP in time-series analysis for each of the 115 countries between 1950 and 1980, and cross-sectional analysis among the 115 countries. Ram utilized a recently generated internationally comparable data (GDP, government expenditures, etc.) compiled by Summers and Heston (1984). Ram's study represents the most comprehensive test of elasticities of government expenditures with respect to national income. Its use of internationally real data should improve cross-sectional comparisons.

Neither the time-series nor the cross-section results seem to yield a conclusive test of Wagner's hypothesis. Ram concluded that Wagner's hypothesis appears to have been supported in about 60 percent of the countries and refuted in the remaining 40 per cent. Slightly less than half the results are statistically significant at the 5 per cent level (pp.198 and 203).

We detect two problems with Ram's study: a) the lumping of results for countries at different levels of development, and b) the use of a bivariate model. This lumping process led Wagner and Weber (1977) to similar and inconclusive results as those of Ram's. Wagner and Weber concluded "While there are countries for which Wagner's Law seems to be aptly descriptive of government, there are many other nations in which Wagner's Law clearly does not hold" (p.67). In regard to the second problem, Ram like many other researchers before him uses a bivariate model in which the share of government expenditure in national income is related to GDP (or GNP). This approach yields an incomplete test of Wagner's hypothesis. It should be remembered that this hypothesis was formulated in the context of economic development and industrialization (see Bird, 1971). Development is a multidimensional process, involving institutional and structural changes in the economy and society. Government expenditures, on the other hand, are the result of political decisions that involve political institutions and variables (see, Mueller, 1987; Abizadeh and Yousefi, 1988). Although Ram's study as well as others are constrained by the availability of data, the use of GDP per capita, no matter how adjusted, fails to capture the underlying dimensions of development and, thus, yields an incomplete test of Wagner's hypothesis.

Yousefi and Abizadeh (1992) examined the empirical validity of Wagner's law for thirty states in the United States. These authors argued that three conditions put forth by Bird (1972) must be met for the law to be valid. These conditions deal with: a) democratization of polity, b) absence of wars and political conflicts, and c) a rising level of national (state) income. Yousefi and Abizadeh argued that many previous empirical studies of Wagner's law had overlooked these conditions and extended empirical analyses to countries that did not meet them. The novelty of the approach adopted by Yousefi and Abizadeh is that they are able "to retain certain implicit assumptions of Wagner's hypothesis such as cultural similarity, presence of peace and stability, prevalence of democratic institutions, and absence of a significant economic disturbance caused by external factors" (p.325).

Yousefi and Abizadeh introduced variables designed to capture the essence of Wagner's hypothesis. They commented that the conventional empirical models had ignored the administrative and protective functions of government, the question of externalities, the social and cultural considerations, and the notion of causality. The authors argued that these functions assume prominence as the economy develops and the standard of living improves.

Yousefi and Abizadeh employed a log-linear model that related government expenditure ratio to the "desired" expenditure ratio, the ratio of full employment State Gross Product (SGP) to state private income (SGP less government expenditures), the rate of unemployment, and the dependency ratio (the sum of young and old as a fraction of total population). They maintained that the real test of Wagner's law rests on the size of long run income elasticity of demand for public expenditures being in excess of unity. On the basis of results of their time-series (1950-1985) they found empirical verification of Wagner's law. They concluded that the long run "income elasticity of government expenditures with respect to SGP" is in excess of one "in twenty-one of possible thirty cases." Thus, in their view this implied "that Wagner's law is confirmed" (p.337).

B. CROSS-SECTIONAL STUDIES

While time-series studies are generally supportive of Wagner's law, cross-sectional studies have produced conflicting evidence. For instance, Musgrave (1969, p. 123) noted that the positive relationship between the ratio of current government expenditure to GNP and per capita income disappears "once the sample is divided into low and high income groups. Taking a per capita income of about $300 as the dividing line, the relation breaks down for the low group." On the other hand, Williamson (1961, p. 49) stated that "when we use current expenditure and total revenue as measures of the public share in gross national product, there is a definite positive correlation between per capita income and the government share."

Lall (1969) in his examination of 46 LDCs found no significant relationship between government share in GNP and per capita GNP. He also found no significant relationship between total current government expenditure and per capita income. Finally, expenditure on "Social Services as a whole showed no significant tendency to increase as a portion of total expenditure or of G.D.P. with rising incomes" (p. 415). There are other studies which have produced conflicting evidence for Wagner's law. This prompted Gandhi (1971, p. 48) to state that conflicting results are more likely "when one uses a cross-section sample of less-developed countries as against that of a sample containing both developed and less developed countries."

Wagner and Weber (1977) investigated the growth of government spending for 34 countries. The countries included in this study were as diverse as the U.S. and Ethiopia in terms of institutional arrangements and income levels. Although recognizing the need for the use of time-series data as an appropriate test of Wagner's Law, Wagner and Weber conducted a cross-sectional analysis. These authors used two measures of government activities: (a) government consumption (excluding transfers and capital outlays), and (b) government expenditure, including transfers and outlays on capital formation but excluding expenditure by local governments.

Wagner and Weber specified a model of the following form

$$(B1) \quad \text{Log } G_t = \beta_0 + \beta_1 t + \beta_2 \text{ Log } Y_t^P + \text{Log } \varepsilon_t$$

In equation $(B1)$, β_0, β_1, and β_2 are parameters and ε is an error term. Variables G_t and Y_t^P refer to per capita government spending and permanent per capita income. The use of Y_t^P reduces "the simultaneous equation bias that results because current government spending is a determinant of current income...." Further, the inclusion of t variable "allows for influences other than economic progress to affect the level of government expenditure" (p. 62).

Wagner and Weber also used a similar model without the t variable. The choice of either model depends on the best fit as measured by the standard error of estimate. They reject or accept Wagner's law on the basis of:

$$H_o : \beta_2 \geq 1$$
$$H_1 : \beta_2 < 1$$

Due to a high rejection rate of the null hypothesis, Wagner and Weber conclude "that Wagner's Law can hardly be considered a `law' at all" (p. 65).

A different kind of cross-sectional analysis was undertaken by Kelley (1976). The essence of this study was the analytical linkages between demographic change and government spending shares. Using cross-section data for 27 countries ranging in per capita income from $250 to $2,250 (1961-63 data), Kelley focused on the impact of demographic factors such as the age distribution of population, urbanization, population density, size, and dependency burden on the demand for public service.

Kelley employed a "traditional" model of Wagner's law as well as (a successively) demographically augmented model. A comparison of the results showed that "not only does the explanation of the total variance in government expenditure shares increase greatly in the demographically-augmented models ... but the size of income per capita terms, as well as their statistical significance, declines progressively ..." (p. 1065). Kelley also found that the introduction of demographic variables reduces the size of expenditure elasticity of income per capita. Kelley's analysis is interesting since it implicitly recognizes that Wagner's law is not necessarily an economic law.[11]

A variation of demographically augmented model was presented by Goffman and Mahar (1971). In a study of six Caribbean nations these authors found that the age structure of population affects public spending. One such affected area is the demand for public education. Diamond (1977), however, found contrary results. In his cross-sectional analysis of 41 countries he found that demand factors such as population and population change, urbanization, and per capita gross product did not offer a comprehensive explanation of inter-country expenditure ratios. Thorn (1967, p.24), on the other hand, argued that the "rising portion of urban population to total population accompanying development, all other things being equal, alone is sufficient to raise the relative level of public expenditure."

Gupta (1967) undertook a cross-sectional study of 53 countries which were diverse in institutional arrangements and per capita income. He posited a polynomial regression function of the following form:

$$(B2) \qquad Y = .227 + .065\,X + .286\,X^2 - .061X^3$$

In equation (B2), $X = \log Yc$ and $Y = \log G/Y$. The terms Y_c, G, and Y refer to per capita income, government expenditures, and national income respectively. The ratio G/Y indicates government's share in national income. On the basis of his results, Gupta asserted that: a) an increasing rate of G/Y relative to Y_c is possible for poor countries; b) the relationship between G/Y and Y_c diminishes as development proceeds; and c) once Y_c exceeds $1,750 level, the fitted "curve approaches an asymptote parallel to the X-axis and such a curve ... is perfectly compatible with the hypothesis of diminishing rate of G/Y ..." (p.35).[12]

Why are cross-sectional studies of Wagner's law so conflicting? To begin with, the problem may stem from the impercission of the law itself. This impercission has resulted in the development of a number of different interpretations. Gandhi (1977), for instance, identified five different versions of the law. A second problem has to do with measurement errors or misspecified equations. Third, as Goffman and Mahar (1971) pointed out the influence of institutional arrangements inherent in cross-sectional studies may not be justified.

Fourth, cross-sectional studies do not necessarily prove or disprove Wagner's hypothesis. As Bird (1971, p.10) suggested the essence of Wagner's law "is a postulated change over time in a particular country." Viewed in this context, cross-sectional studies are irrelevant to the test of

Wagner's hypothesis. This criticism is far more serious for studies which use a mixture of data for Developed and Less Developed Countries.

Fifth, the pattern of development may influence the level of public spending. For this reason, Diamond (1977) suggested the interesting proposition of reversing Wagner's chain of causation.[13] Diamond examined this proposition empirically by regressing the average rate of income of LDCs on the ratio of total public spending to GDP. For the sample as a whole he found a strong and statistically significant relationship between these variables. "However, this significant relationship breaks down for our geographical groupings...which may throw doubt on the usefulness of our scheme for desegregating the total sample" (p.52).

Sixth, complications arise from the use of nominal as opposed to real variables. In his 1982 study, Beck observed that once data are adjusted for inflation, "the share of government is increasingly found to be a stable or declining function of economic growth" (p.163). On the other hand, an earlier study by Goffman and Mahar (1971) found that deflating public expenditures by CPI or WPI did not significantly alter the time pattern of public spending growth.

Finally, problems may arise from the proper measure of public spending. For example, should transfer payments be excluded from government expenditures if the government is considered a consumer of resources? Transfers may, however, play a major redistributive role in the economy. Beck (1982, p.163) observed that "in many countries transfer outlays dominate public expenditure, nominal or real; and government's role as a supplier of public good is being surpassed by its function as a redistributor of income."

Despite the foregoing problems, practical considerations may be a reason for the use of cross-sectional studies. For instance, the paucity of reliable time-series data, particularly for LDCs, may force researchers to rely on cross-section data. As seen earlier, researchers have used per capita income as an index of economic development. The underlying assumption for this is that the differences in per capita income of different countries capture the essence of social, institutional, and economic problems of different societies. A study by Abizadeh and Gray (1985) overcame this problem by classifying countries according to their ranking of Physical Quality of Life Index (PQLI). These authors identified three classes of economies: Developed, Developing, and Less Developed. Based on their results, Abizadeh and Gray concluded that Wagner's law holds for the Developing countries. This, they maintained, is consistent with what Wagner viewed as industrializing countries.

C. OTHER STUDIES

There are a number of other studies which cannot be classified as either time-series analyses or cross-sectional analyses. A study by Andre and Delmore (1978) focused on French expenditure data. This study led the authors to conclude "that the displacement effect reduces in the French case to a simple threshold effect, the validity of which is heavily dependent upon the lengths of time periods..." (Andre and Delmore, 1978, p. 59). This study suggested a possible emergence of stage three (of Herber's hypothesis) for the national government of France. Oshima (1957) put forth an argument which is analogous to the "displacement effect" hypothesis; although the concept was not formulated until some time later. Oshima's analysis led him to conclude that in a developing economy, "it takes a major event (wars, depression, etc.) to raise government expenditures beyond previous levels." After these major events, however, "the percentage share of the government does not recede to the previous low levels" (p. 386). Underdeveloped economies do not experience the same phenomenon since these economies do not enjoy high levels of productivity and growth. Further, in these countries government expenditure falls behind productivity.

Pryor (1965) set out to empirically examine governmental budgetary expenditures for a socialist economy (East Germany), and by means of comparison, for a capitalist country (West Germany). The purpose was to "illuminate certain aspects of problems related to such expenditures which have been hitherto neglected" (p. 301). Pryor examined a set of hypotheses which may be termed as modifications of Wagner's Law. Generalizations about the time-pattern of expenditures in East and West Germany are not meaningful unless data are disaggregated "to take account of heterogeneous nature of different governmental expenditures" (p. 341).

Pryor found the hypotheses that predict "all governmental expenditures have income elasticity greater than unity" to be wrong for the period (1950-62) examined. This turned out to be the case for all expenditures except defense, research and development, and perhaps health. Pryor also examined a second set of hypotheses which relate the relative levels of expenditures to GNP. He found that political considerations explain the ratio of expenditure to GNP for security purposes. Further, the hypotheses that assume social welfare expenditures are higher in East Germany are found to be groundless. Finally, Pryor examined a set of hypotheses which deal "with the level of government at which certain expenditures were made" (p. 345). These hypotheses failed in their predictions; the underlying causes of failure were partly political, partly institutional, and partly due to differences in the two countries.

Abizadeh and Yousefi (1988) examined the growth of government expenditures in Canada for the period 1945-1984. They adopted a model which relates government expenditure ratio (ER) to openness (OP), the dependency ratio (DR), unemployment rate (U), preferences of political elite (PF), and public sector employment (LFGR).

Abizadeh and Yousefi used two measures of ER: a) total government expenditure ratio, defined as total public sector spending divided by GNP, and b) net government expenditure ratio, defined as public spending less transfer payments divided by GNP. Although this study is not a direct test of Wagner's hypothesis, it incorporates many of the implicit assumptions of Wagner's studies. For instance, variables such as openness, growth, and changes in the demographic composition of population are incorporated in the hypothesis. Openness is defined as the ratio of the sum of the exports and imports divided by GNP . The purpose of this variable is to reflect the economy's diversification. The dependency ratio is defined as the sum of young (0-15 years of age) and old (those over 65) as a fraction of total population. The inclusion of this variable is intended to reflect changes in the age distribution of population. The unemployment variable is used as an index of perceived national economic problem (or lack thereof). The most innovative variable used by Abizadeh and Yousefi is a political factor index. This index is designed to measure the percentage of liberal or conservative members of the House. The variable LFGR is intended to reflect the productivity of the public sector and, indirectly, the extent of logrolling and elite preference.

On the basis of their results, the authors contended that the distinction between nominal and real values of government spending does not make a perceptible difference in their conclusions. Second, they discovered that the distinction between exhaustive and nonexhaustive expenditures significantly affect their results. Third, they discovered an evidence of political elite preference for public spending in Canada. Fourth the size of public expenditures is affected by the dependency ratio. Finally, they discovered an indication of a positive income elasticity of demand for public goods.

IV. CRITICISMS AND COMMENTS

Wagner's law was formulated for industrializing economies. The empirical studies of the law have been extended to developed as well as less developed countries. This seems to be inconsistent with the intent of Wagner's hypotheses. Additionally, as Bird (1971) has noted, Wagner's law is predicated on three conditions: rising per capita income, technological change, and democratization of the polity. Even if there is a consensus in regard to the first two conditions, the political climate of many LDCs does not satisfy the third condition. Consequently, cross-sectional studies of Wagner's hypothesis are extremely flawed in this regard.

Second, Bird (1971, p. 20) suggests the law is not really a theory at all but rather a kind of generalization about history. Once cast in this mold, an "attempt to `test' it necessarily does violence to the facts by adjusting them to the preconceived theory ... The fundamental preconception underlying the `law' ... is that the process of evolution is inherently similar at different historical periods. ..." Bird considers Wagner's law akin to some grand speculation--being incapable of a rigorous and meaningful test.

Third, Wagner's hypothesis is not necessarily one of economics. It is formulated in general terms encompassing social, political, and institutional factors. Thus, even a good statistical "fit" of G/Y ratio and per capita income ignores the influence of important demographic and social factors.

There are specific criticisms which may be raised against econometric studies of Wagner's law. Ideally, as Peacock and Wiseman (1979) point out, the problem of using an econometric technique has three characteristics: 1) the lack of ambiguity about the general nature of the causal relationship, 2) the ability of the model to explain all potential explanations, and 3) "the forecasting `test' is an adequate basis for choosing between alternative `explanation"' (p. 18). Peacock and Wiseman are quick to point out that the study of public expenditure growth scores badly on all counts. Clearly, empirical tests of Wagner's law are not any exception.

The econometric studies of Wagner's law are fraught with many shortcomings. Both time-series and cors-sectional studies use highly aggregated data. Pryor and others have explained the difficulties with such data. The time-series studies often rely on bivariate models which may yield a good statistical "fit" but fail to produce unombiguous results. The problem with cross-sectional studies is more serious. For instance, they implicitly assume the existence of similar institutional setups in all countries. Further, as Bird (1971, p. 10) states there is nothing in any formulation of Wagner's law which states "country A must have a higher government expenditure ratio than country B simply because the level of average per capita income is higher in A than in B in a particular point in time." Inferences drawn from cross-sectional studies are irrelevant to Wagner's law, the essence of which is a dynamic change.

What alternatives are possible. One possibility is case studies of countries whose social, economic, and political conditions are consistent with Wagner's intentions. For a more meaningful of test of Wagner's law, allowance must be made for the parameters of a nation's decision-making process. Allowance also must be made for public perception of the role of government, demographic factors, international demonstration effect for public goods (particularly in the case of developing countries). Herber (1983, p. 331) offers thirteen independent variables, as a partial list, toward the explanation of a positive theory of public expenditure represented by Wagner's hypothesis.

ENDNOTES

1. This, however, seems to contradict the country studies alluded to earlier. Canada, the United Kingdom, Norway, and Sweden seem to be in the post-industrial stage by whatever criteria used. Yet, Wagner's law has been vindicated for these countries.

2. In modern parlance this means that the "income" elasticity of demand for government expenditures is greater than unity.

3. A new version, according to Bird (1971), relates the activities of the government to the changing structure of the economy. Elements of this thesis are to be found in J.K. Galbraith's *The New Industrial State*. For details, see Bird (1971). Crowley (1971) provides a more remote variation of Wagner's law. This study is an attempt to vindicate the work of Henri Pirenne, the Belgian economic historian. Crowley's conclusion is "that researchers concerned with long-term growth in government should be cognizant of the possibilities of declines in the role of government. Existing theories, ... are likely to be in error if extrapolated to the past or future" (Crowley, 1971, p. 42).

4. Peacock and Wiseman point out that the government, in areas of defense and environmental services, has been a leading innovator.

5. Herber cites Beck (1976) and Beck (1982) as evidence of slowdown in public sector growth in Western industrial economies.

6. Martin and Lewis (1956, p. 206) point out that the basic reason why LDCs "now spend relatively more on public spending ... is not that they are richer, but that they have a different conception of the duties of state ..." Musgrave (1969,p. 72) argues along the same line. Pryor (1965) argues that very few changes in terms of public expenditures are explained by aggregate income changes. Instead, "change in the ratios to output, he argues, must be explained disaggregatively and then not necessarily in terms of income, but also in terms of economic, demographic, social, and institutional variables" (Goffman and Mahar, 1971, p. 66). See also Williamson (1961) who argues that the rising government share is due to productivity lag in the public sector.

7. A detailed criticism of all statistical methods will be given later.

8. Enweze recognizes the possibility of autocorrelation. The limited number of observations does not allow for D-W statistic test of autocorrelation. Enweze states that his concern is not with the degree of predictiveness. Instead, he is concerned with the estimate of elasticity; coefficient b in (A2).

9. As Goffman Maher (1971, p. 70) point out, in many LDCs, "internal dictatorship or pressure from a foreign power or even international agency may reduce the role of the ballot box and introduce instead a different set of constraints ..."

10. See Peach and Webb (1983). Cooley and Leroy (1981), Mayer (1981), and Pesaran (1974) for criticism to goodness of fit and other problems of econometric studies.

11. Kelly's position is supported by Diamond (1977,p.43) who argued that "Wagner framed his 'law' in general terms, encompassing institutional changes, industrialization, democratization, etc."

12. For criticisms of Gupta's conclusion, see Bird (1971).

13. Diamond discusses, at length, the views of two opposing groups in regard to the impact of public sector expansion on economic growth. One group whose ideas has currency in LDCs argues that public

spending raises the rate of economic growth. On the other hand, another body of opinion finds a deleterious effect, at least for industrially advanced countries, on economic growth of increased public spending. For details, see Diamond (1977, pp. 47-54). See also, Beck (1982) for views on the role of public spending in the industrially advanced countries.

REFERENCES

Abizadeh, S. and J. Gray, (1985), "Wagner's Law: A Pooled Cross-Section and Time Series Comparison," *National Tax Journal* 38:209-218.

Abizadeh, S. and M. Yousefi, (1988), "Growth of Government Expenditures: The Case of Canada," *Public Finance Quarterly* 16:78-100.

Andre, C. and R. Delmore, (1978), "The Long-Run Growth of Public Expenditure in France," *Public Finance* 33:42-67.

Baumol, W.J., (1967), "The Macroeconomics of Unbalanced Growth," *American Economic Review* 57:415-26.

Baumol, W.J. and W.H. Oates, (1975), *The Theory of Environmental Policy*.

Beck, M., (1982), "Toward a Theory of Public Sector Growth," *Public Finance* 37:163-77.

Beck, M., (1979), "Public Sector Growth: A Real Perspective," *Public Finance* 34:313-56.

Bird, R.M., (1971), "Wagner's `Law' of Expanding State Activity," *Public Finance* 26:1-26.

Cooley, T.F. and S.F. LeRoy, (1981), "Identification and Estimation of Money Demand," *American Economic Review* 71:825-44.

Crowley, R.W., (1971), "Long Swings in the Role of Government: An Analysis of Wars and Government Expenditures in Western Europe since the Eleventh Century," *Public Finance* 26:27-43.

Diamond, J., (1977), "Wagner's `Law' and the Developing Countries," *The Developing Economies* 15:37-59.

Enweze, C., (1973), "Structure of Public Expenditure in Selected Developing Countries: A Time Serie's Study," *Manchester School of Economics and Social Studies* 41:430-63.

Gandhi, V.P., (1971), "Wagner's Law of Public Expenditure: Do Recent Cross-section Studies Confirm It?" *Public Finance* 26:44-56.

Ganti, S. and B.R. Kolluri, (1979), "Wagner's Law of Public Expenditures: Some Efficient Results for the United States," *Public Finance* 34:223-33.

Goffman, I.J., (1968), "On the Empirical Testing of `Wagner's Law': A Technical Note," *Public Finance* 23:359-64.

Goffman, I.J. and D.J. Mahar, (1971), "The Growth of Public Expenditures in Selected Nations: Six Caribbean Countries," *Public Finance* 26:57-74.

Gupta, S.P., (1967), "Public Expenditure and Economic Development - A Cross-Sections Analysis," *Finanazarchiv* 28:26-41.

Herber, B.P., (1983), *Modern Public Finance* Homewood, Irwin.

Hook, E., (1962), "The Expansion of the Public Sector - A Study of the Development of Public Expenditures in Sweden During the Years 1912-1958," *Public Finance* 17:289-312.

Johansen, L., (1968), *Public Economics* Chicago, Rand McNally.

Kelley, A.C., (1976), "Demographic Change and the Size of the Government Sector," *Southern Economic Journal* 43:1056-65.

Lall, S., (1969), "A Note on Government Expenditures in Developing Countries," *Economic Journal* 79:413-17.

Lotz, J.R. and E.R. Morss, (1970), "A Theory of Tax Level Determinants for Developing Countries," *Economic Development and Cultural Change* 18:238-41.

Mahar, D.J., (1971), "The Growth of Public Expenditures in Selected Developing Nations: Six Caribbean Countries 1940-65," *Public Finance* 26:57-74.

Mann, A.J., (1980), "Wagner's Law: An Econometric Test for Mexico," *National Tax Journal* 33:189-201.

Martin, A.M. and W.A. Lewis, (1956), "Patterns of Public Revenue and Expenditure," *The Manchester School of Economics and Social Studies* 24:203-44.

Mayer, T., (1975), "Selecting Economic Hypotheses by Goodness of Fit," *Economic Journal* 85:877-83.

Michas, N.A., (1975), "Wagner's Law of Public Expenditures: What Is The Appropriate Measurement for a Valid Test?" *Public Finance* 30:77-84.

Mueller, D.C., (1987), "The Growth of Government: A Public Choice Perspective," *IMF Staff Papers,* 34:115-49.

Musgrave, R.A., (1969), *Fiscal Systems* New Haven, Yale University Press.

Oshima, H.T., (1957), "The Share of Government in Gross National Product for Various Countries," *American Economic Review* 47:381-90.

Peach, J.T. and J.L. Webb, (1983), "Randomly Specified Macroeconomic Models: Some Implications for Model Selection," Journal of Economic Issues 17:697-720.

Peacock, A.T. and J. Wiseman, (1967), *The Growth of Public Expenditure in the United Kingdom London, George Allen & Unwin.*

Peacock, A.T. and J. Wiseman, (1979), "Approaches to the Analysis of Government Expenditure Growth," *Public Finance Quarterly* 7:3-23.

Pesaran, M.H., (1974), "On the General Problem of Model Selection," *Review of Economic Studies* 61:153-71.

Pryor, F.L., (1965), "East and West German Governmental Expenditures," *Public Finance* 20:300-59.

Ram, R., (1987), "Wagner's Hypothesis in Time-series and Cross-section perspectives: Evidence from `Real' data for 115 Countries," *Review of Economics and Statistics*, 68:194-204.

Summers, R. and A. Heston, (1984), "Improved International Comparisons of Real Product and Its Composition: 1950-80," *Review of Income and Wealth* 30:207-62.

Thorn, R.S., (1967), "The Evolution of Public Finance During Economic Development," *The Manchester School of Economics and Social Studies* 35:19-53.

Wagner, R.E. and W.E. Weber, (1977), "Wagner's Law, Fiscal Institutions, and the Growth of Government," *National Tax Journal* 30:59-68.

Williamson, J.G.,(1961), "Public Expenditure and Revenue" An International Comparison," *The Manchester School of Economics and Social Studies* 29:43-56.

Yousefi, M. and S. Abizadeh, (1992), "Growth of State Government Expenditures: Empirical Evidence from the United States," *Public Finance* 47:322-39.

CHAPTER TWO

TAX CHANGES AND ECONOMIC DEVELOPMENT: A CRITICAL REVIEW[1]

Mahmood Yousefi & Sohrab Abizadeh

I. INTRODUCTION

A major preoccupation of most governments is broadening the existing tax base and creating new tax sources to raise revenue. The reasons for this preoccupation differ between more developed countries (MDCs) and less developed countries (LDCs). In LDCs, tax revenues are needed to develop necessay infrastructure for economic development while providing incentives in the private sector for increased investment and output. However, most MDCs need higher tax revenues to finance their rising expenditures on social programs and programs designed to correct market failure and externalities. Regardless of the level of economic development almost every country strives to raise its tax revenue.

For this reason, in the last three decades interest has grown both, theoretically and empirically, in the construction of tax system and tax structure changes. Observers such as Hinrichs (1966) and Musgrave (1969) have noted that MDCs are characterized by a higher ratio of tax revenues to national income than LDCs. Others have questioned the association of tax revenues and national income for LDCs at various stages of development. For example, Mironski and Schwartz (1982-83) argue that corporate income tax burden has become smaller in selected OECD countries; an indication of change in the composition of taxes as economies grow. Before reaching the performance level of MDCs, most LDCs need to secure a larger tax base to support their economic development initiatives.

Among many common characteristics of LDCs one may include low levels of living, low levels of productivity, high rates of growth of population, high and rising levels of unemployment, interdependence in international relations, etc. Low levels of living are evident by low levels of per capita income. Not only are living standards low in LDCs but, there is a manifest growing gap between the rich and the poor as well. Low living standards are directly linked to low levels of labor productivity. This, in turn, is attributed to many causes including the absence or severe lack of "complementary" factors such as physical capital. Investment and capital resources may be mobilized through domestic channels such as saving. Other alternatives include measures such as accepting foreign assistance, induced inflation, and raising taxes.

An analysis of tax structure change in LDCs helps us understand their development problems. Hinrichs (1966) observes that during the course of development, LDCs face an expenditure-revenue gap. The main causes of the gap are as follows. First, the rate of indicators of social mobilization exceeds the rate of adjustment capabilities. The outcome "is a strain on social organization" and a corresponding increase in demand "for government services that cannot yet satisfactorily be met by government" (p. 48). Second, conventional economic growth theory requires "a shift in saving, say from 5 to 12 percent of GNP that cannot easily be met by private or public saving without either inflation or external borrowing" (p. 48). Third, there is a changing role of government consonant with "Wagner's general theory of rising government expenditures with the sociopolitical lag in increasing...tax rates and in shifting tax base..." (p. 49).

The implication of an expenditure-revenue gap is that it "may be filled by internal and external borrowing or grants. If not, the gap may result in some degree of inflation..." (p. 49). In order to speed up the closure of this gap, tax rates may be increased and/or tax base may be broadened. Further, society's saving ratio may be altered through government's tax and expenditure policies. For instance, the government can affect the propensity to save by altering income and consumption related (indirect) taxes. In the same vein, it can affect the level of investment by altering (or introducing) a system of profit taxes.[2]

Because capital accumulation is a major concern of many LDCs, an important consideration in public finance is a system of fiscal policy design which addresses that concern. Development economists who address the issue of tax structure change, implicitly assume that LDCs aspire economic growth. These economists argue that in order to ensure a desired rate of growth, LDCs must enhance their productive capacity. Therefore, capital accumulation is a necessary ingredient of the growth objective. However, there are many obstacles to raising the level of private saving. They include such things as low levels of income, demonstration effect, political misgivings, and so on. Yet, national saving may be mobilized and its growth secured if it is increased compulsorily by raising taxes, thereby reducing consumption. In other words, "taxation becomes a form of saving and involves postponement of consumption. The problem then becomes one of ability to postpone current consumption" (Musgrave, 1969, p. 161). Raising domestic saving through a budgetary policy avoids the complications alluded to earlier. Revenues raised this way accommodate development objectives so long as they are not used for government expenditure on defense, social services, etc. Please (1967, p. 25) points out that this preoccupation with raising revenues through taxes was so significant "in the eyes of many people and institutions interested in economic development that the ratio of tax revenue to gross national product (GNP) [became an exceedingly] important criteria for measuring and judging a country's economic performance."

If the objective of tax policy is to maximize tax yield, the logical question is what system of tax design would satisfy that objective. One way to ensure an automatic increase in the ratio of government revenues to GNP (or GDP) is to design a tax structure in which the marginal ratio exceeds average ratio; i.e., a progressive tax system. At the same time, the disincentive effects of such a tax structure should not be ignored. On practical grounds, there are limitations to the scope of progressive taxes in LDCs. The dilemma developing countries face in designing a tax system is one which will provide adequate resources for growth purposes while not inhibiting (or distorting) incentives in the private sector.

II. THEORETICAL FRAMEWORK

Many economists have addressed the problem of tax structure change and economic development. Musgrave (1969) and Hinrichs (1966) have provided much of the theoretical framework, while others have presented the bulk of empirical evidence. In this section we present a brief summary of discussions put forth by Musgrave and Hinrichs.

Musgrave suggests that there are two ways in which economic factors affect tax structure. First, as economic development takes place, "the nature of tax base changes... [and, thus,] the 'handles' to which the revenue system may be attached." Second, "the economic objectives of tax policy

vary with the stages of economic development, as do the economic criteria by which a good tax structure is to be judged" (p. 125).

In the early stages of development, the economic conditions impose
severe limitations on the structure of tax system. Since agriculture is the
predominant form of economic activity and it is extremely difficult to
reach it through income taxation, Musgrave stresses the importance of
land taxes. In the manufacturing sector, the effective tax base is limited to
a few selected products of large establishments. It is possible to increase
the revenue base through the pricing policies of public enterprises. Additionally, in the early stages, the effectiveness of personal income taxes is
"limited to the wage income of civil servants and employees of large
firms" (p. 127). Since the determination of business income is exceedingly
difficult, business income tax becomes, in effect, "a sales tax, with ad valorem rates varying with the average margin or the industry" (p. 127).

Later, as the economy develops, it is possible to impose income taxes
on a broader base; thereby allowing the effective taxation of personal as
well as business income. The implication is that the prospects for an increase in the share of direct taxes improve with economic development.
Drawing from the experience of the U.S. and other industrialized countries, Musgrave suggests that the development of tax structure change in
modern times has been characterized by the rise of direct taxes, especially
income taxes. Further, the U.S. experience suggests that over time a larger
fraction of population is subject to income tax coverage. Both in the U.S.
and U.K. with the rising importance of income taxes, there has been a
concomitant decline in the importance of property taxation. Similarly,
sales and excise taxes have declined in relative importance.

Hinrichs (1966) is more ambitious than Musgrave. He proposes a
"general theory" of tax structure change and purports "that his empirical
analysis reveals an `ideal type' of tax structure for each level of economic
development" (Tanzi, 1975, p. 200). In his empirical generalizations, Hinrichs "attempts to prove.... that the tax burden defined as the ratio yield
to gross national output, is on the whole lower in the less developed countries than in the developed countries, and that it is lower in the less developed countries than what it ought to be" (Andic, 1973: p. 157). Further,
Hinrichs identifies "openness" as the major determinant of government
revenue share of GNP. Openness is a key determinant of both the size of
the government revenue share and its composition for LDCs with a per
capita income of less than $300 (Hinrichs, 1966, p. 98). Two reasons ex-
plain the importance of openness. First, foreign trade is the chief source of
revenue for over two-thirds of governments of LDCs. These revenues are
derived from import duties, taxes on exports, government marketing

board arrangements, etc. Second, foreign trade is the sector through which the ability to collect taxes permeates the economy. In Hinrichs' words, "there is a spillover effect of the foreign trade sector size on ability to collect taxes elsewhere in the economy. The greater the size of foreign trade sector, ... the greater the degree of monetization of the economy, the predominance of `cash' crops..., and the extent of urbanization and industrialization" (p. 20).

Recognizing that the government revenue share of GNP increases with economic development, Hinrichs, associates different types of taxes with different stages of development. For instance, in traditional societies where trade, commercialism, and urbanization have not developed to any great extent, government revenues are derived essentially from traditional sources (e.g. taxes on land or livestock). The transitional stage consists of two phases. In the first phase, old values begin to crumble; government becomes consolidated and centralized; and money, trade, and transport develop. In this phase, revenues are obtained by taxing trade and the rising mercantile group. Gradually, traditional sources of revenue lose significance "and are in part replaced by indirect taxes in general and foreign trade taxes in particular" (Tanzi, 1975: p. 200). In the second phase, the country has achieved political consolidation and the government has gained dominance "over the regional landed interests, and the spirit of nationalism predominates" (Hinrichs, 1966, p. 93). In this phase, the import competing sector replaces imports in response to a deliberate policy of import substitution. Since taxes on imports are replaced by internal indirect taxes, foreign trade taxes are either stable or falling. In this phase modern taxes are brought to the forefront so that by the end of this phase these taxes constitute 20-40 percent of total revenues. In the transitional stage, there is a positive relationship between government revenue share and per capita income.

A government revenue share of 18 percent is necessary, though not sufficient, for a move to development. Upon the emergence of modern society, the government revenue share of GNP is about 20-35 percent. In this stage, modern taxes replace traditional taxes and modern direct and internal indirect taxes become predominant. In this stage tax styles are not so much shaped by economic consideration as they are by the socio-political considerations. In essence, "the socio-political ideologies and additions will tend to become more important than economic structure in shaping the nature of the tax system" (1966, p.93).

Can we generalize from these theoretical considerations? Generalizations about tax structure change seem to be difficult in view of many countries, many time periods, and myraids of exceptions. Hinrichs (p. 97) contends that "Even though tax structure change during development may seem to resemble a multi-colored tapestry, ... a general theoretical pattern does emerge." This pattern may be considered an ideal type which is not "a system that must follow for all cases under all circumstances. [Instead,] it is a heuristic device that establishes a framework in which to fit disparate pieces."

III. EMPIRICAL EVIDENCE

The objective of empirical analyses of tax ratio changes is the quantification of determinants of tax effort. This would be useful if it enabled the policy-maker to estimate the effect of changes in variables that affect taxes. Andic (1973, p. 155) contends that these empirical analyses are "very seldom carried out in a macro-economic sense, in checking the correspondence of a tax system,..., to the development objectives...." Instead, these analyses are global in scope "... in that inter-country global tax ratios and performances are compared and related to global proxy variables such as per capita income, the degree of openness...." Further, as Tanzi (1973) points out most of the statistical studies are contradictory. They try to explain "statistically how a particular tax (or often a group of taxes) changes in cross-section sample when one varies per capita income or...other variables such as monetization..." (p. 199).

A common argument in the literature of tax structure change and economic development is "that high per capita income levels lead to high tax ratios because of both the correspondingly high capacity to pay taxes and high income elasticity of demand for public goods" (Chelliah, 1971: p.280). Using per capita income as an explanatory variable of revenue/tax ratio changes, however, poses a problem recognized by Bird. In such an analysis an identification problem is involved because "income is surely as much a `demand' as it is a `supply' factor ..." (Bird, 1978: p. 43). The identification problem is particularly serious if an extended time-series is used.

In several empirical studies which have tried to examine the relationship between tax structure change and economic development, it is generally argued that as development proceeds the government revenue share of national income rises. This increased share is accommodated by increases in taxes which rise faster than income and by changes in the overall composition of taxes. In other words, as development takes place, the resulting changes in the commercialization of the economy, urbanization, and modernization imply that more taxes are levied and collected. Not only do taxes rise as development takes place, but the type of taxes imposed change as well. For instance, sales and excise taxes gain at the expense of foreign trade taxes. Due and Meyer (1989) posit that relative importance of import duties and export taxes declines as a country's per capita income rises. In addition, personal and corporate income taxes come into more prominence (for evidence, see Chelliah, 1971; Chelliah et al., 1975; and Thorn, 1967). Tanzi's (1983) conclusions are consistent with the foregoing observations. Due and Meyer (1989, p.48) summarize Tanzi's conclusions as follows:

1. Personal income taxes rise as a percentage of tax revenue as GNP per capita increases.
2. Corporation income taxes show a higher correlation between the relative reliance on these taxes and per capita GNP for developing countries. This relationship is reversed for industrialized countries.
3. For developing countries there is no relationship between indirect taxes and per capita GNP, i.e., one observes a wide variation in these taxes among different countries with similar economic conditions.
4. As per capita income rises relative reliance on import duties and export taxes decline.

Attempts to formulate policy prescriptions through studies of tax ratio differences and changes in tax components have taken different forms. Martin and Lewis (1956), for instance, compared the revenues and expenditures of 16 countries at different levels of economic development. Their objective was twofold: first, to delineate patterns of expenditure and sources of revenue with respect to stages of development, and second, portray patterns of taxes and expenditures most appropriate to various levels of development. Logically, it is difficult to infer from such statistical relationships that a growing trend in tax ratios reflects economic development. One would need to pay close attention to the structure of tax systems as well as the underlying conditions of development. For instance, it is important to know how the fruits of economic progress are divided among the population of a country.

Oshima (1957) assessed the taxable capacity of a country by analyzing the relationship between government expenditures and economic development. Based on evidence obtained for selected developed and less developed countries, he found a direct link between the percentage share of government expenditures in gross domestic product and the degree of economic development. He argued that an explanation for the link may be found in the relative productivity of different countries. This link implies that the greater the productivity, the larger will be the relative margin of incomes above strictly physical subsistence. Further, the larger this margin the greater, generally speaking, the potential taxable capacity of the economy.

Hinrichs (1965) questioned the findings of previous studies and tried to present a "better" explanation for tax changes using a multiple regression analysis of 60 different countries. The time period for which data were collected was 1957-60. Hinrichs' implicit assumption was that per capita income is reflective of economic well-being. However, if indices other than per capita income explain tax ratio changes more satisfactorily, the validity of the conclusion that tax ratios (taxes/GDP) are related to states of development (as reflected in per capita income) would become less meaningful. Hinrichs himself states that:

> ... conventional wisdom holds that government revenue shares of gross national product increase with economic development. This is obvious when contrasting the level of government revenue shares between developed and less-developed countries. However, when observing differences among less-developed countries only, this proposition is misleading at best or worst just plain wrong (p. 564).

Hinrichs (1966), in a more thorough study of taxes, attempted to deal with both tax ratio and tax component changes within the course of economic development. The objective was to identify the sources of government revenues and their relationship to GDP (or GNP). Hinrichs accepted the hypothesis that there exists a direct relationship between total tax ratio and the degree of economic development. He further suggested that, in developing countries, tax level differences are correlated to some extent with the "degree of openness" measured by imports as a percentage of GNP. However, while Hinrichs listed a few possible reasons for his findings, he did not offer much empirical support for his reasoning. Abizadeh (1979) provided support for the general theory of a direct relationship between total tax ratio and the degree of economic development.

Musgrave (1969) presented a series of bivariate regression equations (a cross-sectional view) to substantiate his arguments regarding tax structure change and economic development. He offered two hypothesis concerning the share of indirect taxes in GNP. First, the ratio of indirect taxes (T_{id}) to total taxes (T) is inversely related to per capita income. This is expected since the economic structure of low income countries is not suited to the imposition of direct taxes. Further, indirect taxes (including customs duties) can be imposed more readily. Second, the ratio T_{id}/T is positively related to "the T/GNP ratio, or to the overall level of tax rates. The proposition is that direct taxes .... .resorted to increasingly after direct tax rates have reached higher levels" (p. 149). Musgrave's empirical evidence vindicated the first hypothesis. However, the second hypothesis was not borne out by evidence.

Lotz and Morss (1970) claimed to have given detailed consideration to some of the factors likely to affect tax levels in developing countries. The authors arbitrarily chose $800 of per capita income as the dividing line between developed and developing countries. The cross-section study by Lotz and Morss contained data on 52 developing countries. The authors chose the export ratio (X/GNP) as a measure of openness. Lotz and Morss hypothesized that the degree of monetization is measured by per capita money holding. Three measures of money supply used were: coins and currency in circulation (C^p), M_1 defined as the sum of C^p and demand deposits (DD), and M_2 defined as M_1 plus time deposits (TD). These authors paid some attention to different types of taxes and the degree of centralization of the government. Lotz and Morss concluded that tax levels in developing countries are:

1. importantly affected by the availability of taxable bases; and
2. kept down by the limited availability of taxable bases.

Though intuitively appealing, this study fails to recognize that some countries are more favorably placed (in term of income) to levy taxes. In other words, some countries simply have a greater taxable capacity than others. In regard to openness one should not merely concentrate on the secular trends of exports and imports. It is important that we trace dynamic changes in the composition of exports and imports. Exports could rise and imports fall while a country pursues a restrictive trade policy. In regard to the monetization process, it is not sufficient to look at some measures of monetary aggregates. We need to pay attention to the development of financial markets. In many LDCs where a barter system prevails in rural areas, simple per capita money holding fails to reflect the dynamics of monetization process. The distribution and composition of money and deposit holding in various sectors of the economy should be considered as well.

Chelliah (1971) recognized that the general practice of using the T/GNP ratio, where T is inclusive of all tax and tax like changes (e.g.

royalties on minerals), has certain problems. For one thing, it "does not indicate anything about the proportion of national output generated in the public sector..." Nor does T portray "a reliable index of the relative importance of public sector as a final purchaser or goods and services" (p. 257). According to Chelliah what the T/GNP ratio measures is the relative share of national income which "is `compulsorily' transferred from private hands into the government sector for public purposes" (p. 258). Conceptually, the tax ratio is affected by four groups of factors. Two groups of factors related to the demand side for government services are: "a) the need for services arising out of `objective' conditions and b) the preferences of people between public and private services...." Two groups of factors postulated on the supply side are: "a) the ability of people to pay taxes and b) the ability of government to collect taxes" (p. 292).

Observing trends for countries included in his study, Chelliah found that there had been a shift from property and poll taxes to taxes on income. From these trends one may conclude that these tax changes conform to the general theoretical framework put forth earlier. However, direct taxes constitute a minor part of total revenues in LDCs. The experience of these countries suggests that the share of direct taxes does not rise with per capita income until a certain minimum level of income has been reached. Once this threshold has been attained, there seems to be a positive relationship between the share of direct taxes and per capita income.

The foregoing arguments suggest that each country decides for itself what level of taxes to impose, in accordance with its own constraints. Nevertheless, "policy-makers inevitably make comparisons with the level of taxation and the experiences in other countries in a similar stage of development" (p. 299). The usual approach to the determination of tax effort and tax capacity has been to regress variables affecting tax capacity on the tax ratio. The predicted ratio "is what the country concerned would have had if it had made the average tax effort" (p. 299). Tax effort may be defined as "the quotient of the actual tax ratio divided by the tax ratio estimated according to" the following equation,

$$T/y = 10.05 + 0.0031 (Yp - Xp) + 0.3973Ny + 0.00881Xy$$

$$(7.48) \quad (0.77) \quad (5.55) \quad (1.89)$$

$R^2 = 0.393$, where
T/y = tax ratio (excluding social security contributions),
Yp = per capita income in U.S. dollars,
$Yp - Xp$ = per capita nonexport income in U.S.dollars,
Ny = the share of mining in GDP,
Xy = the export ratio excluding mineral exports.

Chelliah (p. 30) derived the indices of relative tax effort on the basis of the above equation "as well as the actual ratios for 49 countries in the sample...." Considering the actual tax ratios, only "21 of the 49 countries have tax ratios above average..." On the other hand, tax effort indices indicate that "roughly about the same proportion of countries...making above average tax effort...," that is 25 out of 49.

Mann (1980), being skeptical of cross-sectional studies, undertook a time-series analysis of Mexico. He rationalized his statistical analysis of Mexico's tax structure changes by raising questions about the relevance and validity of cross-sectional studies. His main objection to this type of study was that it relies on the results generated for a specific point in time and that these results are frequently used to infer past and future trends in the tax structure-economic development relationship. Mann's time-series analysis of Mexico covered the period of 1895-1975. The rationale was that by concentrating on Mexico for the entire period, the same country is observed ever time at *different levels of development*, thereby obviating a principal defect of cross-section studies of this nature.

In his paper, Mann reported the results of 32 bivariate regression equations. In most cases R_f/Y (the share of federal government revenues in GDP), R/Y (the share of government revenues of all levels in GDP), and T/Y (total taxes as a fraction of GDP) separately served as the dependent variable. Per capita income, sectoral share of manufacturing in GDP, sectoral share of the primary sector in GDP, and an index of openness separately served as independent variables. Two measures of openness were: imports share in GDP and the sum of exports' and imports' share in GDP.

The regression equations satisfied all the usual conditions of statistical significance. On the basis of these results, Mann concluded that openness and per capita income have statistically significant associations with revenue/tax ratios. He suggested that his results were consistent with those of cross-sectional studies. However, he cautioned the reader against generalizations based on time-series analysis. These studies are subject to exceptions which may often be merely a function of time period and/or subperiod selected.

Abizadeh and Yousefi (1985) undertook a multivariate analysis of tax structure change. Although they recognized the importance of international trade taxes, their analysis incorporated variables other than openness measures. The focus of their study was two groups of countries designated as: "least developed"; comprised of countries such as Somalia, Malawi, Ghana; and "developing"; including such countries as South Africa, Brazil, Portugal, etc. They used Physical Quality of Life Index (PQLI), an index developed by Morris (1977), to classify countries into these groups. Abizadeh and Yousefi (1985) concluded that during the course of economic development, the relative importance of international trade taxes diminishes. Further, such taxes play a more important role in the revenue structure of the least developed countries than that of the developing countries.[3] Essentially, Abizadeh and Yousefi corroborated findings of earlier research.

IV. ASSESSMENT

The empirical studies of tax structure change do not reveal much about their economic significance. Carl Shoup (1972, p. 140) observes that "too often the information is hardly more useful, directly, than data on the proportion of taxation imposed on inhabitants over six feet in height." As a guide to policy, these studies are inadequate. Bird (1978, p. 40) observes "that a great deal...of variations in national tax ratios are statistically associated with the shares of agriculture, mining..." though interesting, add little to our knowledge of evaluating fiscal performance.

An inherent problem of studies on LDCs, is a lack of consensus about the meaning of economic development and how it is measured. A large number of these studies use proxies such as the share of total output in agriculture or manufacturing to indicate that a country has passed certain thresholds in its development process. By using per capita income or similar proxies as indices of development, these studies, inadvertently, treat economic growth and economic development synonymously. Flammang (1979, p. 47) observes that though these two concepts are related, they are "two different...processes which are both counterparts and competitors...and the distinction is important from both theoretical and policy-making standpoint."

One needs to go beyond the facade of terminology to determine the implication of, say, per capita income for employment opportunities, demunition of poverty, improved health, etc. Since per capita income does not tell us much about development, we need a concept expressed "in terms of the reduction or elimination of poverty, inequality, and unemployment within the context of a growing economy"[4] (Todaro, 1985, p.84). Though economic growth is necessary for economic development, growth by itself is not sufficient. Morris (1977), recognizing the inadequacy of per capita income as a development index, has constructed the Physical Quality of Life Index. This index "does not measure all 'development' nor does it measure freedom, justice, security, or other intangible goods. It does... attempt to measure how well societies satisfy certain specific life-saving social characteristics"[5] (p. 4).

A second problem of empirical studies of tax structure change is the implied assumption that a higher tax ratio indicates more development. Please (1967) points out that the record of many LDCs in channelling more of "domestic resources into economic development" is depressing. Drawing from the experience of India, Sri Lanka, and Peru, Please observes that increases in tax efforts in these countries were matched, more or less, by persistent decline in saving. Please finds tax effort prescription relevant if "the government can prevent its expenditure from rising as fast as its income" (p. 27). As a guide to policy, tax effort prescription must be cognizant of possible adverse effects of a high tax rate on investment, production, and work effort.

A third problem, common in many empirical studies of tax structure change, is their failure to establish causality between taxable capacity and government's share of GDP. The public sector share of GDP may be relatively high even in the absence of a corresponding change in taxable capacity. It is not too uncommon for governments to resort to deficit spending. Additionally, Bird (1978, p. 43) observes that "The successful measurement of taxable capacity used in these studies depended critically on the *a priori* justification of the explanatory variables as affecting only taxable capacity and not at all either demands for higher public expenditures or willingness to tax."

A final problem is that taxable capacity and tax efforts are not the same thing. If tax effort is measured by the actual tax collection, we need to recognize the inadequacy of fiscal machinery in LDCs. Unskilled tax agents, rudimentary methods of record keeping, and wholesale tax evasion (because of tax "loopholes") retard tax collection efforts. Further, the exercise of political power may undermine tax efforts. Thus without requisite changes in the social, economic, and political institutions of LDCs, the adoption of modern tax systems (e.g. corporate income taxes or personal income taxes) may lead to wholesale evasion of these taxes.[6]

In sum, the empirical studies of tax changes do not tell us whether tax ratio increases are attributed to: a) efficiency in tax collection; b) changes in tax rates; c) the development of new taxes; d) increased tax base, or e) inflation. Prest (1978, p. 15) aptly summarizes the inference to be drawn from these empirical studies:[7]

> ...The ratio of taxation to GNP is some sort of national virility symbol, and that they should try to emulate the ratios of developed countries, or, or at any rate, that those developing countries occupying low positions

in their own league table should try to mend their ways and increase their ratios, so that they are closer to those of the leaders.

ENDNOTES

1. An ealier version of this chapter was published in the *Bulletin for International Fiscal Documentation* 44 (March, 1990). We extend our thanks to S.M.C. Lyons, the editor of the *Bulletin*, for his permission to use this source.

2. It is important to note that higher tax revenue does not always cause higher government expenditures. Hoover and Sheffrin (1992) have found that taxes appear to cause spending before the mid-1960's while after that time taxes and spending are found to be casually independent.

3. Khan (1988) using time series data for two and a half decades for Pakistan concludes that a direct relationship between fiscal dependence on trade taxes and economic development exists in a dynamic setting. This is both the case for aggregated and disaggregated levels

4. Todaro correctly contends that economic development is "a multi-dimensional process involving major changes in social structures... as well as acceleration of economic growth, the reduction of inequality, and the eradication of absolute poverty" (Todaro, 1985: p. 85). See Sen (1983: pp. 753-54) for a clear discussion of some thematic deficiencies of traditional development economics.

5. Even in a highly industrialized and monetized economy, GNP is not an accurate measure of total welfare. Many productive activities are excluded and many intangibles such as justice, freedom, leisure, etc. are not allowed for in GNP calculations. Since GNP is an index of production and not consumption and, assuming that the ultimate goal of economic activity is consumption, hypotheses using GNP per capita as the sole index of development should be amended.

6. None of the existing empirical studies have explicitly included political and social factors in their analyses. Studies of tax structure change should emphasize the role of politics and social factors in shaping the tax structure of a country.

7. It is the view of the authors that research in this area is incomplete and scarce and there is much room for new development in this field.

REFERENCES

Abizadeh, S., (1979), "Tax Ratio and the Degree of Economic Development." *Malayan Economic Review* 24:21-34.

Abizadeh S. and M. Yousefi, (1985), "International Trade Taxes and Economic Development: An Empirical Analysis," *International Review of Economics and Business* 32:736-749.

Andic, S., (1973), "Tax Problems of Developing Countries," *Finanzarchiv* 32:155-159.

Bird, R.M., (1978), "Assessing Tax Performance in Developing Countries," in J.F.J. Toye, Ed. *Taxation and Economic Development*, London: Cass.

Chelliah, R.J., (1971), "Trends in Taxation in Developing Countries," *IMF Staff Papers* 18:254-331.

_____ Bass, J.J.1 and M.R. Kelly, (1975), "Tax Ratios and Tax Effort in Developing Countries, 1969-71, *IMF Staff Papers* 22:187-205.

Due, J.F. and C., Meyer, (1989), "Major Determinants of tax Structures of Market Economy Countries," *Tanzania Journal of Economics*, 1:47-65.

Flammang, R.A., (1979), "Economic Growth and Economic Development: Counterparts or Competitors," *Economic Development and Cultural Change* 17:47-61.

Hinrichs, H.H., (1965), "Determinants of Governments Revenue Shares Among Less Developed Countries," *Economic Journal* 75:546-556.

_____ (1966), *A General Theory of Tax Structure Change During Economic Development*. Cambridge, MA: Harvard Law School.

Hoover, K.D. and S.M. Sheffrin, (1992), "Causation, Spending and Taxes: Sand in the Sand Box or Tax Collector for the Welfare State," *American Economic Review*, 82:225-248.

Khan, A.H., (1988), "Fiscal Dependence on Trade, Taxes and Economic Development: A Case Study of Pakistan," *Public Finance*, 43:96-112.

Lotz, J.R. and E.R. Morss, (1970), "A Theory of Tax Level Determinants for Developing Countries," *Economic Development and Cultural Change* 18:328-41.

Mann, A.J., (1980), "Economic Development and Tax Structure Change: Mexico, 1895-1975," *Public Finance Quarterly* 18:291-306.

Martin, A.M. and W.A. Lewis, (1956), "Patterns of Public Revenue and Expenditure," *Manchester School of Economics and Social Studies* 24:203-244.

Mirowski, P. and A.R. Schwartz, (1982-83), "The Falling Share of Corporate Taxation," *Journal of Post Keynesian Economics*, 5:245-256.

Morris, M.D., (1977), *Measuring the Conditions of the World's Poor*. New York, N.Y.: Pergamon Press.

Musgrave, R.A., (1969), *Fiscal Systems*. New Haven, CT: Yale University Press.

Oshima, H.T., (1957), "The Share of Government in Gross National Product for Various Countries," *American Economic Review* 47:381-90.

Please, S., (1967), "Saving Through Taxation--Reality or Mirage?" *Finance and Development* 4:24-32.

Prest, A.R., (1978), "Tax Effort in Developing Countries: What do Regression Measures Really Measure?" in J.F.J. Toye, Ed. *Taxation and Economic Development*, London: Cass.

Sen, A., (1983), "Development: Which Way Now?" *The Economic Journal* 93:745-762.

Shoup, C., (1972), "Quantitative Research in Taxation and Government Expenditure," in *Public Expenditures and Taxation*. New York, N.Y.: National Bureau of Economic Research.

Tanzi, V., (1973), "The Theory of Tax Structure Change During Economic Development: A Critical Survey," *Rivista de Diritto Finanziano e Scienza delle Finanze* 32:199-208.

Tanzi, V., (1983), "Quantitative Characteristics of the Tax Systems of Developing Countries," *International Monetary Fund Document*.

Thorn, R.S., (1967), "The Evolution of Public Finance During Economic Development," *Manchester School of Economic and Social Studies* 35:19-51.

Todaro, M.P., (1985), *Economic Development in the Third World*. N.Y.: Longman.

CHAPTER THREE

THE PUBLIC SECTOR ECONOMICS OF JAPAN

Donald G. Cummings

I. INTRODUCTION

The purpose of this chapter is to discuss the public sector economics of Japan. Section I briefly examines the economic performance of Japan since World War II and possible causes of the rapid growth it has experienced. Growth of the public sector relative to GDP is outlined in Section II. The structure of the Japanese government, the national budget, and the budget making process are described in Section III. Trends in aggregate national and local tax revenues and the major taxes are discussed in Section IV. This is followed in Section V with an examination of aggregate public expenditures and major expenditure programs. Section VI analyzes budget deficits and the national debt. Budgetary policy of the central government during the high growth era of 1950 and 1973 is examined in Section VII. Finally, Section VIII discusses Japanese budgetary policy since 1973.

II. THE ECONOMIC PERFORMANCE OF JAPAN SINCE WORLD WAR II

The period 1950 to 1973 is known as the high economic growth era in Japan (See Lincoln and Kosai, 1986). From 1960 to 1969 the average annual real GNP growth rate was 12 percent. In comparison, the U.S. growth rate averaged 4 percent during this period. While Japan's growth rate slowed from 1970 to 1973, it still averaged 7.5 percent, compared with 3.2 percent for the United States (Lincoln, 1988, p.3). Since 1973 Japan's growth rate has slowed even more (3.8 percent from 1974 to 1985), but it still has managed to outperform the major industrial countries of the world.

How was Japan able to achieve this phenomenal growth? In land area Japan is slightly smaller than California, but larger than Italy and half again as large as the United Kingdom. Four-fifths of the terrain is rugged and mountainous with only 13 percent arable land. Japan has a great variety of climatic conditions since the four main islands (Hokkaido, Honshu, Shikoku, Kyushu) have the same range of latitudes as Maine to the Gulf of Mexico on the East Coast of the United States (Reischauer, 1977, p. 11-13). The population of approximately 124 million is concentrated on the seacoasts and is roughly one-half that of the United States, but twice that of countries such as the United Kingdom, Italy, and France. Japan has the highest population density per square mile of habitable land than any country in the world, with the exception of city states such as Hong Kong and Singapore. Of the over 60 million person labor force, 8 percent is engaged in agriculture, forestry, and fishing. Japan has little in the way of natural resources and imports most of the coal, oil, iron ore, and other natural resources it uses.

The economic performance of Japan is all the more impressive when one considers the state of its economy immediately after World War II: Two to three million Japanese lost their lives, 40 percent of Japan's capital stock was destroyed, 50 percent of the labor force was unemployed, one-half of those employed were in agriculture, industrial production was less than one-tenth of 1930 production, the yen was almost worthless, and there were shortages of consumer goods, food, and housing. In addition, there was a collapse of morale since the Japanese people had lived through eight years of military dictatorship and war. The economic recovery was slow at the beginning. It took a decade for per capita production to reach the mid-1930s level.

Many reasons have been given for Japan's phenomenal growth that began in the 1950s. Denison and Chung (1976) stress the role of the factors of production (pp. 101-138). They contend that the growth of the capital stock, the absorption and adaptation of foreign technology, and the excess labor in agriculture that moved into manufacturing and heavy industry stimulated investment and increased productivity. Also, high private sector savings fed strong investment demand. In addition, there were gains from economies of scale since much of the new investment went into larger scale production. Furthermore, Denison and Chung emphasize the

importance of the economic and political heritage of Japan that was based
on a private market economy and a stable political system (pp. 101-138).

Edward J. Lincoln (1988), in his book *Japan: Facing Economic Maturity*,
cites several economic and noneconomic factors to explain Japan's rapid
economic growth (pp. 15-21). He contends that the destruction of the war
led to a strong social commitment by the Japanese people to economic
growth as a national goal. Japan's tradition of hard work, support of education, loyalty to the group, and a homogeneous society led to the willingness of the Japanese people to forego leisure, consumption, and social
amenities for the national goal of economic growth. In addition, postwar
occupation by the U.S. provided impetus for growth by the promotion of
land reform, legalization of labor unions, dissolution of business conglomerates, establishment of antitrust laws, and the provision of a defense
umbrella. Lincoln further maintains that in the postwar period Japan
benefitted from a favorable world environment that featured trade liberalization, worldwide economic growth, and stable raw materials prices;
all of which enabled Japan to increase its exports. Lincoln concludes, "As
a result of these years of growth, by the early 70s Japan was transformed
from a impoverished, war-devastated nation into a prosperous, industrialized country" (p. 21).

What role did the government play in Japan's economic success?
While numerous studies have examined the significance of central planning and industrial policy in the promotion of Japan's economic growth,
the purpose here is to focus on the national government's budgetary policy during the period of high economic growth and its aftermath.

III. Growth of the Government Sector

There was a significant increase in the relative size of the government sector in the industrialized countries after World War II, as measured by the
ratio of government expenditures to gross domestic product (GDP). Table
1 shows expenditure/GDP ratios for OECD countries from 1960 to 1989.
The average expenditures/GDP ratio for OECD countries increased from
29.4 percent during the 1960-67 period to 40.7 percent during the 1980-89
period.

Japan has experienced a dramatic increase in the expenditure/GDP
ratio since 1970. While the ratio remained below 20 percent during the 60s
and was only slightly above 20 percent by the mid-70s, it increased to 28.4
percent during 1974-79, and by 1989 the ratio was over 33 percent. Never-

theless, the size of Japan's public sector, as measured by this ratio, is still smaller than that of most OECD countries. Table 1 indicates that the expenditure/GDP ratio during the 1980-89 period averaged 36 percent for the U.S. and 33 percent for Japan. It has been argued that Japan's small public sector relative to other industrialized nations results from a lag between the introduction of an expanded social security system in the 70s and the actual increase in outlays. As the system matures and the aging of the population accelerates, it is predicted that the size of the Japanese government will catch-up with many OECD countries (Noguchi, 1987, p. 191).

Table 1 Total Government Expenditures, Japan and Other Countries, Selected Years, FY 1960-1989 (Percent of GDP)

Country	Total Government Expenditures			
	1960-67	1968-73	1974-79	1980-89
Japan	18.7%	20.5%	28.4%	33.2%
United States	28.3	31.1	32.6	36.0
Germany	35.7	39.8	47.5	47.6
France	37.4	38.9	43.3	50.3
United Kingdom	34.7	39.5	44.4	44.9
Italy	31.9	36.0	42.9	48.7
Canada	29.3	34.7	39.2	45.0
Average of above	**29.7**	**32.3**	**36.3**	**39.9**
Austria	37.6%	40.2%	46.7%	51.0%
Denmark	29.1	40.1	49.1	58.9
Netherlands	37.8	44.8	52.8	59.6
Sweden	34.8	44.3	54.4	62.8
Total EEC	**33.9**	**37.1**	**43.1**	**48.1**
Total OECD (Europe)	**33.1**	**36.5**	**43.1**	**48.0**
Total OECD (-USA)	**30.3**	**32.9**	**39.4**	**44.2**
Total OECD	**29.4**	**32.1**	**36.6**	**40.7**

Source: OECD. *Economic Outlook: Historical Statistics, 1960-1989*, p. 68.

IV. THE STRUCTURE OF GOVERNMENT AND THE BUDGET SYSTEM

A. THE GOVERNMENT SYSTEM

Japan's system of government is based on the Constitution of 1946. The Constitution transferred sovereign power from the Emperor to the people and provided that the Diet shall be the legislative branch of government. The government is based on a parliamentary system. The Prime Minister is selected from the Diet by its members. The Cabinet consists of the Prime Minister and 20 Ministers of State appointed by the Prime Minister. A Cabinet Minister heads one of the 12 Ministries (Justice, Foreign Affairs, Finance, Education, Health and Welfare, Agriculture, International Trade and Industry, Transportation, Post and Telecommunications, Labor, Construction, and Home Affairs), or one of the agencies under the Prime Minister's Office.

If there is a vote of non-confidence by the House of Representatives the Prime Minister and his Cabinet may resign at once, or the Prime Minister may dissolve the House of Representatives and call for a national election, in which case the Prime Minister and the Cabinet must resign as soon as a new house is elected.

The Diet (Legislature) is the highest level of government power and the only law-making body. It consists of two houses, the House of Representatives (512 seats) and the House of Councillors (252 seats). Members of the House of Representatives are elected for a four year term. Members of the House of Councillors are elected for a six-year term, with one-half elected every three years. One hundred of the members of the House of Councillors are elected by party proportional representation, while the remainder are elected by prefectional constituencies. Japan is divided into 47 local administrative districts or prefectures. Within these prefectures are cities, towns and villages, considered as local government entities. Members of the House of Representatives are elected by 130 constituencies which are multi-member constituencies of two to six members, depending on the size of the population. The voting age is 20 years and above. Each of the two Houses of the Diet establishes standing and special committees, with each Diet member assigned to at least one committee. A bill is enacted into law when approved by both Houses of the Diet. However, in the case of the budget, the approval of treaties, and when the decision of the two Houses differ the vote of the House of Representatives prevails.

The judiciary system is independent of the executive and legislative branches. The system consists of the Supreme Court, eight high courts, a district court in each of the prefectures (except Hokkaido which has four), and a number of summary courts. Also, there are many family courts that deal with domestic complaints. The Supreme Court is composed of a Chief Justice and 14 other Justices. The Chief Justice is appointed by the Emperor after designation by the Cabinet, while the other 14 Justices are appointed by the Cabinet. Lower court judges are appointed by the Cabinet from a list of persons nominated by the Supreme Court. There are no local government courts, and judges (not juries) are the decision makers. The appointment of Supreme Court Justices is subject to review in a national referendum, first at the time of the general election following their appointment, and then at a general election after the lapse of 10-year periods. They may be impeached by the Court of Impeachment which consists of members of both Houses.

B. THE BUDGET SYSTEM

The Japanese national government has three types of budgets: a general account budget, special account budgets, and government agency budgets. When the term "government budget" is used in Japan it usually refers to the general account budget. (See Tables 4 and 5 for FY 1986-90 general account budgets.) Similarly, when the term "budget deficit" is used it refers to the excess of expenditures over receipts in the general account budget.

Special accounts are established for specific projects such as highway and airport construction, or they may be established for programs with specific revenues such as the social security account. In addition to receiving funds from tax revenues (either directly or as transfers from the General account), special accounts acquire funds from interest on loans, the sale of bonds, enterprise receipts, and other sources (Campbell, 1977, p. 207). In 1991 there were 38 special accounts. These budgets are reviewed by the Ministry of Finance and passed by the Diet, but some argue that once these accounts are established they are scrutinized less rigorously than the General Account and funds are easier to obtain (pp. 207-08).

Finally, there are numerous government-affiliated agencies and special corporations financed by the national government. Nine of these accounts are finance corporations and two are special banks (the Export-

Import Bank and the Japan Development Bank). The privatization in 1987-89 of Japan National Railways and Nippon Telephone and Telegram significantly reduced the size of these accounts from over 22 billion yen in 1981 to 5-6 billion yen in 1988, or approximately 10 percent of the size of the general account budget (Ito, 1992, p. 146).

In addition to the above budgets, there is the Fiscal Investment and Loan Program (FILP), referred to as the "second" or "other" budget. It is not financed through taxes, but rather its funds come from postal savings and insurance funds, governmental pension and other trust funds (including social security), and bond issues. Most post offices in Japan accept savings deposits from individuals and offer demand deposits, time deposits, savings certificates, and annuity/insurance policies. In 1988, the household sector held approximately 20 percent of its financial wealth in post office deposits and insurance policies, although this percentage is decreasing as liberalization of financial markets continues in Japan (Ito, 1992, p. 163). Some of the funds deposited in post offices are transferred by the Ministry of Post and Communications to the special FILP account in the Ministry of Finance (MOF). From this account, money is distributed as loans and capital funds to government agencies, or it is used to finance projects managed in special accounts. Specifically, loans are made to government corporations and special accounts and then these funds are given out as subsidized loans to finance government, household, and business projects (p. 164). As shown in Table 2, in FY 1990 the FILP had funds of 36,274 billion yen, as compared to 66, 273 billion yen in the general account budget (See Table 4). Most of the funds in FILP (34,220 billion yen) came from postal savings and welfare/national pension funds. Major disbursements from FILP involved housing (30 percent), small business (16 percent), improvement of living environment (15 percent), roads (10 percent), transportation and communications (8 percent), and trade and economic cooperation (6 percent). Recent emphasis has been placed on housing and infrastructure improvements, import promotion, and the recycling of funds through the Export-Import Bank of Japan (*Japan Economic Almanac*, 1990, p. 22). The role of FILP has been controversial. Some argue that it is merely a financial intermediary, others contend it disguises government debt, and still others think it has been used by government to facilitate the targeting of certain industries for accelerated development(p. 165). In his book, *Contemporary Japanese Budget Policies*, John C. Campbell (1981) suggests that the Ministry of Finance may use FILP and special accounts to circumvent the general account budget:

The Budget Bureau tends to regard the FILP, along with Special Accounts and government corporations, as another means for satisfying ministry or party demands without expending ordinary budget funds. In some cases, direct provision of investment funds is sufficient; in others, an organization may be granted FILP funds at no or low interest, which it is then allowed to lend at higher interest rates and apply the "profits" to running expenses. Such devices are rather common in times of fiscal stringency, particularly when political pressures during revival negotiations become more intense than expected, and the MOF is hard pressed to protect its announced General Account total (pp. 210-211).

C. THE BUDGET-MAKING PROCESS

The fiscal year in Japan runs from April 1 to March 31, whereas in the U.S. it begins October 1 and ends September 30. The Ministry of Finance (MOF) and its Budget Bureau are legally responsible to the Cabinet for preparing the annual budget. The formal beginning of the budget making process begins in July with the finance minister's budget call to the various government ministries and agencies, at which time deadlines for requests are announced. Budget requests are then submitted by the ministries and agencies to the MOF in late August, after they secure general agreement from the ruling party (Campbell, 1977, p. 43). The MOF Budget Bureau and the ministries negotiate a budget plan during the Fall. In addition, the party in power, draws up and submits its budget program to the Cabinet and the MOF. In mid-December the MOF releases its draft budget. This begins a week of what is referred to as "revival negotiations", during which time ministries appeal to MOF officials. The party in power also submits revival requests during Cabinet-level negotiations between top officials of the party and government (pp. 10-11). The resulting budget, known as the government draft budget, is ratified by the Cabinet (usually in late January or early February) and is sent to the Diet for passage around April 1. If the budget is not passed by the end of the fiscal year, a Provisional Budget must be enacted. The total amount of the budget is usually not changed by the Diet after it is approved by the Cabinet (Ito, 1992, p. 149).

During the fiscal year the budget may be revised by "Supplementary Budgets" to reflect economic and other changes not anticipated in the original budget. For example, these supplements have been used to increase spending on public works in order to stimulate the economy during periods of economic slowdown. Furthermore, they have been used

Table 2

TREASURY INVESTMENT AND LOANS PROGRAMS FOR FY1986-90
(in billions of yen)

Fund resources	FY90	FY89	FY88	FY87	FY86
Industrial Investment Special Account	53.4	85.2	91.2	144.3	61.5
Trust Fund Bureau Fund	34,220.6	26,871.3	26,206.6	24,595.8	20,738.6
Postal savings		8,500.0	7,900.0	7,900.0	7,000.0
Welfare & national pensions		4,3ː0.0	3,500.0	4,450.0	4,300.0
Post-office life Insurance		5,6ː4.0	4,409.4	3,941.2	3,145.0
Government-guaranteed bond and borrowing	2,000.0	2,000.0	2,406.8	2,400.0	3,210.0
Total	36,274.0	34,570.5	33,114.0	31,081.3	27,155.1

Table 2 (continued)

By disbursement

Housing	8,115.8	7,460.0	6,921.5	6,328.2	5,856.2
Improvement of living environment	4,196.5	4,371.3	4,450.9	3,998.7	3,694.5
Welfare	773.5	736.0	661.8	627.7	625.9
Education	615.9	520.2	637.6	784.1	678.2
Small Businesses	4,324.8	4,176.4	4,030.6	3,985.6	3,700.0
Agriculture, forestry and fisheries	860.8	924.4	979.4	907.8	902.1
(Sub total)	18,887.3	18,188.9	17,681.8	16,632.1	15,456.9
Disaster reconstruction	360.0	357.9	409.8	493.0	5422.7
Roads	2,687.9	2,576.8	2,512.1	2,363.0	2,024.4
Transportation and communications	2,285.0	2,361.6	2,229.9	2,264.1	2,015.1
Local Development	679.5	676.6	652.2	657.7	566.1
(Sub total)	6,012.4	5,972.9	5,804.0	5,777.6	5,028.3
Industry and technology	741.3	758.7	687.2	630.9	635.9
Trade and economic cooperation	1,603.0	1,420.0	1,171.0	690.5	1,034.0
Total	27,224.0	26,340.5	25,344.0	23,731.3	22,155.1

Source : Japan Economic Almanac 1990, p. 279.

to increase salaries of government employees, agricultural subsidies, transfers to local governments, and to provide disaster relief from earthquakes and typhoons. In past periods of high economic growth the source of revenue for Supplementary Budgets was the so-called "natural surplus". This "surplus" was defined as the difference between revenues forecast in the budget and actual revenues collected. Tax collections often exceeded projections because of underestimation of economic growth. Since supplemental budgets were frequently procyclical (increasing in boom years and decreasing in slowdown years) and reduced discretionary control over expenditures, the MOF in the late 1960s attempted to reduce the use of these budgets by the inclusion of many supplemental items into the initial budget (Campbell, 1977, pp. 201-207). Nevertheless, supplemental budgets continue to be used in Japan.

Table 3 Growth of National and Local Taxes as a Percent of National Income, Japan FY 1955-90

Fiscal Year	National Income (billion yen) (A)	Total amount of taxes (billion yen)			Tax/National Income Ratio		
		Total (B)	National Tax (C)	Local Tax (D)	Total (B/A)	National Tax (C/A)	Local Tax (D/A)
1955	7299	1318	936	382	18.1	12.8	5.2
1960	13269	2545	1801	744	19.2	13.6	5.6
1965	26380	4828	3279	1549	18.0	12.2	5.9
1970	61030	11524	7773	3751	18.9	12.7	6.1
1975	123991	22659	14504	8155	18.3	11.7	6.6
1980	199335	44263	28369	15894	22.2	14.2	8.0
1985	254395	62467	39150	23317	24.6	15.4	9.2
1987	273248	75011	47807	27204	27.5	17.5	10.0
1988	291942	82311	52194	30117	28.2	17.9	10.3
1989[1]	310300	87868	56503	31365	28.3	18.2	10.1
1990[1]	326900	92510	60820	31690	28.3	18.6	9.7

[1] Estimated
Source: *Japan Statistical Yearbook 1990*, p. 452;
Original Source: *Budget Bureau and Tax Bureau, Ministry of Finance.*

V. THE TAX SYSTEM

Table 3 shows the growth of national and local taxes as a percentage of
Japan's national income. Local taxes include revenues collected at the prefectural, city, town, and village levels. From 1955 to 1975 combined national and local taxes as a percentage of national income remained stable
at 18 percent. During the same period both national and local taxes as a
percentage of national income remained relatively stable at 12 and 6 percent respectively. From 1975 to 1988 the combined tax to national income
ratio steadily increased from 18 percent to over 28 percent. The national
tax to national income ratio increased from 12 percent to over 18 percent,
and the local tax to national income ratio increased from 6 percent to
roughly 10 percent.

The personal income tax and the corporate tax are the major sources
of tax revenue for the Japanese central government. In 1988 the personal
income tax was 34.4 percent of total central government tax revenues, and
the corporate tax was 35.3 percent of revenues, up from 31.2 and 33 percent respectively in 1970 (Japan Statistical Yearbook, 1990, p. 45). For
comparison, in the U.S. the personal income tax was 44.9 percent and the
corporate tax was 10.4 percent of federal revenues in 1989 (Ito, 1992, p.
151). Other sources of national revenue in Japan in 1988 included an inheritance tax (3.5 percent of tax revenues), a liquor tax (4.2 percent), a tobacco excise tax (1.9 percent), a gasoline tax (2.6 percent), a securities
transactions tax (4 percent), and stamp duties (3.7 percent). The commodity tax on luxury items, 3.9 percent of revenues in 1988, was replaced with
a consumption tax in April 1989 (Japan Statistical Yearbook, 1990, p. 452).
The value-added type consumption tax is expected to bring in more than
double the revenues of the old commodity tax. The major taxes in Japan
are discussed below.

A. THE INDIVIDUAL INCOME TAX

All three levels of Japanese government (national, prefectural, and municipal) tax the income of individuals. As of April 1990 the national individual income tax rate system had five brackets with the lowest taxed at
10 percent and the highest at 50 percent. In contrast, the U.S. had three
brackets with the rate varying from 15 percent to 31 percent. Individual
income taxes are collected through a national withholding system. Wages,
salaries, bonuses, fees, interest, and dividends are subject to withholding

at the source of payment. Generally, if an individual's tax liabilities are met by the amount withheld, no tax return needs to be filed. However, if income exceeds 15 million yen, or if total employment income exceeds 200,000 yen, a tax return must be filed. Commonly, when a return is filed, it is filed at the national tax office and a separate return need not be filed with the prefectural or municipal tax offices (Handbook, 1991, pp. 57-58).

Capital gains on different types of assets are treated differently. Taxpayers with capital gains from stocks and convertible bonds may elect to either have 1 percent (0.5% for convertible bonds) of the sales value withheld at the time of sale, or pay a 26 percent income tax on net gains when their income tax return is filed. Capital gains from land and buildings held less than 5 years is considered as short-term and taxed as ordinary income. Gains from these assets held longer than 5 years is treated as long-term gains and a deduction of a minimum of 1 million yen is allowed on these gains. Capital gains from assets other than land, buildings, stocks, and convertible bonds that have been held longer than five years, are taxed on only one-half of the long term gains (Handbook, 1991, p. 71).

Personal deductions for the taxpayer, a spouse, and dependents are allowed, with increased amounts for the physically handicapped, the aged, widows, widowers, divorcees, and working students. For example, as of April 1990, the basic deduction for a dependent was 350,000 yen, but if the dependent was 70 or older and living with the taxpayer, the deduction increased to 550,000 yen, and to 850,000 yen if the aged dependent was also seriously handicapped (Handbook, 1991, p. 115). Retirement income, including lump sum retirement payments, is taxed separately from ordinary income. Taxable retirement income is computed as one-half of retirement income after deductions for each year of service. Deductions are based on length of service. For example, a 400,000 yen deduction for each year of service up to 20 years is allowed. For each year of service over 20 years a 700,000 yen deduction can be taken. Social insurance premiums paid by the taxpayer are fully deductible. Social insurance includes Japanese health insurance, welfare pension insurance, and employment insurance. Life insurance premiums and payments into individual pension plans are partially deductible (Handbook, p. 74).

In addition to the national income tax, individuals are subject to a inhabitant tax at both the prefectural and municipal levels. This tax has two parts, the per capita levy and the income levy. At the beginning of FY 1990 the per capita levy at the municipal level varied from 1500 to 3200 yen depending on population level, while at the prefectural level the per capita levy was a uniform 700 yen. The income levy varied from 3-11% at the municipal level, and from 2-4% at the prefectural level, depending on the taxable income level. The calculation of taxable income is similar to that used for the national tax, except deductions and tax credits are different. Usually, salary earners pay the inhabitant tax through the monthly withholding system.

Finally, an enterprise tax is levied at the prefectural level on the business income of the individual. A standard deduction of 2.3 million yen is allowed. Depending on the type of business or profession, tax rates vary from 3 to 5 percent (Handbook, 1991, p. 75).

B. THE CORPORATE INCOME TAX

Corporate income is also subject to a national tax, an enterprise tax, and an inhabitant tax. The sum of these tax rates on taxable corporate income (April 1990) was approximately 52 percent for large corporations (Handbook, 1991, p. 61). The comparable rate for the U.S. was approximately 40 percent (Ito, 1992, p. 156). After adjusting for differences in rates of depreciation, expenses, investment tax credits, and other provisions it has been estimated that the real corporate tax burden was 50 percent in Japan and 31 percent in the United States (p. 156). The national corporate tax rate varies with level of capitalization and the amount of taxable income. As of April 1990, corporations with capitalization of less than 100 million yen are taxed at 28 percent on taxable income up to 8 million yen, and 37.5 percent on income over that amount. Businesses with income over 100 million yen capitalization are taxed at 37.5 percent of taxable income.

The enterprise tax on corporate income is levied by prefectures on all types of business conducted by corporations in the prefectures where the corporation has a place of business. Rates vary from 6-12 percent depending on the prefecture. The inhabitant tax on corporate income is assessed by both prefectures and municipalities. The tax is computed as a percentage of the national corporate income tax. In 1989, this rate varied from 17.3-20.7 percent. Also, assessment for a per capita tax, ranging from 50,000 to 3,750,000 yen based upon the company's capitalization and number of employees, is included in the inhabitant tax return (Handbook, 1991, pp. 60-61). Corporations are required to file tax returns with the national tax office and the prefectural and municipal tax offices where the corporations have places of business.

C. THE CONSUMPTION TAX

In April 1989 the commodity tax on luxury goods was replaced with a general consumption tax. The consumption tax used in Japan is similar in nature to the value-added tax used by countries in the European Community. In the case of goods, a 3 percent tax is levied on the difference between the sale price and cost at each stage of distribution from manufacturing to wholesale to retail. The tax paid to suppliers is credited against the tax charged on sales.

The consumption tax is highly controversial in Japan. Supporters of the tax contend that it will: (1) alleviate some inequities caused by loopholes in the income tax, (2) supply additional revenues to cover future increases in social security expenditures, (3) eliminate economic distortions caused by the old commodity tax on luxury goods, and (4) help eliminate national deficits. Critics of the tax express concern over the regressive nature of the tax and inequities created by certain provisions of the new tax. Food and clothing are not exempt from the consumption tax. Transactions that involve sale or lease of land, sale of securities, interest on loans, insurance premiums, and foreign exchange are exempt. Businesses with annual sales of less than 30 million yen are exempt. Companies with sales under 500 million yen may use a simplified formula based on a fixed percentage of sales (20% for retailers and 10% for wholesalers) to calculate their value-added, thereby reducing bookkeeping costs. Recently, proposals have been introduced to exempt from the value-added tax not only food and clothing, but also rents, textbooks, baby deliveries, and funerals. Also, many would like to eliminate the favorable treatment of some companies. The projected revenue from the consumption tax for fiscal year 1989 was 3.6 trillion yen (6% of total tax revenue of 56.5 trillion yen), and for fiscal year 1990, 5.3 trillion yen (8.9% of total tax revenue of 60.8 trillion yen). (Japan Statistical Yearbook, 1990, p. 452).

D. OTHER TAXES

In Japan, the inheritance tax, instead of being imposed directly on the descendants estate as is the case in the United States, is imposed on the value of property beneficiaries acquire by the inheritance (Handbook, 1991, pp. 75-76). The tax paid by each beneficiary is calculated by first determining the total value of the estate, then the aggregate tax, and finally each beneficiary's share of the tax. A progressive rate schedule is applied to the taxable value of the property. The result is that the greater the number of heirs the lower the total estate tax. The taxable value of property in the estate is generally based on 30-50 percent of the market value (Ito, 1992, p. 158). This low assessment ratio stems from the high price of land in Japan. The Diet in 1991 enacted a national land tax to curb high land prices. The new tax was set at an annual 0.2 percent of the assessed value of land beginning January 1992, and will be raised to 0.3 percent in 1993. The tax is to be reviewed after three years.

The aggregate inheritance tax is the sum of each beneficiary's tax. Japanese law requires that the calculation of each heir's tax share be based on the statutorily determined distributive share of each heir, and not the actual distribution (p. 76). For example, under the concept of "statutory heir", half of an estate goes to the spouse and each child receives an equal share of the remainder. If the spouse is deceased, each child divides the estate in equal shares. The law in Japan guarantees a spouse and the children a minimum of 50 percent of their "statutory share", regardless of how the will specifies the distribution (Ito, 1992, p. 159).

A securities transaction tax is levied on the transfer of securities at rates of 0.01% to 0.3% of the sale price, depending on the nature of the transaction and the type of securities. The stamp tax ranges from 200-600,000 yen based on the type of documents and the amount involved. The stamp tax law specifies the documents that require stamps (Handbook, 1991, p. 54).

Finally, regarding regional and local governments, the Japanese prefectural governments rely on inhabitant and enterprise taxes (described above) for revenue. Municipal governments raise most of their revenue from a local inhabitants tax and a property tax. Japanese local government's are less fiscally independent than those in the United States. While the Local Tax Law is administered by local government authorities, the law is enacted by the Diet and is under the supervision of the Ministry of Finance. For example, taxes on property are assessed at the prefectural and municipal levels, but tax rates on property (1.4% on fixed assets and land-holding as of April 1990) are set by the central government and are uniform throughout Japan (p. 54).

VI. EXPENDITURES IN THE GENERAL ACCOUNT BUDGET

Table 4 displays the general account draft budgets for fiscal years 1986-90, and Table 5 provides a breakdown of FY 1990 general account expenditures. Total general account budget expenditures in FY 1990 were 66,273.6 trillion yen. For the year 1990 the three major items of expenditures were tax grants to finance local governments (23 percent), debt servicing (21.6 percent), and social security (17.5 percent). Other major areas of expenditures were public works (9.4 percent), education (7.6 percent), and defense (6.2 percent). In comparison, major U.S. federal government expenditures in FY 1990 included defense (23.9 percent of total expenditures), social security (19.9 percent), debt servicing (14.7 percent), and grants in aid (10.5 percent). Total budget expenditures were 1.8 trillion dollars (*Economic Report of the President*, 1992).

Some of the major expenditure programs included in the Japanese general account budget are discussed below.

Table 4 General Account Budget For FY1990
(Draft budget; in billions of yen)

	FY1990	FY1989	FY1988	FY1987	FY1986
Revenues					
Taxes and stamps	58,004.0	51,010.0	45,090.0	41,194.0	40,560.0
Bonds	5,630.0	7,111.0	8,841.0	10,501.0	10,946.0
NTT proceeds	1,300.0	1,300.0	1,300.0	-	-
Other revenues	1,339.6	993.2	1,468.7	2,406.0	2,582.6
Total	**66,273.6**	**60,414.2**	**56,699.7**	**54,101.0**	**54,088.6**
Expenditures					
Social Security	11,614.8	10,894.7	10,384.5	10,089.6	9,834.6
Education,science promotion	5,112.9	4,937.0	4,858.1	4,849.7	4,844.5
Debt servicing	14,289.3	11,664.8	11,512.0	11,333.5	11,319.5
Pensions	1,837.5	1,855.7	1,879.9	1,895.6	1,850.1
Finance for local autonomous bodies	15,275.1	13,368.8	10,905.6	10,184.1	10,185.0
Defense	4,159.3	3,919.8	3,700.3	3,517.4	3,343.5
Public works	6,214.7	6,197.4	6,082.4	6,082.4	6,223.3
Economic cooperation	784.5	727.7	682.2	649.2	623.2
Promotion for smaller businesses	194.3	194.2	195.2	197.3	205.2
Energy measures	547.6	527.4	461.6	495.2	629.7
Food control	395.2	418.2	448.2	540.6	596.2
Public works financed by NTT proceeds	1,300.0	1,300.0	1,300.0		
Others	4,198.3	4,058.1	3,939.8	3,916.3	4,083.7
Reserves	350.0	350.0	350.0	350.0	350.0
Total	**66,273.6**	**60,414.2**	**56,699.7**	**54,101.0**	**54,088.6**

Breakdown(%)					
Social security	17.5	18.0	18.3	18.6	18.2
Education, science		8.2	8.6	9.0	9.0
promotion	7.6				
Debt servicing	21.6	19.3	20.3	20.9	20.9
Pensions	2.7	3.1	3.3	3.5	3.4
Finance for local autonomous bodies	23.0	22.1	19.2	18.8	18.8
Defense	6.2	6.5	6.5	6.5	6.2
Public works	9.4	10.2	10.7	11.2	11.5
Economic cooperation	1.2	1.2	1.2	1.2	1.2
Promotion for smaller businesses	0.3	0.3	0.3	0.4	0.4
Energy measures	0.8	0.9	0.8	0.9	1.2
Food control special account	0.6	0.7	0.8	1.0	1.1

Source: *Japan Economic Almanac 1990*, p. 279.

Table 5 General Account Budget For FY1990
(Draft Budget; In Billions Of Yen)

	FY1990
Revenues	
Taxes and stamps	58,004,000
NTT proceeds	1,300,000
Other revenues	1,339,611
Bonds	5,630,000
Total	**66,273,611**
Expenditures	
Social Security	
Public assistance	1,108,748
Social welfare	2,405,588
Social insurance	7,194,692
Public health service	558,674
Measures for unemployed	347,116
Sub-total	11,614,818
Education, science promotion	
National government's share of compulsory education expenses	2,485,160
Transfer to the national schools' special account	1,199,785
Promotion of science and technology	475,460

Public school facilities	243,830
School education assistance	625,195
Scholarships on loan basis to students	83,440
Sub-total	5,112,870
Debt servicing	14,289,304
Pensions	
For civil servants	107,800
For veterans and war-bereaved families of soldiers	1,580,523
Administrative expenses for pension payments	8,011
Aid to war-bereaved families and families of the un-repatriated	141,173
Sub-total	1,837,507
Finance for local autonomous bodies	15,275,090
Defense	4,159,341
Public works	
Erosion and flood control	1,085,739
Road improvement	1,788,127
Improvement of harbors, fishing ports and airports	514,624
Promotion of housing construction	764,097
Improvement of environmental sanitation	957,397
Improvement of conditions for agricultural production	869,633
Forest roads, water for industrial use, etc.	157,766
Adjustment works	10,605
(Total)	6,147,988
Disaster reconstruction	66,271
Sub-total	6,214,709
Economic cooperation	784,480
Promotion for smaller businesses	194,349
Energy measures	547,590
Food control	395,225
Public works financed by NTT proceeds	1,300,000
Others	4,198,328
Reserves	350,000
Total	**66,273,611**

Source: *Japan Economic Almanac 1990*, p. 278.

A. LOCAL GOVERNMENT GRANTS

The high percentage of the budget allocated to local government grants reflects the central role that the national government plays in local government public finance. A fixed percentage of national tax revenues are earmarked for local tax grants, thus the amount paid out increases automatically as tax receipts increase. In the mid 1980s this percentage was set at 32 percent of the total of income tax, corporation tax, and liquor tax revenues (Noguchi, 1987, p. 201).

B. Social Security

The Japanese social security system is similar to many systems in other industrialized countries. The system consists of three major programs: social insurance, social welfare, and public assistance. (See Table 5.) Of these programs, social insurance, which consists of health insurance, public pensions, and unemployment compensation, is the largest.

The social insurance system is complex in that different employees may belong to different programs and each program may be administered and financed differently. In the case of the public pension program, employees of private firms belong to the Employee's Pension Fund, the self-employed to the People's Pension Fund, and government employees to the Cooperative Pension Fund. Most programs in the social insurance system, including the public pension program, are financed by both social insurance contributions from employers and employees held in a separate trust fund, and by government subsidies that appear in the general account budget. Approximately one-half of the receipts of the Employee's Pension Fund come from the government (Lincoln, 1988, p. 94). After large increases in the 1970s, benefits from the Japanese system are roughly comparable to those of the U.S. social security system (Campbell, 1981, p. 209).

C. Health Insurance

Virtually all Japanese are covered by some type of compulsory health insurance program. The programs vary as to how they are administered and financed, the group covered, and the level of benefits. National Health Insurance covers farmers, the self-employed, retired workers, and those without jobs. Participants make monthly payments to a local government office.

The central government operated Employee's Health Insurance covers most private salaried employees, and is financed by matching employer-employee contributions and some government financial support. Most firms with over 1000 employees have formed Health Insurance Societies within the Employee's Health Insurance system. In these programs it is common for the firm to pay a larger portion of the costs than the employee, and benefits are more extensive (Campbell, 1981, p. 208). Finally, Mutual Aid Associations are set up for various groups of government employees. In general, employees working for government and larger firms receive more extensive benefits and incur lower costs from the medical insurance program than do the self-employed and the employees of small firms (p. 208). It should be noted that while health care insurance is provided through a government system, the Japanese health care delivery system is provided by the private sector. Most Japanese doctors are in private practice and often run small hospitals and clinics.

D. PUBLIC WORKS

In the area of public works, expenditures were 9.4 percent of the FY 1990 general account budget, and averaged 10.5 percent of the budget over the period of 1985 to 1990. (See Tables 4 and 5.) However, the average annual rate of growth during this period was a negative 0.5 percent. It should be noted that the general account budget does not include all public works expenditures. Local governments, partially through revenues received from central government grants and the Fiscal Investment and Loan Program, allocate funds to public works.

Of those public works expenditures appearing in the FY 1990 general account budget, the major programs were road improvement (27 percent of the total public works expenditures), erosion and flood control (16 percent), improvement of environmental sanitation (15 percent), improvement of agricultural production (14 percent), promotion of housing construction (12 percent), and improvement of harbors, fishing ports and airports (8 percent). Japan pledged in the 1990 Structural Impediments Initiative with the U.S. to increase public works expenditures by 430 trillion yen over the next 10 years. Total national public works spending was projected to increase 2 trillion yen to a total of 27 trillion yen in FY 1992. Of this amount, half was expected to come from local governments. In FY 1991, local government total spending was 70 trillion yen, of which 13.3 trillion yen went into public works. Public works expenditures by local governments was projected to increase 11.5 percent in 1992. Of the 32 trillion yen Fiscal Investment and Loan Program FY 1991 budget, 5.2 trillion yen was earmarked for public works projects (*Far Eastern Economic Review*, Jan. 9, 1992, p. 38).

E. NATIONAL DEFENSE

The small portion (6 percent) of Japan's general account budget allocated to national defense continues to be a controversial subject both inside and outside Japanese borders. As a percentage of GDP, Japan's defense expenditures have remained stable at roughly one percent. In comparison, U.S. defense expenditures in FY 1990 were 23.9 percent of federal budget expenditures, and 5.4 percent of GDP (*Economic Report of the President*, 1992). Other major industrial countries spend 2 to 5 percent of GDP on national defense. In absolute terms, however, Japan's defense budget is the third largest in the world, after the U.S. and the former Soviet Union.

As part of the post-World War II demilitarization program, the U.S. Occupation required Japan to renounce war. Accordingly, Article 9 of the new Japanese Constitution stated, "The right of belligerency of the State will not be recognized." In light of the disintegration of the Soviet Union, Japan is in the process of redefining the role of its military forces (referred to in Japan as Self Defense Forces). The subject is extremely controversial within Japan. Some have taken the position that the mere existence of the Self Defense Forces and the Security Treaty with the United States contradicts Article 9. Others want to continue with a military build-up, but based on a revised strategy. Some would recognize the demise of the Soviet Union as a military threat, but would emphasize possible regional threats to Japan. Others, however, see the independent countries of the former Soviet Union and recent changes in Western Europe as possible future military threats to Japan. A recent defense program proposal would have cut the number of military personnel (148,413 in March 1991) by 30,000, but would have continued with current plans to increase military hardware expenditures. Local government jurisdictions with military installations were strongly opposed to such changes (*Far Eastern Economic Review*, Feb. 20, 1992, p. 11).

The U.S. and other countries have put pressure on Japan to increase its share of the defense burden. In response to a U.S. request in 1990 for Japan to pay a greater share of the cost of maintaining U.S. forces in Japan, the Japanese Government increased its share of the wage bill for Japanese nationals working at U.S. bases. In addition, Japan contributed over $11 billion, partially funded from a temporary corporate tax, to the multinational Gulf War effort. Furthermore, in 1992, Japan passed a bill that allows Japanese troops to be deployed overseas. The legislation allows up to 2,000 troops to participate in United Nations peacekeeping operations, but not as combat troops. While indications are that most Japanese want to increase contributions to international peace, many continue to express concerns about the political, economic, and legal implications of any offensive military involvement.

The draft budget for FY 1992 increased Japan's military budget to 4.55 trillion yen, an increase of 3.8 percent, the smallest rate of increase since 1960. Proposals to revise the current five-year Defense Plan (1991-95) include a reduction of 100 billion yen over the period, or 0.44 percent of the defense budget (*Far Eastern Economic Review*, Feb. 20, 1992, pp. 10-11).

F. FOREIGN AID

While the rate of increase in Japan's defense expenditures slowed somewhat in the early 90s, foreign aid expenditures, referred to as official development assistance (ODA), have accelerated. This program approached 800 billion yen in FY 1990 (1.2 percent of general account expenditures), and grew at an average annual rate of roughly 6 percent from 1986 to 1990. (See "economic cooperation" expenditures, Table 6.) These expenditures have increased in recent years because of Japan's international commitment to spend $50 billion in ODA during 1988-1992. Some political leaders called for an "international contribution tax" to finance these expenditures. In FY 1992, ODA was expected to rise by 7.8 percent to 952 billion yen (*Far Eastern Economic Review*, Jan. 9, 1992, p. 38). Much of this aid is in the form of debt relief to developing countries, food aid, and low interest loans.

VII. BUDGET DEFICITS AND THE NATIONAL DEBT

Table 6 shows Japan's general account budget expenditures, revenue, deficits, deficit/expenditure ratios, and deficit/GNP ratios for the years 1960-84. Generally, from 1945 until 1965 the general account budget was balanced, or had a small surplus. The deficit/expenditures ratio remained low at 4-5 percent during the last half of the 1960s, increased to the 11-16 percent rage during the 1971-74 period, jumped to 29 percent in 1976, peaked at 34.7 percent in 1979, and ranged from 32.6 percent in 1980 to 24.8 percent in 1984. This ratio continued to drop during the rest of the 1980s, reaching 9.5 percent in FY 1990 (*Far Eastern Economic Review*, Jan. 9, 1992, p. 38). As a percentage of GNP, deficits varied from 1-2 percent of GNP in the early 70s, increased to 3-5 percent in the later 70s, peaked at 6.1 percent in 1979, and fell back to 4.3 percent in 1984. Since 1984, the deficit/GNP ratio has continued to fall from 3.8 in 1985 to 1.8 in 1989 (Ito, p. 168). By 1990 this ratio had decreased to 1.5 percent (*Far Eastern Economic Review*, Jan. 9, 1990, p. 38).

The figures for deficits discussed above are based on the difference between expenditures and revenues that appear in the general account budget. However, only a portion of public works expenditures are financed through this budget. A large portion of public works outlays are provided through the Fiscal Investment and Loan Program (FILP) which is funded from postal savings and state pension revenues, not general tax revenues. Because of this overlap between the general account budget and FILP concerning public works, and other public works programs that appear in special accounts, the general account deficit may understate the overall deficit position of the central government. Therefore, changes in national government debt rather than current account deficits may be a more accurate indicator of the financial position of the central government. For example, from 1940 to 1945 Japan's war expenditures were not included in the general account budget, but rather appeared in a special account. Consequently, the national debt increased by greater amounts than did deficits in the general account. Furthermore, from 1947 to 1951 the general account showed surpluses but the national debt continued to increase, an indication that the central government's net deficit position had increased (Scott, et. al., 1983, p. 94). In light of this problem of accurately measuring deficits, the discussion that follows concentrates on the national government debt of Japan.

Table 6 General Account of the Central Government,
Final Settlement Figures, Selected Fiscal Years, 1960-84

	Expenditures	Revenue	Balance	Ratio of deficit to expenditures (percent)	Ratio of deficit to GNP (percent)
1960	1,743	1,961	218	0	...
1965	3,723	3,526	- 197	5.3	0.6
1970	8,188	7,841	- 347	4.2	0.5
1971	9,561	8,374	- 1,187	12.4	1.5
1972	11,932	9,982	- 1,950	16.3	2.1
1973	14,778	13,012	- 1,766	12.0	1.6
1974	19,100	16,940	- 2,160	11.3	1.6
1975	20,861	15,580	- 5,281	25.3	3.6
1976	24,468	17,270	- 7,198	29.4	4.3
1977	29,060	19,499	- 9,561	32.9	5.2
1978	34,096	23,422	-10,674	31.3	5.2
1979	38,790	25,318	-13,472	34.7	6.1
1980	43,405	29,235	-14,170	32.6	5.9

1981	46,921	34,021	-12,900	27.5	5.0
1982	47,245	33,200	-14,045	29.7	5.2
1983	50,635	37,149	-13,486	26.6	4.8
1984	51,481	38,700	-12,781	24.8	4.3

Source: Edward J. Lincoln. Japan: Facing Economic Maturity, p. 93. Original Sources: Ministry of Finance (Fiscal Statistics, 1986) and Economic Planning Agency, Annual Report on National Accounts, 1987.

Table 7 shows the outstanding central government debt of Japan for selected years from 1965 to 1988. The debt is classified into domestic bonds and foreign currency bonds depending on whether they are issued in Japan or abroad. Also the debt is classified into long-term, medium-term, and short-term bonds. Short-term bonds are issued to cover temporary financial shortages. To further complicate matters, but not shown by the table, the government distinguishes between construction bonds that finance public works and that are issued under the provisions of the Public Finance Law, and special government bonds (deficit bonds) that cover revenue shortages in the current account that involve operating expenses and that are issued under provisions of the Special Government Bond Law (Japan Statistical Yearbook, 1990, p. 437). As indicated by Table 7, from 1965 to 1985 there was a rapid increase in the national debt, especially after 1975 when the government first began to issue deficit bonds. Internal bonds issues by the central government jumped from 688 billion yen in 1965 to 3, 597 billion yen in 1970 (a 5-fold increase), from 1970 to 1975 it increased from 3,597 to 15,776 billion yen (a 4.5 fold increase), from 1975 to 1980 it increased from 15,776 to 71,906 billion yen (4.5 fold increase), and from 1980 to 1985 the debt increased from 71,906 to 136,611 billion yen (a 4.5-fold increase). Since 1985 the rate of increase of the debt has significantly slowed. From 1985 to 1988 the internal bond debt increased from 136,611 to 159,095 billion yen, a 16 percent increase. The total amount of national bonds outstanding in FY 1991 is expected to be around 170,000 billion yen (Far Eastern Economic Review, Jan. 9, 1992, p. 38). In FY 1990 Japan issued no new deficit bonds, the first time since 1975, and cut its dependence on bonds to 8.5% of total revenues, the first single-digit figure in 15 years (p. 38).

Table 7
OUTSTANDING NATIONAL GOVERNMENT DEBT (FY1965-88)

(in billions of yen)

Breakdown by kind

End of fiscal year	Total	Government bonds		Short-term government securities			Borrowings	Temporary borrowings	Total	Internal bonds
		Internal bonds	Foreign-currency bonds	Finance Ministry notes	Food certificates	Foreign exchange fund securities				
1965	1 767	688	57	0.4	406	312	302	-	809	92
1970	6 226	3 597	54	-	1 293	648	633	2.3	2 438	1 190
1975	22 795	15 776	33	-	1 304	2 819	2 860	-	7 572	3 031
1980	95 012	71 906	15	-	2 233	9 626	11 231	-	30 369	14 018
1985	163 571	136 611	0.8	-	1 339	8 922	16 699	-	58 436	40 902
1986	184 689	147 326	0.7	-	1 472	12 990	22 901	-	74 148	48 432
1987	198 612	154 113	0.5	-	1 184	17 820	25 494	-	84 961	58 804
1988	206 206	159 095	0.5	-	806	19 669	26 635	-	92 428	60 807

Breakdown by holder and lender

End of Fiscal Year	Government		The Bank of Japan			Other				
	Short-term government securities	Borrowings	Total	Internal bonds	Short-term government securities	Total	Internal bonds	Short-term government securities	Foreign currency bonds	Borrowings
1965	494	224	293	208	86	664	389	139	57	78
1970	691	557	1 882	1 203	679	1 906	1 204	572	54	76
1975	1 720	2 821	7 455	5 592	1 863	7 768	7 154	540	33	41
1980	5 161	11 190	14 241	9 077	5 164	50 402	48 811	1 534	15	41
1985	877	16 657	12 378	4 442	7 936	92 757	91 266	1 449	0.8	41
1986	2 857	22 859	12 474	3 635	8 839	98 068	95 260	2 766	0.7	41
1987	4 704	25 453	17 014	5 817	11 197	96 637	93 493	3 103	0.5	41
1988	5 027	26 594	17 615	3 289	14 325	96 163	94 999	1 123	0.5	41

Source: Japan Statistical Yearbook, 1990, p. 456. Original Source: Financial Bureau, Ministry of Finance.

VIII. JAPANESE BUDGETARY POLICY
IN THE HIGH GROWTH ERA: 1950-73

Ackley and Ishi maintain that budgetary policy in post World War II Japan was based on three principles: (1) a balanced-budget rule, (2) annual adjustments in tax schedules to keep combined national and local tax revenues at roughly 20 percent of national income, and (3) the use of fiscal and monetary policies to control aggregate demand so as to promote economic growth and price stability (p. 212).

In 1949 the U.S. government shifted its policy toward Japan from demilitarization and democratization to the promotion of a self-supporting Japanese economy capable of serving as a deterrent to totalitarian threats in the Far East. In an effort to stabilize the Japanese economy, U.S. occupation authorities adopted the "Dodge Plan", proposed by Joseph Dodge, then president of the Detroit Bank. In order to help dampen inflation that had developed after the war, one facet of the plan called for a balanced budget. Any surpluses in the budget were to be used for debt retirement. Concern over Japan's war and prewar debts had led to passage of the 1947 Public Finance Law that prohibited the issuance of national bonds. However, "hidden deficits" continued to occur through the use of the special accounts. To offset developing inflationary pressures, the FY 1949 general account budget was to have a surplus, to be obtained by holding down expenditures and tightening up on tax collections. This deflationary budget policy was coupled with action by the Bank of Japan that reduced loan rates to banks. Referring to this seemingly inconsistent set of policies to deal with inflation Kosai states:

> This testifies to the Japanese government's ambivalence, submitting to Dodge's policies on the one hand and resisting them on the other; and somehow it also seemed to have the understanding and support of the occupation authorities in Japan, who were not necessarily always of the same mind as the U.S. government officialdom in Washington (p. 63).

However, this practice of tempering restrictive fiscal policy with relaxed monetary action carried over into future government policy. Kosai concludes:

> It might be stated parenthetically that the technique of supplementing the fiscal balance from the monetary side also became a special feature of the Ikeda public finance policies in the first half of the 1950s and

left a trail as the subsequent practice of "flexible use" of treasury loans and investments (p. 63).

The Japanese economy was faced with a recessionary crisis in 1949, but the outbreak of the Korean War in 1950 resulted in an economic boom as Japan became a procurement base for the U.S. armed forces. From 1951 to 1953 the budget was in balance as called for by the Dodge Plan.

From 1955 to 1960 Japan experienced rapid growth. Economic policy goals as stated in the first five year economic plan stressed growth, investment, and exports. Growth and modernization in industry was needed to absorb the underemployed in agriculture and small enterprises. This growth required rapid increases in investment in plant and equipment and thus a high rate of national saving. In addition, the plan required rapid expansion of export markets because the increased output could not be absorbed domestically, and also because the earnings from exports would be needed to pay for the increase in the imports of raw materials. Specifically, the goals of the five year plan called for a 5 percent annual growth of real GNP, and an 8.8 and 7.4 rate of growth for exports and imports. Each of these goals were exceeded; the growth of real GNP averaged 9 percent between 1955 and 1960, exports grew at the rate of 12 percent and imports grew at 16 percent. In addition, the rate of growth of private plant and equipment and productivity averaged 22.5 and 7.4 percent respectively (Kosai, 1986, pp. 158-161).

Japan experienced sharp economic expansions in 1956-57 and again in the period from 1959 to 1961. Both of these expansions ended with inflation, increased imports and trade balance deficits. The Bank of Japan, concerned about the attainment of trade surpluses, turned to a tight money policy to control inflation and decrease imports. On the other hand, Prime Minister Tanzan (1956-57) implemented an expansionary fiscal policy that included a 100 billion yen tax cut and a 100 billion yen increase in expenditures. The tax reduction occurred mainly in the personal income tax, and the expenditures increase concentrated on the development of social capital--roads, housing, and transportation. Referring to the purpose of such tax cuts and expenditure increases, Kosai (1986) asserts:

> The intent of the tax reduction and the increased fiscal spending was to launch a cyclical process whereby the fruits of rapid growth could on the one hand revive the private sector and on the other remove obstacles to growth and, in so doing, stimulate further growth. This way of thinking set the pattern for public finance policy during the period of rapid growth (p. 102).

In 1960 the Ikeda government (1960-65) came to power and empha-sized programs for doubling income, liberalization of trade, and the re-duction of interest rates. However, in 1961 as the economy again experi-enced inflation and a movement toward trade deficits, the government used restrictive fiscal and monetary policies. But in 1963, as the economy slowed, monetary expansion was used to reduce the discount rate and increase the money supply by 35 percent over what it had been the previ-ous year (Kosai, 1986, p. 144). Tax revenues lagged due to the economic slowdown and government spending was held down to balance the budget.

Although the annual rate of growth of real GNP had averaged 9.7 percent between 1960 and 1965, the year 1965 was considered a recession year because the growth rate dropped to 5.7 percent, up to that time the lowest in the postwar period. Prime Minister Sato (1965-72), who suc-ceeded Ikeda, abandoned the policy of balanced budgets. In 1966 the gen-eral account budget included an increase in expenditures to 4.3 trillion yen and a tax cut of 310 billion yen (p.144). As a result a deficit occurred in the general account and special bonds were issued. Thus ended the bal-anced budget rule that had been in effect for 15 years since implementa-tion of the Dodge Plan.

From 1965 to 1970 the real GNP growth rate accelerated to 11.6 per-cent, peaking at 13 percent in 1967. The annual rate of growth in plant and equipment expenditures averaged 21 percent and productivity grew at 10.4 percent (Kosai, pp. 158-60). Japan's trade surplus was $1900 million in 1965, dropped to $800 million in 1967, increased to $3900 million in 1970, and by 1972 was $8900 million (p. 177). The money supply grew at an av-erage annual rate of 16.5 percent, but with the increase in productivity, consumer prices increased an average of only 5.5 percent annually. De-spite the change to deficits in the general account and the growth of gen-eral account expenditures that averaged 17 percent during this period, the deficit to government expenditure ratio remained low at 4-5 percent dur-ing the latter half of the 1960s (Lincoln, 1988, pp. 22-43).

An abrupt change in the growth rate came in the early 70s. By 1970-73 the average annual real GNP growth had slowed to 7.5 percent. In 1974, for the first time in the postwar period, the growth rate became negative (-1.4 percent), and in 1975 the growth rate was only 2.7 percent. Whereas the rate of increase in the consumer price index had averaged 5.5 percent during 1965-70, it jumped to 11.8 percent in 1972 and 24.3 percent in 1973. The percentage change in the wholesale price index increased dramati-cally from 0.8 percent in 1971 to 15.9 percent in 1972, and 31.3 percent in

1973. Japan had moved into a period of stagflation--simultaneous high inflation and recession (Lincoln, 1988, pp. 22-43).

What had changed to cause this problem? Lincoln (1988) contends this slower growth rate was caused primarily by the following: (1) Capital formation slowed as Japan's technology caught up with foreign technology. While real capital investment grew at a real annual rate of nearly 20 percent from 1960 to 1973, it averaged only 3.9 percent from 1974 to 1985. (2) Real energy costs accelerated with the big increases coming during the oil shock years of 1973 and 1979-80. Since Japan depended on imports of oil for much of its total energy needs it lost revenues to the oil exporting countries as import prices rose relative to export prices, and energy intensive industries had to adjust, which meant a period of lower productivity and loss of international competitiveness for some. (3) Slower economic growth in the rest of the world and protectionist measures resulted in an slowdown of export growth. (4) Finally, there was a shift in priorities away from economic growth to broader social goals. A heightened concern for pollution, social welfare, health, and social infrastructure resulted in reduced economic growth as investment was shifted into these areas that had lower productivity potential. In addition to the above reasons for Japan's economic slowdown, monetary authorities in an attempt to offset the possible negative effect on net exports caused by the 1971 yen revaluation, increased the rate of growth of the money supply. In the first quarter of 1972 the rates of growth of both M1 and M2 reached 24 percent. Recognizing that inflation was a problem, monetary authorities increased the discount rate from 4 percent at the beginning of 1973 to 9 percent by the end of the year. By 1974-75 the rate of growth of the money supply had been reduced to roughly 11-14 percent (Lincoln, 1988, pp. 41-68).

IX. BUDGETARY POLICY SINCE THE MID-1970S

Fiscal policy from 1974 to 1979 was marked by rapid increases in general account deficits. The deficit to expenditure ratio which had ranged from 11 to 16 percent during the period 1971-74, jumped to 29 percent in 1975 and peaked at 34.7 percent in 1979. In 1975, deficit bonds were issued for the first time. (See Section VI.) The rapid build-up of deficits in the last half of the 70s was due to increased government expenditures and lagging tax revenues caused by slower economic growth. From 1974 to 1979 central government's nominal expenditures grew at an average annual rate of 17.4 percent, while during the same period tax revenue grew at a rate of only 11.7 percent (Lincoln, 1988, pp. 92-93). Much of the increase in expenditures was due to the expansion of social programs that included free medical care for the aged, increased health insurance and pension benefits. In addition, there were increased expenditures on public works, education, defense, and debt-servicing. The slower growth of tax revenues was due not only to slower economic growth, but also to the continuance of the traditional annual personal income tax cuts in 1974, 1975 and 1977.

Beginning in 1979, the Ministry of Finance (MOF), concerned with the growth of deficits and the increased debt-servicing burden, sought to reestablish a balanced general account budget policy and eliminate the use of deficit bonds. Initially, the MOF proposed to reduce deficits by the introduction of a value-added-tax (VAT). When this tax faced strong public opposition, various other tax reforms were proposed and some passed from 1980 to 1987. The annual reduction in personal income tax rates was eliminated until 1984. Various excise taxes on liquor, official stamps, automobiles, and cigarettes were increased. The 1985 and 1987 tax reform bills, while they did not include a VAT, did reduce marginal tax rates, eliminate tax-free savings accounts, and plug several loopholes in the corporate income tax. The MOF also tried to reduce deficits by setting limits on increases in discretionary spending. Furthermore, the three major government-owned corporations (Nippon Telegraph and Telephone, Japanese National Railways, and Japan Tobacco and Salt) were privatized. While the increase in nominal spending was 15.2 percent in 1979, it averaged less than 3 percent for the years 1982-86 (Lincoln, 1988, p. 113).

Generally, the central government of Japan continued to follow a program of fiscal austerity in the 80s and early 90s, despite periodic internal and external pressures to relax this policy. With the rapid rise in the value of the yen in 1985-86, there was internal concern that if the foreign sector surplus decreased it would require increases in domestic demand and fiscal policy would have to be more expansionary. However, there was little change in fiscal policy. In the first half of the 1980s, business, the bureaucracy, and the Liberal Democratic Party continued to support a fiscal policy based on the reduction of deficits by expenditure cuts and without tax increases (Lincoln, 1988, p. 122). However, there was some internal support for expansionary fiscal policy in order to stimulate domestic demand and address foreign criticism of Japan's large foreign account surplus. Kiichi Miyazawa, who eventually became prime minister in 1992, proposed in 1984 an expansionary policy based on plans to increase spending on housing, sewers, urban parks, and expressways. Miyazawa's 1984 challenge to then Prime Minister Nakasone failed and with it his plan for fiscal expansion. Furthermore, in 1986 a report by the Advisory Group on Economic Structural Adjustment for International Harmony, known as the Maekawa Report, called for a policy with less emphasis on exports and more emphasis on increased domestic demand, flexibility in fiscal policy, and the elimination of deficit bonds. However, those who continued to advocate tight fiscal policy proposed an alternative program based on "private-sector vitality". (Referred to as "minkatsu".) This led to legislation in 1986 to promote joint ventures between prefectural and municipal governments and local business in the construction of research centers for high-technology industries, international exchange facilities, and telecommunications infrastructure. These projects were to receive low-cost loans, exemptions from local taxes, special depreciation allowances, and loan guarantees from the central government (Lincoln, 1988, p. 125). During this time the MOF and the government continued to adopt budgets based on the reduction of deficits. On this matter, Lincoln concludes:

> While the debate may have been lively, little action resulted from the government other than the minkatsu-ho. MOF budget guidelines continued to aim at a 10 percent reduction in discretionary spending (and 5 percent in capital expenditures) for fiscal years 1985, 1986, and 1987. When compiled, all three budgets anticipated a reduction in the gap between spending and revenue (p. 127).

It should be pointed out that while the general account budgets adopted in the 80s and early 90s were based on the idea of reducing deficits, supplementary budgets were sometimes used to modify initially tight fiscal budgets.

Japan experienced a four year economic expansion from 1987 to 1990. This growth was due to expansion of domestic demand, especially business investment. The result was that in FY 1990 tax revenues increased so that government spending could increase "at its fastest pace in nine years without ever needing to issue deficit-financing bonds" (*Japan Economic Almanac*, p. 20). Thus, as noted earlier, for the first time in 15 years the general account budget was balanced and no new deficit bonds were issued. The government's dependance on bonds (construction bonds) was cut to 8.5 percent of expenditures (pp. 20-21). The national debt of Japan stood at roughly 160 trillion yen in FY 1990. (See Section VII.)

In addition to the elimination of general account deficits, the increased tax receipts in FY 1990 were used to reduce so-called "hidden debts". These debts were past deferrals of certain expenses that ordinarily would be in the general account budget. These included past suspensions of fixed-rate annual transfers from the general account to the debt consolidation fund (a pool of funds for the redemption of outstanding government bonds), and deferrals of other expenses. As of FY 1989 the suspended transfers to the debt consolidation fund was 15.573 trillion yen and deferrals of other expenses amounted to 10.579 trillion yen (Japan Economic Almanac, pp. 20-21). These hidden debts were partially reduced in 1990 in a supplementary budget where the government appropriated 2 trillion yen out of 3.217 trillion yen in excess revenues (those above what was estimated, commonly referred to as a "natural increase") for payment of deferred government contributions to the welfare pension fund and to interest subsidies for the Housing Loan Corporation. The government also resumed in FY 1990 fixed rate transfers to the debt consolidation fund, suspended in 1982 because of fiscal constraints. Thus, the debt servicing expenses in the FY 1990 general account budget shows a rise of 22.5 percent (p. 22).

Kiichi Miyazawa's first budget (FY 1992) as prime minister proposed a 2.7 percent increase in spending, the smallest increase in five years. Tax revenues were projected to increase 1.2 percent based on an assumed GNP growth rate of 3.5 percent (*Far Eastern Economic Review*, Jan. 9, 1992, p. 38). This appeared overly optimistic in light of projections that called for a continuation of the economic slowdown in Japan that began after 1990. Despite projections that the economic growth rate would be 2 percent or less in 1992, the MOF continued to support a policy of fiscal restraint. However, as a result of Japan's deepening economic crisis in mid-1992, the government implemented a plan to increase government spending, mostly on public works and loans to small and medium-sized businesses. This increase in expenditures coupled with reduced tax collections would likely require the issuance of more bonds and make it difficult for the government to achieve its debt reduction goals.

In summary, from the mid-1970s to the mid-1980s Japan's general account deficits and the national debt increased rapidly. This was due to increased expenditures on social programs and public works, and slower growth of tax collections. Since the early 1980s Japan's budgetary policy has been based on a plan for "fiscal consolidation." The core of this plan has included programs for budget deficit reduction, slower public sector growth, tax reform, and privatization of public enterprises. To reduce growth of the public sector the MOF established growth rate guidelines of minus 10 percent for some current expenditures and minus 5 percent for public investment. Also, as a result of the Structural Impediments Initiative (SII) agreement with the U.S. to open its domestic markets, Japan planned to restructure government expenditures so as to place emphasis on public investment expenditures that improve the quality of life (especially expenditures on parks, sewers, public sanitation, and transportation). In the latter half of the 1980s tax reform was enacted for the purpose of reducing the burden of direct taxes, correcting inequities, and reducing marginal income tax rates. A general consumption tax (VAT) of 3 percent was introduced in 1989.

In FY 1990 no new deficit bonds were issued, the first time since 1975. The bond-dependency ratio (new government bond issues as a proportion of total expenditures) was reduced to 8.5 percent, from a peak of 35 percent in 1979. The national (central) government's deficit in FY 1990 was about 1 1/4 percent of GNP, or less than half the average for the major industrial countries (OECD, 1990/91 *Economic Survey: Japan*, p. 47). On the other hand, the national government's debt and debt interest payments remained relatively high. The initial budget for FY 1991 showed interest payments of 16,036 billion yen; 22.8 percent of total expenditures, or 3.7 percent of GNP. Gross debt (includes central government construction bonds and deficit-financing bonds) as a percentage of GNP was 38 percent, or 45 percent if off-budget items (government corporations and special accounts) are included. In contrast, in the early 1980s Japan's debt/GNP ratio was only 25 percent and the interest payment/expenditure ratio was 9 percent. For comparison, the U.S. gross debt/GNP ratio which includes off-budget items such as social security, was 58 percent in 1990, while the interest payment/GNP ratio was 4.9 percent. However, these percentages from 1988 to 1990 decreased for Japan and increased for the United States (p. 50).

A primary objective of recent Japanese fiscal policy has been to further reduce the central government's debt-dependency ratio and debt interest payments by the reduction of new construction bond issues and the use of any surpluses in the general account budget to retire outstanding bonds. However, further reduction of the debt burden may be delayed as the government increases expenditures to cope with Japan's economic slowdown.

REFERENCES

Ackley, G. and H. Ishi, (1976), "Fiscal, Monetary, and Related Policies." In *Asia's New Giant*, eds., H. Patrick and H. Rovousky, pp. 232-47.

Campbell, J.C., (1974), *Contemporary Japanese Budget Politics*, Berkeley: University of California Press.

Campbell, J.C., (1981), "Japan's Social Welfare System," in *Business and Society In Japan*, eds., Bradley M. Richardson and Taizo Veda, pp.207-

214, (East Asian Studies Program, Ohio State University), Praeger Publisher.

Denison, E.F. and W.K. Chung, (1976), "Economic Growth and Its Sources," in *Asia's New Giant*, eds., H. Patrick and H. Rovousky, pp. 63-151.

Handbook: Doing Business in Japan, Ernst and Young (Jan. 1, 1991), International Business Series.

International Monetary Fund. *World Economic Outlook*, May 1991.

Ito, T., (1992), *The Japanese Economy*, Cambridge, Mass: The MIT Press.

Japan Statistical Yearbook, (1990), Japan, Management and Coordination Agency.

Kosai, Y., (1986), *The Era of High-Speed Growth: Notes on the Postwar Japanese Economy*, Tokyo: University of Tokyo Press.

Lincoln, E.J., (1988), *Japan: Facing Economic Maturity*, Washington, D.C.: The Brookings Institution.

Noguchi, Y., (1987), "Public Finance," in *The Political Economy of Japan*, Vol. 1, eds., K. Yamamura and Y. Yasuba., pp.186-122, Stanford University Press.

Organization for Economic Co-Operation and Development (OECD). *Economic Outlook: Historical Statistics, 1960-1989.*

Patrick, H. and H. Rovousky, (eds.), (1976), *Asia's New Giant: How the Japanese Economy Works.* Washington, D.C.: The Brookings Institution.

Reischauer, E.O.,(1977), *The Japanese*, Cambridge, Mass: Harvard University Press.

Scott, B.R., J.W. Rosenblum, and A.T. Sproat, (1980), *Case Studies in Political Economy: Japan 1854-1977*, Boston: Harvard Business School.

ECONOMY AND PUBLIC FINANCES IN TURKEY IN THE 1980s[1]

Bülent Uyar

I. INTRODUCTION

Turkey is a bridge between Europe and Asia. It is located in the Middle East and extends into the southeast corner of Europe. Its area is 300,948 square miles. About 95 percent of the land mass is in Asia and the rest is in Europe; the continents are separated by two straits, called, the Bosphorous and the Dardanelles. According to the 1990 census, the population of Turkey was slightly over 56 million. Ankara is the capital city. It has a population of over 3 million. The two other major cities are Istanbul and Izmir, with populations of 8 and 2.5 million, respectively.

The (nominal) gross national product (GNP) of Turkey in 1990 was about 150 billion U.S. dollars. The ratio of public spending to GNP was 23 percent. About half of public expenditures was for current expenditures and only 13 percent was for public investment projects. The ratio of government revenues to GNP was slightly over 19 percent. The individual income tax and the Value Added Tax (VAT) together generated half of the total public sector revenues. (See OECD, *Economic Surveys: Turkey*, various issues.)

The main objective of this chapter is to examine the public finances of the central government of Turkey against the political developments in the 1980s and the early 1990s. The reason for focusing on this period is that the events of the early 1980s proved to be a turning point in Turkey's

socio-political development and economic evolution. One person more
than any other, namely, the late Turgut Özal, is identified with this decade. Özal had been involved in shaping the course of the Turkish economy since the late 1960s. Most importantly, he was instrumental in usher-
ing a departure in both the strategy and the approach to development in
Turkey in the 1980s, as compared to earlier periods. The elections of November 1991 resulted in a change in government. This obviously reflects
public unhappiness with some of the policies followed in the 1980s. Thus,
the agenda for the rest of the 1990s will be different. Still, there are signs
that the new government recognizes that some of Özal's policies entailed
rather irreversible changes in public's economic expectations and atti-
tudes.

In the remainder of this chapter, I will first review the basic economic
and political features of the years prior to 1979. Next, I will provide an
overview of the economic conditions in the 1979-1983 period. Against this
background, I will examine the developments in the public finances in
Turkey in the 1980s. In the final section, I will offer summary observations.

II. PRE-1979 PERIOD[2]

Since the establishment of the Republic in 1923, the Turkish political system has evolved from a single- to a multi-party system. All along, the
main concern of the governments was, and still is, to promote economic
development. In practice, this has meant economic growth and industrialization through the strategy of import substitution.[3] Depending on the
political orientations of governments and the circumstances, the policies
followed differed. Yet all had the imprint of certain political, and socio-economic themes which Hershlag (1988, p. ix) calls "conceptual patterns."

One such conceptual pattern was the avoidance of foreign capital and
assistance. The reasons were rooted in the events of the early 1920s, after
the War of Independence. The leaders of the time were concerned that
such economic ties could eventually threaten the sovereignty of the new
Republic as they had its predecessor, the Ottoman Empire. Such concerns
dominated the economic-political scene until Turkey's transition to a
multi-party system in the late 1940s. Also under the Lausanne Treaty of
1923, and as another price for international recognition, Turkey agreed to
impose no tariffs or customs duties until 1929. So, the leaders were denied

access to some important sources for much needed revenues. (See Barkey, 1990, pp. 43-51.)

These developments were responsible for yet another and more lasting pattern, namely, etatism. Etatism is the notion that the public sector assumes leadership in economic life until or unless the private sector is able to do so.[4] By the time the Republic was established, most of Turkey's infrastructure and economic base had been destroyed as a result of a decade of wars (including the two Balkan Wars, World War I, and the War of Independence). Since Turkey did not have the entrepreneurial class with sufficient capital to assume economic leadership, etatism emerged as the Turkish approach to development in the early 1930s. The inability of the developed countries to deal adequately with the Great Depression also strengthened the resolve of the officials to rely on etatism and planning.[5] It was during this period that the first State Economic Enterprises (SEEs) were established and agricultural price supports were introduced. Growth through industrialization via import substitution meant interventionist and protectionist (inward-oriented) policies.[6] Etatism continues to play a role in Turkey's development strategy though not to the same extent it did until the late 1970s.

Turkey's development history reveals some similarities from the mid 1950s to 1980. They include: civilian governments' inability to sustain economic growth and control inflation; their failure to undertake structural reforms; increasing inequity; political instability; and military *coup* (in 1960, 1971, and again in 1980). I now turn to an overview of these developments.

Transition to a multi-party system culminated in the Democratic Party (DP) winning the elections in 1950, and the transfer of power from the Republican Peoples Party (RPP). The RPP was founded by the leaders of the Turkish War of Independence. It was always dominated by the intellectuals, the technocrats, the bureaucrats, and the retired members of the armed forces. The DP's platform attracted the industrialists, merchants, and mainly the residents of the rural areas; groups which felt disenfranchised during the single-party system under the RPP. The DP's platform was anti-etatist; it promised to sell the SEEs to the private sector, and promote a free market economy. Under DP, the domestic markets were opened to international flow of capital. Most of the public investment in the early 1950s was in much needed infrastructure and other capital-intensive projects with long gestation periods. Therefore, in spite of increased economic participation by the private sector, the public sector continued to dominate the economy. The DP underestimated the potential inflationary impact of its approach, deficit spending, in financing public expenditures. A prudent approach would have been to reform the tax system and to finance such projects mainly with tax proceeds.[7] Attempts at tax reform, particularly those aimed at direct taxation of agricultural incomes for the first time since 1925, failed because of political pressures.[8] Continued exemption of the agricultural sector from the income tax meant "... 77 percent of (the) population and 40 percent of (the) gross national product" was effectively excluded from the tax base in the mid-1950s (Barkey, 1990, p.54.). The tax burden was mainly on the nonagricultural workers and the wage-and-salaried employees whose taxes could be withheld at the source. Another adversely affected group was the industrial sector; the bookkeeping requirements and the relatively small number of relatively large firms made it easy for the authorities to monitor their taxable incomes. The industrialists maintained that widespread tax evasion by the commercial sector (consisting mainly of small, sole proprietorships in retail and services) added to their tax burden. (p. 58 n43 and pp. 128-9.) In order to increase the revenue base, the government in 1954 imposed a number of ad valorem tariffs, including customs, stamp, and wharf duties, and municipal taxes. Some of these taxes were as high as 2000 percent but they "were reduced and even eliminated if the government thought it was necessary to support a specific industry or enterprise" (p.92, 71.) The actual revenues collected from these taxes varied with fluctuations in imports.

The industrialists and the merchants could co-exist within the DP in the early 1950s because of the favorable international and domestic economic conditions. By the late 1950s, Turkey had a capital-intensive, underutilized industrial sector which was heavily dependent on imported intermediate goods. The tax system was skewed heavily in favor of indirect taxes and was inefficient. The SEEs operating deficits had become a burden on the budget. The economy was beset by balance of payments problems, high inflation, high unemployment, increasing disparity in the distributions of income and wealth, and chronic budget deficits.[9] The DP's response was increased intervention through price and exchange rate controls and regulatory measures. These measures threatened the interests of the aforementioned economic groups. These groups sought control over economic policy in order to secure their own survival. The resulting power struggle fractured the political base of the DP and paralyzed the government. The failure to implement some of the measures in a timely manner worsened the economic problems which led to political demonstrations and street violence. Even the internationally supported stabilization package of 1958 was not sufficient to improve the economy and stem the tide of violence. In May 1960, the DP was forced out of power, and eventually disbanded, by a military *coup* (Chs. 2-6).

The military government only stayed in power until the general elections of 1961. Some of the policies adopted during its brief reign set the stage for future reforms. The military government instituted the policy of "wealth declaration," revised the property and real estate taxes, and declared agricultural incomes to be taxable.[10] Socio-economic concerns of the military rulers were reflected in the Constitution of 1961, drafted with their sponsorship. For instance, Article 2 cited "social state" as a characteristic of the Turkish Republic. As defined in other articles, "social state" denoted a "welfare state." The 1961 Constitution also specified measures to promote that welfare state. Article 61 stated that everyone is obliged to pay taxes according to his ability to pay. Other articles acknowledged the "right to social security" and medical care, and made it the state's obligation to establish or assist "the establishment of social security and social welfare organizations" and "to assure ... adequate housing facilities for the poor and low income families." (Özbudun, 1980, p.66.) Yet, by linking the fulfillment of such obligations to the availability of public resources, the Constitution provided an escape hatch for the governments. After the elections in October 1961, the civilian governments in general undermined these reforms.[11] Still, the Constitution of 1961 provided the philosophical guidelines for future discussions on such issues.[12]

From 1961 to 1969, Turkey had coalition governments none of which had the parliamentary strength to implement economic reforms. The political parties were trying to expand their respective power bases by attracting the groups which previously had supported the DP. The Justice Party (JP) proved to be more successful in doing so than the other parties, and emerged with the parliamentary majority from the 1969 elections. From 1961 until the 1983 elections, this was the only instance when a party in Turkey had a parliamentary majority. During the summer of 1970, the JP government attempted to rely on its parliamentary strength and pushed for an ambitious stabilization package.

This was in response to increasing street violence arising from economic problems. The stabilization package aimed at making the manufacturing sector more competitive, promoting a more balanced approach to industrialization and growth, liberalizing trade, increasing the foreign currency reserves of Turkey, and reducing the expected deficit by increasing the revenues. In August 1970, the Turkish Lira was devalued. The Central Bank was given increased powers regarding the monetary policy. The discount rate, the interest rates on deposits, and the bank finance charges were increased. Even though some sectors (e.g., agriculture) continued to borrow at preferential interest rates, the measures as a whole were meant to control inflation by stimulating savings and discouraging credit expansion.[13]

The newly introduced taxes were: a purchase tax on motor vehicles; a sales tax on "luxury" consumption; a tax on officially-run football pools; and a increased-value tax on real estate.[14] The rates of some existing taxes were increased. The stabilization package also extended the expenditure tax to assembly industries and various construction activities, the so-called "production" tax. Other measures targeted the inheritance tax, certain business licensing fees, and the real estate purchase tax. Tax rates on petroleum products were raised. The tax rebate system for exports was restructured, and the stamp tax on imports was lowered. The changes in the tax structure increased the share of indirect taxes in total revenues; they also "broaden(ed) the tax base and reduc(ed) the reliance on import duties and other taxes connected with imports" and promoted "a more equitable distribution of the tax burden among social classes" (OECD, *Economic Surveys: Turkey 1970*, p.26.). All in all, the package had provisions for the structural reform of every sector except agriculture.

The government might have been able to weather the reaction to the package if the unity of the JP itself had not been threatened. The reactions to the economic proposals revealed that the JP had pockets of representatives aligned with different economic interest groups. To preserve the unity of the party, the government started making concessions on the stabilization package almost immediately after it was introduced. The concessions did nothing to stop street violence. Against this background, the military issued an ultimatum in March, 1971, and forced the resignation of the JP government.

Until the elections in 1973, Turkey had a succession of governments formed by the civilians who were appointed by the military. The 1970s witnessed a proliferation of parties. Most were founded by the splinter groups from the JP, and were aligned with various economic interest groups. During the 1973-1979 period, there were five elected civilian governments. All were coalition governments; none had the strength or the tenure in office required for structural transformation of the economy through institutional, fiscal, and monetary measures.

Tables 1-7 show the trends in major economic variables in light of the events and developments outlined above. For instance, Table 1 shows that the share of Gross Domestic Product (GDP) originating in the agricultural sector declined from 27 to 22 percent between 1970 and 1980. Over the same period, the combined shares of the manufacturing and the "Other Industrial" sectors increased from 22 percent of GDP to 26 percent. Table

2 shows that the growth in employment in the manufacturing and the "Other Industrial" sectors over the same period was not sufficient to absorb the workers released from the agricultural sector.[15] One important reason for this was the nature of the import-substitution strategy of industrialization. In part as a result, the unemployment rate increased from 5 percent in 1970 to almost 12 percent in 1980; this is shown in Table 3.[16]

In support of the import-substituting strategy, the Turkish governments followed a fixed exchange-rate policy until the early 1980s. Table 4, which traces the value of the Turkish Lira (TL) against the U.S. dollar, shows that the 1970 devaluation of the TL was the first (official) adjustment in the exchange rate in almost a decade.[17] Throughout the years, the overvalued currency had discouraged exports by the (protected) manufacturing sector as well as the nonmanufacturing sector. The resulting shortages in foreign currency meant difficulty in importing the intermediate goods needed by the manufacturing sector itself. Increasingly, the governments had to rely on foreign borrowing to relieve the foreign currency shortage. Foreign borrowing coupled with higher prices of imported oil were two factors which contributed to inflation.

Table 5 shows that the inflation rate, as measured by the annual percentage change in CPI (Consumer Price Index), jumped from about 7 percent in 1970 to about 16 percent in 1971. It remained rather stable until 1977 when it started increasing again and reached 110 percent in 1980. The sudden increase in the rate of inflation during 1970-71 initially was due to Turkey's inability to meet the increased demand for her exports following the 1970 devaluation. Eventually, the devaluation helped boost Turkey's foreign currency reserves through increased overseas remittances and increased exports.[18] These increased reserves enabled the coalition governments to meet the first international oil crisis of 1973-1974 without a significant impact on the economy in general and on the domestic oil prices in particular. However, by 1977, the foreign currency reserves had been severely depleted and the Lira once again was overvalued. The second oil price increase in 1978-80 affected Turkey very seriously. Her exports and foreign exchange earnings declined because of the impact of the oil crisis on Turkey's Western trading partners; at the same time, her import bill rose because the prices of imported finished and semi-finished products increased.

Table 1: GDP - Percent Distribution by Type of Activity

	Total	Agricultural	Manufacturing	Other Industrial*	Construction	Wholesale & Retail	Transportation & Communication	Other Activities**
1970	100.0	27.0	19.0	3.0	7.0	12.0	8.0	23.0
1975	100.0	27.0	19.0	3.0	5.0	13.0	8.0	22.0
1979	100.0	22.0	22.0	2.0	5.0	14.0	9.0	23.0
1980	100.0	22.0	22.0	4.0	5.0	15.0	10.0	22.0
1981	100.0	21.0	24.0	4.0	5.0	16.0	10.0	21.0
1985	100.0	18.0	25.0	7.0	4.0	17.0	10.0	18.0
1986	100.0	17.0	26.0	7.0	4.0	17.0	10.0	18.0
1987	100.0	17.0	26.0	6.0	4.0	17.0	10.0	18.0
1988	100.0	16.0	27.0	7.0	4.0	17.0	10.0	18.0
1989	100.0	15.0	26.0	7.0	4.0	17.0	10.0	19.0

* Other Industrial Activities: Mining, Electricity, Gas, Water
** Other Activities: Financial & Community Services, Producers of Government Services, & other Producers

Source: UN (1991). National Accounts Statistics: Analysis of Main Aggregates: 1988-1989. New York. Table 3.

Table 2: Percentage Distribution of Civilian Employment
by Type of Activity.

	Total	Agricultural	Manufacturing	Industrial *	Other Services**
1970	100.0	66.5	9.8	4.5	19.2
1975	100.0	62.8	10.9	5.0	21.3
1979	100.0	55.1	12.0	7.0	25.9
1980	100.0	54.9	11.8	7.1	26.2
1985	100.0	52.7	12.7	6.9	27.7
1986	100.0	51.8	13.0	7.1	28.1
1987	100.0	51.0	13.2	7.3	28.5
1988	100.0	48.3	13.8	6.9	31.0
1989	100.0	49.2	14.2	6.3	30.3
1990	100.0	47.8	14.0	5.9	32.3

Note: Numbers may not always add up to 100.0 due to rounding.
* "Other Industrial" consists of Mining, Electricity, Gas, Water.
** "Services" is defined to include Construction, Wholesale & Retail Trade, Transportation & Communication, And Other Activities.

Source: OECD. *Historical Statistics* (various issues)

Table 3: Labor Market - Selected Years.

	Population in 000s	Civilian Labor Force in 000s	Number of Unemployed in 000s	Unemployment Rate %
1970	35605	14544	724	5.0
1975	40348	16040	1342	8.4
1980	44737	17479	2703	11.9
1988	54074	19674	1581	8.0
1989	55260	20139	1663	8.3
1990	56086	20163	1482	7.4
1991	57182	20145	1476	7.3

Source: OECD. *Economic Surveys: Turkey.* (var. issues)

Table 4: Exchange Rate - TL per US dollar

1961	9.00
1969	9.00
1970	11.50
1971	14.92
1972	14.15
1973	14.15
1974	13.93
1975	14.44
1976	16.05
1977	18.00
1978	24.28
1979	31.08
1980	76.04
1981	111.22
1982	162.55
1983	225.46
1984	366.68
1985	521.98
1986	674.51
1987	857.21
1988	1422.35
1989	2121.68
1990	2608.64
1991	4171.80
1992a	5686.50

a. preliminary

Sources: IMF (1992). *International Financial Statistics Yearbook: 1992*. Washington, D.C. pp.700-1.
OECD (1992). *Economic Surveys: Turkey 1991/1992*. p.155.

Note: These are the rates the IMF reports as series 'rf' (*par rate/market rate*). The IMF uses these rates to find the US$ equivalents for "trade and other flow or average statistics...they are period average market rates wherever available, i.e., period average rates in the market of the country or, if these are not available, official rates" (IMF, *International Financial Statistics Yearbook: 1992*, p.4). In Turkey, the rates have been adjusted daily since May 1, 1981 according to market rates. So, the figures from 1981 on are annual averages of the daily rates. Prior to May 1, 1981, were four devaluations in 1981.

Table 5: Annual Percentage Change in CPI

1970	6.9
1971	15.7
1972	11.7
1973	15.4
1974	15.8
1975	19.2
1976	17.4
1977	27.1
1978	45.3
1979	58.7
1980	110.2
1981	36.6
1982	30.8
1983	31.4
1984	48.4
1985	45.0
1986	34.6
1987	38.8
1988	73.7
1989	63.2
1990	60.3
1991	66.0
1992a	78.4

a. preliminary

Source: IMF (1992). *International Financial Statistics Yearbook: 1992.* pp.106-7.
OECD (1992). *Economic Surveys: Turkey 1991/1992.* Table 5.

In January 1990, new weights for the consumer price indices were introduced as of 1988.

Other factors contributing to inflationary pressures since the mid-1970s include: union demands for higher wages to keep up with inflation; credit expansion encouraged by an interest rate policy which by the end of the decade resulted in the negative real rate of 35-40 percent; overspending by the government; and the monetization of the deficit. Table 6 shows the trends in the consolidated budget of the central government. It reveals that there was a significant increase in expenditures in 1977 which continued throughout the rest of the 1970s. The reasons are increased defense spending as a result of the military operation in Cyprus, increasing deficits of the SEEs, and the pay raises given to the public employees. Finally, Table 7 shows that even though the nominal GDP increased by a factor of 3.4 from 1978 to 1980, it actually declined in real terms; the last

column of the Table shows that real GDP per capita declined by three percent in both 1979 and 1980.

The overwhelming sense of frustration and despair associated with
these conditions were reflected in continued street violence and anarchy
in the 1970s. By 1979, when by-elections were held, the economy was experiencing stagflation: increasing unemployment and high inflation.[19]

III. REFORM YEARS: 1979-83

No party emerged with a simple majority in the 1979 elections. For the
first time in her democratic history, Turkey had a minority government,
formed by the JP and with support from two other parties. Süleyman
Demirel, the leader of the JP and the Prime Minister, had managed to re-
absorb some of the splinter parties formed following the unsuccessful
stabilization scheme of 1970.

In January 1980, a new stabilization package was proposed. One of its
architects was Turgut Özal, the Chief of the State Planning Organization
(SPO). The international financial community offered to extend credit and
reschedule Turkey's foreign debt in exchange for the stabilization package.[20] The proposed measures aimed at controlling inflation, improving
the distribution of income, opening the economy to international competition, and replacing the import-substitution based approach to growth
and development with an export-oriented policy. The stabilization package proposed devaluation of the Lira. It deregulated the interest rates on
certain time deposits, expressed a commitment to a tight monetary policy,
and adjusted the prices of some SEEs products in order to reduce their
operating deficits. The primary reason for the stabilization policy was the
instinct for survival. Economic factors were behind the rising and increasingly indiscriminate violence. The rising violence was undermining political stability and leading to anarchy.

In spite of the urgency of the situation, the parliament still did not
approve the tax-reform component of the stabilization package. The
measures which were approved and implemented adversely affected the
economy in the short run. The credit crunch stemming from tight monetary policy worsened the recession and unemployment. By the end of
1979, the rising oil prices following the Iranian revolution worsened the
inflationary situation even more.

Segments of the private sector quickly realized that each might be the
victim of any economic restructuring. Encouraged by the initial support of
the international agencies, and doubting the ability of a minority govern-

ment to withstand political pressure, these segments pressed for economic concessions. Consequently, parliamentary squabbles became the order of the day. Prolonged strikes, continuing violence, widespread anarchy in spite of martial law, and general public discontent with the economy paved the way for the military *coup* of September, 1980.[21]

The military disbanded the parliament and suspended all political activity. By selecting Turgut Özal as their Deputy Minister in charge of the economy, the *coup* leaders indirectly endorsed the stabilization measures and the program of economic liberalization. The military viewed its job as facilitating economic transformation by "restructuring the Turkish political system." (Barkey, 1990, p. 179.) To that end, it changed the election laws, making it more difficult for fringe parties to gain seats in the parliament.[22]

Table 6: Consolidated Budget for Selected Years
Billions of Current TL

	Revenues	Expend.	Balance	Rev/GNP %	Exp/GNP %	Bal/GNP %
1971	41	47	-6	21.8	25.3	-3.5
1974	72	80	-8	17.5	19.4	-1.9
1976	143	153	-10	21.5	23.1	-1.6
1977	188	240	-52	21.8	27.8	-6.0
1978	287	340	-52	22.6	26.7	-4.1
1979	507	595	-88	23.5	27.6	-4.1
1980	912	1078	-166	20.6	24.3	-3.7
1981	1392	1516	-124	21.2	23.1	-1.9
1982	1445	1602	-157	16.5	18.3	-1.8
1983	2300	2613	-313	19.9	22.6	-2.7
1984	2805	3784	-979	15.3	20.6	-5.3
1985	4515	5313	-798	16.2	19.1	-2.9
1986	6754	8165	-1411	17.2	20.7	-3.6
1987	10089	12696	-2607	17.2	21.7	-4.5
1988	17016	21006	-3990	16.9	20.9	-4.0
1989	30379	38051	-7672	17.8	22.3	-4.5
1990	55239	67194	-11955	19.2	23.4	-4.2
1991a	97000	129345	-32345	21.3	28.4	-7.1

Source: OECD. *Economic Surveys: Turkey.* (various issues.)

Note: a. preliminary

A number of changes were made in the Budget Law and the budgetary process in Turkey. Most of these took place in the early 1980s and also during the 1986-87 period. As emphasized in this chapter, these changes limit the comparability of the data over time.

Table 7: Gross Domestic Product (GDP)

	GDP in Bil Curnt-TL	GDP in 1985 Prices	Annual % Change *	GDP per CAP in 1985 US$ **	Annual % Change
1960	47.0	7637.4	...	527.0	...
1970	145.5	13259.7	...	713.0	...
1971	187.1	14461.4	9.1	758.0	6.3
1972	232.1	15411.7	6.5	787.0	3.8
1973	295.5	16092.5	4.4	802.0	1.9
1974	409.7	17462.8	8.5	849.0	5.9
1975	519.2	19016.6	8.8	903.0	6.4
1976	663.9	20669.0	8.6	968.0	7.2
1977	863.0	21564.4	4.3	988.0	2.1
1978	1274.8	22178.0	2.8	993.0	0.5
1979	2155.9	21982.7	-0.9	963.0	-3.0
1980	4328.0	21818.9	-0.8	934.0	-3.0
1981	6413.6	22769.4	4.3	951.0	1.8
1982	8620.4	23906.2	4.9	974.0	2.4
1983	11531.8	24791.4	3.7	985.0	1.1
1984	18212.1	26213.8	5.7	1016.0	3.2
1985	27551.8	27551.8	5.1	1042.0	2.6
1986	39288.0	29842.1	8.3	1107.0	6.2
1987	58299.0	32049.3	7.3	1164.0	5.2
1988	100825.0	33298.4	3.8	1182.0	1.6
1989	167770.0	33613.2	0.9	1165.0	-1.4
1990	282800.0	36703.2	9.1	1230.0	5.6

* "Annual % Change" in GDP in 1985 Prices.
** At the prices and the exchange rates of 1985.

Source: OECD (1992). *National Accounts: Main Aggregates, 1960-1990.* (vol.1) various tables.

In the economic arena, the military allowed the price of Lira to be determined by market forces as of May 1, 1981. This was after four devaluations in the first four months of 1981, bringing the total to 30 devaluations since January, 1973. Interest-rate limits on time deposits were eliminated and the financial markets were deregulated. The deregulation of the financial markets was not orderly, however. Given the prevailing economic conditions, there was no time for a "market culture" to develop. Speculative frenzy and greed overrode caution and discretion, resulting in a crash in mid-1982.[23]

The critics portrayed the crash as an outcome of rapid economic liberalization. By then, Özal who was associated with liberalization, was being criticized for two other reasons as well. First, he was criticized for his refusal to make concessions on the stabilization package. Second, the critics were dismayed by his insistence that the long-run success of the package required administrative coordination through his office. Disagreements over these led to his resignation from the government in 1982.

The Motherland Party (MP), which Özal had organized after his resignation, won the elections in November, 1983. For the first time since 1969, Turkey had a civilian majority government. As the Secretary General of the winning party, Özal became the Prime Minister.[24] The election victory gave Özal the administrative control and the mandate to continue with the economic reforms.

Table 8: Deficits of State Economic Enterprises (SEEs), and
Total Public Sector Deficits, as a percent of GNP

	SEEs Deficit as a % of GNP	Public Sec Deficit as a % of GNP
1980	-5.8	-10.5
1981	-2.9	-4.9
1982	-2.4	-4.3
1983	-2.7	-6.0
1984	-2.3	-6.5
1985	-3.1	-4.6
1986	-3.4	-4.7
1987	-4.2	-7.8
1988	-2.8	-6.2
1989	-2.6	-7.2
1990	-5.3	-10.5
1991a	-4.3	-12.6

Source: OECD (1992). *Economic Surveys: Turkey, 1991/1992.* p.38.

Note: a. preliminary

"Public Sector" figures include the SEEs, the Central Government, Local Administrations, Revolving Funds, etc.

His 1984 stabilization measures went beyond the 1980 package.[25] Laws governing foreign exchange transactions were liberalized further; residents and nonresidents alike were allowed to open foreign exchange accounts, with no stipulations concerning their use. Foreigners who imported their capital could buy real estate, participate in domestic investment projects, open branch offices of foreign companies, and buy stocks in Turkish companies. Restrictions on the repatriation of profits, dividends, and the proceeds of sales by foreigners doing business in Turkey were abolished. The bureaucratic formalities regarding exports were simplified; a public Fund was established to subsidize investments in export-oriented endeavors. Government proposed measures to keep its expenditures and deficits in check. These measures included additional reforms in the tax system (as discussed below), and pursuing a market-based pricing policy for the SEEs so that their subsidies could eventually be eliminated. In order to limit the growth of domestic demand, wage increases were to be kept below the inflation rate; this had become a viable policy option because of the changes in the labor law which the military had implemented earlier. The government also announced its resolve to keep the growth of money supply in check. The succeeding events have demonstrated that not all of these goals were achieved.

IV. PUBLIC FINANCES IN THE 1980S

In this section, I will discuss the expenditures and revenues of the public sector during the 1980s. The discussion will be in the context of the reforms implemented, as proposed in the 1980 and 1984 stabilization packages.

Table 6 shows that, from 1980 on, both the (nominal) revenues and the expenditures of the central government increased steadily, as did its deficits. The ratio of deficit-to-GNP, however, averaged only about 4 percent. Although this ratio is comparable to that of the US over the same period, the comparison is misleading because of the budgetary process in Turkey. As discussed in greater detail later, Turkey has a large number of public institutions, funds, and administrative and economic units which have their own budgets. By law, their economic activities are not included in the budget statement of the central government, called the consolidated budget.

Table 8 gives a more accurate picture of the total public sector deficits in the 1980s. Table 8 shows that the total public sector deficit including those of the SEEs, the extra-budget funds, the revolving funds, *and* the central government has averaged about 7 percent of the GNP, in the 1980s. The annual deficits of the central government were exceeded often by the combined deficits of the "rest" of the public sector and, on occasion, by the deficits of the SEEs. By the end of the 1980s, the total public deficit again was over ten percent of the GNP, as it was in 1980.

A. EXPENDITURES

Before discussing the trends in the specific components of public expenditures, an overall view is in order. During the 1970s, the expenditures of the central government averaged about 24 percent of the GNP. (OECD, *Economic Surveys: Turkey*, various reports.) As shown in Table 6, the trend continued through 1980-81. Between 1982 and 1988, these expenditures were reduced to an average of 20-21 percent of GNP. Since then, they have been increasing again, and exceeded 28 percent in 1991.

Table 9: Consolidated Budget Expenditures: Selected Years
in Billions of TL

	Total Expenditures	Current Expenditures	Interest on Total Debt	Investment	Transfers
1970	31.0	15.0	1.0	7.0	8.0
1975	113.0	57.0	3.0	25.0	28.0
1980	1078.0	464.0	28.0	220.0	366.0
1981	1516.0	603.0	67.0	360.0	486.0
1982	1922.0	823.0	93.0	463.0	543.0
1983	2613.0	1062.0	181.0	478.0	892.0
1984	3784.0	1488.0	375.0	677.0	1244.0
1985	5313.0	2095.0	675.0	1030.0	1513.0
1986	8165.0	3051.0	1331.0	1624.0	2159.0
1987	12696.0	4538.0	2266.0	2295.0	3597.0
1988	21006.0	7444.0	4978.0	3141.0	5443.0
1989	38051.0	16607.0	8259.0	5067.0	8118.0
1990	67194.0	33381.0	13966.0	8902.0	10945.0
1991a	129345.0	60900.0	24153.0	16600.0	27692.0

a. preliminary

Source: OECD. *Economic Surveys: Turkey*. (various issues.)

Tables 9 and 10 present the distribution of these expenditures by type.
Table 10 shows that only the interest payments on total debt constituted a
steadily rising share of the total expenditures during the 1980s. This share
increased from less than 3 percent of the total public spending in 1980 to
about 20 percent in 1990. This is related to Table 11 which shows the trend
in the public sector deficits as well as the change in the methods of financing them. Because of agreements with the Treasury, the Central Bank
played a smaller role than usual in monetizing the deficits at the end of
the 1980s. The significance of this point is that government borrowing at
high and rising rates, has been an important reason for the increasing
burden of interest payments during most of the 1980s.

Table 10 shows that during the period 1980-1991, the ratio of current
spending to total expenditures by the central government averaged about
41 percent, compared to about 46 percent during the decade of the 1970s.
(OECD, *Economic Surveys: Turkey*, various reports.) Table 10 shows also
that after declining steadily during the period 1982-88, the current expenditures increased to about fifty percent of the total central government
expenditures by 1990. The most important reason for the reversal in the
trend was the wage increases given to the public employees after 1988.

Table 10: Percentage Distribution of Consolidated Budget Expenditures

	Total Exenditures	Current Expenditures	Interest on Total Debt	Investment	Transfers
1970	100.0	48.4	3.2	22.6	25.8
1975	100.0	50.4	2.7	22.1	24.8
1980	100.0	43.0	2.6	20.4	34.0
1981	100.0	39.8	4.4	23.7	32.1
1982	100.0	42.8	4.8	24.1	28.3
1983	100.0	40.6	6.9	18.3	34.1
1984	100.0	39.3	9.9	17.9	32.9
1985	100.0	39.4	12.7	19.4	28.5
1986	100.0	37.4	16.3	19.9	26.4
1987	100.0	35.7	17.8	18.1	28.3
1988	100.0	35.4	23.7	15.0	25.9
1989	100.0	43.6	21.7	13.3	21.3
1990	100.0	49.7	20.1	13.3	16.3
1991a	100.0	47.1	18.7	12.8	21.4

a. preliminary

Source: Derived from Table 10.

In order to keep aggregate demand in check, the real wages of public employees had been allowed to decline steadily by about 50 percent between 1980 and 1988. (Barkey, 1990, p.186). So, the wage increases given after 1988 were justified on equity grounds. Yet, the magnitude of the wage increases, coupled with the fact that the increases happened over a very short period of time, appears to have contributed to the inflationary pressures at the end of the decade.[26]

Public investments in Turkey historically have tended to be inflationary in the short run due to the long gestation periods of such projects, the shortage of skilled labor, and various bottlenecks in the production process. But in the long run, such investments help increase productivity and alleviate inflationary pressures. Table 10 shows that, in spite of a rather sharp decline after 1987, investment expenditures averaged about 18 percent of the total public expenditures during the period 1980-1991; this is slightly below the average of 19 percent during the 1970s. (OECD, *Economic Surveys: Turkey*, various reports.) There are three main reasons for the decline in the share of investment expenditures. The increasingly active role played by the private sector in the 1980s is the first reason. A possible structural shift in the allocation of public resources, particularly towards the end of the 1980s is the second reason. The third reason for the apparent decline in the share of investment in total public spending is the restructuring of the budgetary process, beginning in 1986. Until 1986, most public investment projects were undertaken by the executive branch through its Ministries. By definition, expenditures by the executive branch are included in the consolidated budget. Karluk (1994, pp. 49-50) mentions that as of the 1986-87 period, the officials began financing some large-scale investment projects through the "extra-budget funds" instead.[27] Since the consolidated budget statements do not include the "extra-budget funds," Tables 10 and 11 understate both the actual amount and also the share of public expenditures devoted to investment after 1986-1987.[28]

The "Transfers" entry in Tables 9 and 10 includes: funds appropriated for capital injection into the SEEs; intergovernmental transfers; transfers to a number of social security and social insurance agencies; and income tax rebates. As discussed in the "Revenues" section below, the tax reform of the 1980s included provisions allowing for an increase in the income tax rebates. As a result, the actual amount of income tax rebates is likely to have been increasing over time. Since there is no published data on the specific components of the "Transfers" item, it is difficult to be more specific in analyzing its trend. As discussed later, some of the transfers are related to the functional breakdown of public expenditures.

Table 11: Public Sector Borrowing Requirements and Sources of Financing

	Public Sector Deficit (TL Bill.)			Sources of Financing as percent of total			
	Total	Central Government	Other Governments	SEEs	Central Bank	Net Foreign Borrowing	Net Domestic Borrowing
1980	-465	-166	-42	-257	22.2	27.6	50.2
1981	-319	-124	-3	-192	12.1	61.7	26.2
1982	-374	-157	-11	-206	8.7	56.1	35.2
1983	-687	-313	-72	-302	10.5	16.6	72.9
1984	-1194	-979	206	-421	11.2	54.1	34.5
1985	-1267	-798	401	-870	27.3	1.7	71.0
1986	-1866	-1411	865	-1320	14.1	58.0	27.9
1987	-4544	-2607	533	-2470	20.4	44.2	35.4
1988	-6226	-3990	569	-2805	15.8	43.3	40.9
1989	-12162	-7672	-70	-4420	3.7	15.3	81.0
1990	-26239	-11955	-3168	-11116	1.1	11.9	87.0

Source: OECD. *Economic Surveys: Turkey.*(var. issues)

Table 12 shows the distribution of the central government expenditures by function during the 1980s. The share of defense in total public expenditures was about 15 percent during the early 1980s, the same as it was during the decade of the 1970s. We see from Table 12 that this share declined after 1981 and the ratio of defense expenditures to total expenditures averaged slightly less than 13 percent a year during the period 1980-1990. Because of tradition and also her membership in Nato, Turkey has always spent a significant share of public funds for defense. She has one of the larger armed forces in the world; historically, a substantial portion of her defense spending has been for personnel. The declining trend in the share of defense expenditures is not due to a reduction in **total** defense spending at all. Geopolitics of the region rule out any sizeable reductions in total defense spending in Turkey. The main reason for the declining **share** is the change in the officials' priorities; the share of public funds allocated to functions other than defense has increased since the 1982-83 period. This is consistent with the objectives of the 1980 stabilization package, and reflects the continuing impact of the 1961 constitutional debates concerning the role of government in promoting social welfare.

Table 12: Percentage Distribution of Expenditures by Function:
Consolidated Budget

	1980	1981	1983	1984	1985	1986	1987	1988	1989	1990
Total	100	100	100	100	100	100	100	100	100	100
General Public Service	26.7	31.2	38.6	49.3	54.0	44.2	31.6	33.5	31.0	25.2
Defense	15.2	15.2	13.2	11.6	10.9	13.5	11.4	10.4	11.6	11.7
Education	14.2	16.8	12.5	10.7	10.0	11.9	12.6	12.7	15.7	19.2
Health	3.6	2.1	1.8	1.6	1.8	2.2	2.4	2.4	2.9	3.6
Social Security	2.0	0.4	0.5	0.4	0.5	0.4	0.7	0.5	0.5	0.6
Welfare	0.6	0.1	0.5	0.5	0.5	0.6	0.7	0.8	1.2	1.5
Housing, Community Development	3.4	8.4	1.1	2.9	2.6	2.8	2.1	1.8	1.5	1.5
Fuel & Energy	4.3	6.7	5.6	4.8	6.3	9.1	7.7	7.2	6.5	5.6
Agriculture, Forest, Fish	1.9	0.6	2.0	1.7	1.3	1.6	1.5	1.5	1.7	2.0
Mining, Manufacturing, Construction	4.9	0.9	0.8	0.7	1.0	1.6	1.7	2.0	0.8	0.9
Transportation, Communication	8.1	6.0	8.6	7.7	8.0	10.4	9.1	7.0	6.9	7.3
Other Economic Activities	14.8	11.5	14.7	8.0	3.0	1.6	3.6	4.5	3.9	2.0
Rest	0.2	0.1	0.1	0.1	0.1	0.0	15.0	15.7	15.9	19.0

Note: There was a change in fiscal year in 1981-82. Through 1981, fiscal year was from March 1 of one year through April 30 of the following year. As a result of the change, fiscal year 1982 was nine months long. Since the figures are not comparable with the other years, they are not shown.

Source: IMF (1991) *Government Finance Statistics Yearbook, 1991*. (derived from data on pp. 567-568.)

Table 12 shows that, in spite of fluctuations, the share of public funds devoted to education averaged about 14 percent during the 1980s but reached almost 20 percent in 1990. Karluk (1994, p. 51) reports that the share was about 20 percent in the early 1990s as well. The previous peak was in the mid-1970s, when almost 17 percent of the public funds were allocated to education. (OECD, *Economic Surveys: Turkey*, various reports.) There are two reasons for the increase in the **amount** of funds devoted to education: a) wage-and-salary increases for teachers and administrative personnel, as of 1988 most education personnel including teachers are public employees; and b) the increase in the number of children attending school. In Turkey, the first five years of schooling is compulsory. The reason for the increase in the **share** of education expenditures in total expenditures is the commitment by the officials to increasing the rate of literacy. Karluk (1994, p. 9) reports that as recently as 1970, the rate of literacy among those who were 6 years old or older was only about 55 percent; it reached 67 percent in 1980, and was 86 percent as of 1990.

Expenditures for health, welfare, housing, and social security are redistributive outlays. As mentioned earlier, state's role in promoting equity was outlined in the Constitution of 1961; equity concerns entered into party platforms in the mid-1970s; and promoting social welfare was among the objectives of both the 1980 and the 1984 stabilization packages. Yet Table 12 shows that during the period 1980-1990 the combined annual share of health, housing, welfare, and social security in total consolidated budget expenditures was only 1.7 percent; this was even less than the 1.9 percent share in the 1970s. (IMF. *Government Finance Statistics Yearbook*, various issues.) These figures understate the actual role played by the public sector in promoting social welfare because they exclude most of such expenditures.

The figures for health, welfare, social security, and housing in Table 12 consist of two components. The first component is inclusive of administrative expenditures of the Government Ministries which oversee these functions. The second component consists of "transfers" from the consolidated budget to the extra-budget funds which are legally responsible for such functions. These extra-budget funds are not included in the consolidated budget; each has its own (earmarked) revenues and budget statement. I now discuss four of these funds. The discussion indicates the full extent of the social welfare programs in Turkey.

The four funds are the Housing Fund (*Konut Fonu*), Government Employees' Retirement Fund (*Emekli Sandigi*), Social Insurance Institution (*Sosyal Sigortalar Kurumu*), and the Self-Employed Retirement Fund (*BAG-KUR*). The Housing Fund (HF) was founded in 1984. Its function is to finance housing for the poor and middle income families. HF receives its resources mainly from certain import surcharges and a special "exit tax" collected from the Turkish **tourists** travelling abroad.

Government Employees' Retirement Fund (GERF) was established in 1949. It provides coverage only for the government employees. Social Insurance Institution (SSI) was founded in 1965. It provides "insurance" for the employees of the state economic organizations, and the private companies and corporations. Participation in both the GERF and the SSI is mandatory. They perform two functions: a) paying retirement pensions to their members, and b) providing medical care to their active as well as retired members, and their dependents. Both the GERF and the SSI are basically pay-as-you-go systems; that is, the benefits paid to current beneficiaries come from the taxes collected from the members who are presently working. Such taxes are the social security tax, the payroll tax, and the manpower tax.

The Self-Employed Retirement Fund (SERF) was established in 1971 as a voluntary annuity fund for retirement. Initially it was only for the self-employed professionals, artisans, and artists; in 1983, it began offering coverage to the self-employed farmers and farm workers as well. In 1985, medical insurance was included among SERF's benefits. Presently, SERF is open to anyone who is not insured by either the GERF or the SSI, and is able and willing to pay the premiums for membership. So far, SERF has been fully funded; that is, the premiums which SERF has collected and invested, and the interest it has earned from such investments, have been sufficient to meet SERF's obligations.

The HF, GREF, SSI, and SERF receive "transfers" from the consolidated budget only when their revenues during a given month or quarter are not sufficient to meet their obligations for that period. The establishment and the growth of HF, GERF, SSI and SERF reflect a strong sense of paternalism on the part of the state. As a group, they constitute a safety net comparable to Social Security, Medicare, Medicaid, and the Low Income Housing programs in the U.S. Karluk (1994, p.51) mentions that, in Turkey, the expenditures for health alone may be as much as seven percent of the total expenditures by all levels of government and extra-budget funds. Obviously, the exclusion of such extra-budget funds from the consolidated budget understates the share of total public expenditures in GNP as well.

When we examine the public expenditures for the other functions, we see from Table 12 that, after reaching a peak in 1986, the share of funds spent for transportation and communication began declining. There are two reasons for this. First, a number of projects, which began in the early 1980s, were completed by the mid-1980s. Second, due to the change in the budgetary process as mentioned earlier, some public investment projects were undertaken through the extra-budget funds, beginning in 1986-87.

Of the remaining items in Table 12, the entry under "Rest" stands out as of 1987. It is not clear what item(s) this category includes. However, a comparison of the figures for the "General Public Services," "Other Economic Activities," and the "Rest" indicates that some public functions may have been reclassified across these three categories beginning in the mid-1980s. The "General Public Services" category traditionally has referred to the expenditures for public order and security, foreign service, and the judicial, legislative, and the executive branches of the government.

B. REVENUES

The early 1980s were characterized by extensive and ambitious tax reforms. These reforms were long overdue reactions to the prevailing inequities of the tax system in Turkey. For instance, in the mid-1970s only 18 percent of the GNP accrued to the wage earners; yet, the wage earners paid two-thirds of all the taxes in Turkey while the merchants, the industrialists, and the professional classes combined paid the remaining one-third of the taxes. (Mumcuoglu, 1980, p.400.) The reasons were the tax structure itself and widespread tax evasion. Özmucur-Çinar (1978) estimated that the Turkish government was able to collect only 57 percent of the potential income tax obligations in 1974. The authors found that the uncollected portion was due to underreporting exclusively by the non-wage-and-salaried classes; it amounted to more than 7 percent of GNP. The tax reforms of the 1980s were designed to encourage compliance and reduce tax evasion.

Article 73 of the 1982 Constitution states: "In order to finance public expenditures, everybody is responsible to pay taxes according to ability to pay. The social objective of fiscal policy is fair and equitable distribution of the tax burden." (Erginay, 1990, p. 11.) This objective served as the impetus for tax reforms whose main features were: the introduction of the Value Added Tax (VAT); changes in the individual and the corporate income taxes, and taxes on foreign trade; the introduction of measures to enforce and encourage compliance, battle tax evasion, and improve efficiency. The tax laws were amended to allow people and businesses to keep one set of records for different taxes. Steps were taken to better computerize the tax system. Additionally, in 1986, an advanced collection scheme was introduced and collection lags were shortened, in order to reduce the inflationary losses in tax revenues.[29] As discussed later, as a result of these reforms, there has been some improvement in the distribution of tax burden. The existing socio-economic conditions make it safe to assume that it might be a while before the rural sectors, small service and trade establishments, and the self-employed individuals bear their respective shares of the burden.

Despite reform, the new tax laws have some shortcomings. The officials' attempts to eliminate these shortcomings resulted in frequent, and even contradictory, changes in the tax laws in the 1980s. Another reason for the changes was that the officials realized that the measures implemented initially under the 1980 and 1984 packages were not sufficient to achieve all of the socio-economic objectives. Consequently, changes in the tax laws sometimes reflected the policy makers' attempts to achieve conflicting objectives and sometimes their indecision. Erginay (1990, pp. 38-42) notes that according to the 1982 Constitution, laws in Turkey cannot be retroactive; but the Constitution has no specific provisions extending this prohibition explicitly to the tax laws. Law makers have taken advantage of this loophole and made some retroactive changes in the tax laws, in order to raise much needed revenues and tax away speculative gains. To the extent that it means taxing legally earned "economic rights," retroactivity adds to the instability and uncertainty in the economy, and undermines public confidence.

Column 2 of Table 6 shows the revenues of the central government. Table 13 and Table 14 present the distribution of these revenues by source. Table 6 shows that the revenues rose from 912 billion TL in 1980 to 97,000 billion TL in 1991. As a percent of GDP, there is not a substantial difference between revenues in 1980 and 1991. We see from Table 6 that the ratio of revenues to GDP averaged about 18 percent in the 1980s; although this ratio fell to 16 percent in the mid-1980s, it has been rising since. The average of 18 percent for the 1980s compares, for example, with 20 percent for the U.S. However, the figures reported in Tables 6, 13 and 14 understate the actual tax collections by the central government in Turkey. (Erginay, 1990, pp. 52-3.) As mentioned earlier, this is due to the budgetary process. Karluk (1994, p. 40) states that only 77 percent of the taxes collected by the central government are reported in the consolidated budget. The central government in Turkey gives 13 percent of the taxes which it collects to the local governments; and the taxes earmarked for the extra-budget funds average about 10 percent of the total collections. Since the central government serves as a "collection agency" for the local governments and the extra-budget funds, the Budget Law does not consider these transactions as "Transfers" from the consolidated budget either. As a result, the overall tax burden in Turkey is much greater than is indicated by the consolidated budget figures.

Table 13: Total Consolidated Budget Revenues - in Billions of Current TL

	1981	1982	1983	1984	1985	1986	1987	1988	1989	1990
INCOME	746	965	1109	1341	1772	3053	4425	6919	13468	23246
Individual	574	713	879	1069	1324	2104	3093	4801	9871	18609
Corporate	125	207	215	272	448	949	1332	2118	3598	4637
Capital Gains	5	7	0	...	...	...	...	...	...	...
Fiscal Balance	42	38	16	...	...	...	...	...	...	...
WEALTH	22	26	40	41	54	53	68	147	177	411
Real Estate	12	14	26	26	30	0	0	0	0	0
Motor Vehicles	6	8	8	9	17	43	51	121	134	329
Inherit./Gift	3	4	5	6	7	10	17	26	43	82
GOODS/SRVCS	308	399	530	602	1098	1853	2768	4487	7641	13667
Domestic Prod.	75	88	123	...	...	...	...	...	...	...
Petroleum	2	3	3	0	46	54	71	159	656	1224
Monopoly Prod.	78	121	122	...	...	...	...	...	...	...
Retail Sales	6	6	9	...	...	...	...	...	...	...

Table 13 (continued)

Sugar Product.	1	1	1	...	...	...	...	...	...	...
MVehicle Prchs	7	8	9	13	21	43	74	127	214	585
RealEst Purchs	14	15	10	...	...	...	...	...	...	...
VAT	...	...	174	567	1040	1563	2661	4176	7650
VAT-MonopGoods	...	...	172	124	178	264	288	461	373
Bank./Insurance	54	65	95	59	58	94	155	374	643	1164
Transportation	3	4	5							
Stamp Duty/Fees	65	83	145	183	282	444	641	878	1489	2673
Communication	4	5	7	...	...	...	...	...	...	...
Construction	1	0	0							
Abolished Taxes	...	...	...	18	159	20	13	7	18	18
FOREIGN TRADE	114	174	254	370	746	993	1777	2672	4246	8057
TOTAL TAX REV	1190	1564	1933	2372	3829	5972	9051	14232	25550	45400
NONTAX&OTHERS	199	194	373	434	686	782	1038	2784	4829	9839
TOTAL REVENUES	1389	1758	2306	2806	4515	6754	10089	17016	30379	55239

Source: OECD. Economic Surveys: Turkey. (various issues)

Table 14: Total Consolidated Budget Revenues - % Distribution

	1981	1982	1983	1984	1985	1986	1987	1988	1989	1990
INCOME	53.7	54.9	48.1	47.8	39.2	45.2	43.9	40.7	44.3	42.1
Individual	41.3	40.6	38.1	38.1	29.3	31.2	30.7	28.2	32.5	33.7
Corporate	9.0	11.8	9.3	9.7	9.9	14.1	13.2	12.4	11.8	8.4
Capital Gains	0.4	0.4	0.0							
Fiscal Balance	3.0	2.2	0.7							
WEALTH	1.6	1.5	1.7	1.5	1.2	0.8	0.7	0.9	0.6	0.7
Real Estate	0.9	0.8	1.1	0.9	0.7					
Motor Vehicles	0.4	0.5	0.3	0.3	0.4	0.6	0.5	0.7	0.4	0.6
Inherit./Gift	0.2	0.2	0.2	0.2	0.2	0.1	0.2	0.2	0.1	0.2
GOODS/SRVCS	22.2	22.7	23.0	21.5	24.3	27.4	27.4	26.4	25.2	24.7
Domestic Prod.	5.4	5.0	5.3							
Petroleum	0.1	0.2	0.1	0.0	1.0	0.8	0.7	0.9	2.2	2.2
Monopoly Prod.	5.6	6.9	5.3							
Retail Sales	0.4	0.3	0.4							

Table 14 (continued)

Sugar Product.	0.1	0.1	0.0	0.5	0.5	0.6	0.7	0.7	0.7	1.1
MVehicle Prchs	0.5	0.5	0.4							
RealEst Purchs	1.0	0.9	0.4							
VAT				6.2	12.6	15.4	15.5	15.6	13.7	13.9
VAT-MonopGoods	3.9	3.7	4.1	6.1	2.7	2.6	2.6	1.7	1.5	0.7
Bank./Insurance				2.1	1.3	1.4	1.5	2.2	2.1	2.1
Transportation	0.2	0.2	0.2							
Stamp Duty/Fees	4.7	4.7	6.3	6.5	6.2	6.6	6.4	5.2	4.9	4.8
Communication	0.3	0.3	0.3							
Construction	0.1	0.0	0.0							
ABOLISHED TXS	0.0	0.0	0.0	0.6	3.5	0.3	0.1	0.0	0.1	-
FOREIGN TRADE	8.2	9.9	11.0	13.2	16.5	14.7	17.6	15.7	14.0	14.6
TOTAL TAX REV	85.7	89.0	83.8	84.5	84.8	88.4	89.7	83.6	84.1	82.2
NONTAX&OTHERS	14.3	11.0	16.2	15.5	15.2	11.6	10.3	16.4	15.9	17.8
TOTAL	100.0	100.0	100.0	100.0	100.0	100.0	100.0	100.0	100.0	100.0

Source: Derived from Table 13.

I now discuss the major sources of revenue, shown in Tables 13 and
14. Table 14 shows that taxes in general have been the major sources of
government revenues. Since 1987, the share of tax revenues has declined
and the share of "non-tax revenues and others" has increased. This does
not reflect a structural shift in revenue sources; rather, it is due to the inclusion of the proceeds from sales of some state properties in the entry,
called, "non-tax revenues and others."

1. Income Taxes

The history of "income" taxes in Turkey goes back to the period of the
Ottoman Empire. The earliest attempt to levy such a tax was in 1863. Its
base was "gains" from employment; it did not generate much revenue. At
the outset of World War I, it was changed to resemble a French levy called
"patente," imposed as a license fee for gainful business and employment.
It was not an important source of revenue in this form either. In 1925, the
"patente" was replaced with "kazanç vergisi" ("revenue tax"), a proportional tax on business revenues and personal incomes alike. With the introduction of tax brackets in 1934, the tax was made progressive.
Hershlag (1968, p.89) reports that the revenues from "kazanç vergisi"
were reported in the budget together with the revenues from the property
tax; the total amount rarely exceeded 15 percent of total public revenues.
The tax reform of 1949 replaced the "kazanç vergisi" with two separate
taxes: Personal Income Tax and Corporate Tax. (For details, see Erginay,
1990, pp.130-133, and Uluatam, 1991, pp.279-280.)

I. Personal Income Tax

The Personal Income Tax Law of 1949 identified the types of income subject to the personal income tax as opposed to the corporate tax, and established personal deductions according to family size. The Law kept the tax
rates and the income brackets the same as they had been since 1934. There
were ten brackets; the first bracket was for the first 2500 T.L. of taxable
income, and the highest bracket included taxable incomes "over 100,000
T.L." The marginal tax rates ranged from 15 percent to 45 percent. There
was no change in the Personal Income Tax Law from 1949 until 1958. In
1958, the highest tax bracket was increased to "over 300,000 T.L." of taxable income; the maximum tax rate was raised to 60 percent. The Income
Tax Law of 1960, which was passed during the military's reign, reaffirmed

the principles of the 1949 Law. It raised the top bracket to "over 500,000 T.L." of taxable income. In addition, the maximum tax rate was increased to 70 percent, but the rate for the first 2,500 T.L. of taxable income was reduced to 10 percent. As discussed earlier, the Income Tax Law of 1960 included specific provisions for the taxation of agricultural incomes as well; but the civilian governments, which succeeded the military, postponed the taxation of agricultural incomes. In 1963, the top income tax bracket was increased to "over 1,000,000 T.L." but the maximum tax rate was reduced from 70 to 68 percent. Finally, in 1964, income derived from agriculture was taxed for the first time since 1925. (See Bulutoglu, 1967, Ch. 14; Hershlag, 1968, pp. 148-9, 241-2; OECD, 1981, *Economic Surveys: Turkey*, pp. 83-4.) In spite of all the changes between 1934 and 1963, the total number of tax brackets remained at ten, and the lowest tax bracket was always defined by the first 2,500 T.L. of taxable income. There were no significant changes in the Personal Income Tax Law between 1963 and 1980. I now turn to the reforms of the 1980s.

In spite of fluctuations in its share, the individual income tax has been the most important source of public revenues in Turkey. Table 14 shows that only twice since 1981 has the share of individual income tax in public revenues been below 30 percent. As is the case with income tax statutes in general, the Turkish Income Tax Law has no definition of "income" per se. Instead, the returns to factors of production are listed as types of taxable incomes. The tax base includes wages, salaries, profits (from sole proprietorships), royalties, rental income, income from various types of investments, and agriculture.[30] Between 1981 and 1983, the tax was based on self-declaration and withholding at the source, depending on the type of income and also the nature of the income generating activity. (For a detailed treatment, see Erginay, 1990, pp.134-220.) However, the extent of tax evasion prompted the authorities to revise the system in 1983. Under the new system, the tax authorities use "some basic rules and indicators" to impute the incomes of certain groups. These groups include the self-employed, self-employed professionals, small retail trade and service establishments, and those engaged in agricultural activities. The higher of the imputed and the self-declared amounts constitutes the tax base. (OECD, *Economic Surveys: Turkey, 1991/1992*, p. 83.)

Table 15: Personal Income Tax Brackets and Rates for Selected Years.

Brackets (TL)	Rates (%) in 1981	Rates (%) in 1985	Brackets (in 1986)	Rates (%) in 1986	Brackets (in 1991)	Rates (%) in 1991
Up to 1 million	40	30	Up to 3 million	25	Up to 12 million	25
Above 1 Million:			3-6 million	30	12-24 million	30
2 to 3	45	36	6-12 million	35	24-48 million	35
3 to 5	50	42	12-24 million	40	48-96 million	40
5 to 10	60	55	24-48 million	45	96-192 million	45
10 to 15	70	60	48 and above	50	192 and above	50
15 to 25	75	65				
Above 25 million	66	60				

Source: OECD (1992). Economic Surveys: Turkey, 1991/1992, p.66.

After the 1980 *coup*, both the income tax rates and the income brackets were also adjusted. The main reason was to rectify the impact which the inflation had on income distribution and tax burdens in the 1970s. Table 15 shows the rates and the brackets for selected years in the 1980s. It shows that the lowest tax bracket for 1981 was defined by the first 1,000,000 T.L. of taxable income; as mentioned earlier, the same amount defined as the top income tax bracket since 1963. The officials reduced the number of tax brackets to seven and changed the marginal tax rates. The rates were progressively reduced through 1985. In 1986, both the brackets and the rates were adjusted again. The rates have remained the same since then but the brackets have been revised upwards every year since 1987. Table 15 shows that, from 1986 to 1991, the brackets were adjusted by a factor of four. The pattern and the timing of the changes in the 1980s indicate that the officials initially tried using the income tax both to stimulate economic activity (from the "supply side") and also to promote equity. However, concerns with the impact of inflation on income distribution, and ultimately political stability, eventually outweighed other factors including using the income tax as an anti-inflationary tool. One impact of the changes in the income tax law has been that the "share of wage earners in personal income tax receipts decreased from 64.4 percent in 1976 to 55.0 percent in 1990." (OECD, *Economic Surveys: Turkey, 1991/92*, p. 65.)

Tax authorities use exemptions, deductions, and withholding provisions to facilitate tax administration, to encourage or discourage various economic activities, and to promote equity. Such provisions also affect the revenue yield. At the time of the 1980 stabilization package, the income tax law had two types of personal exemptions: a "general" allowance for each member in a household, and a higher "special" allowance for the wage earners in the household. These exemptions were not changed from 1981 until 1986, when the "general" exemption was abolished. The "special" exemption was increased annually after 1986, but it has always lagged behind inflation. As of tax year 1991, the legislature has linked it to the minimum wage in effect in a given tax year. (OECD, *Economic Surveys: Turkey, 1991/1992*, p.68.)

Another significant development in the 1980s was the introduction of the "rebate system" in 1984. Initially rebates were allowed to wage earners only, upon submission of invoices for "essential" expenditures. The rebates were subject to an upper limit, and were inversely related to income. One purpose of the rebate system was to strengthen the progressivity of the income tax itself. Another objective of the rebate system was to prepare the public for the Value Added Tax (VAT) which was also scheduled to be introduced in 1984.[31] Over time, the rebate system has been extended to those whose taxable incomes are derived from agricultural activities, professional activities, small (mainly unincorporated) businesses, as well as, various benefits and pensions (such as, retirement, disability, widows, and orphans pensions and benefits). Initially, the only qualifying expenditures were those for heating, education, food, certain durables, and medical treatment. Over time, the list has come to include (in whole or in part) business expenditures for transportation and hotels, and residential rent. As a result, in 1990, the "tax expenditures" due to rebates were more than 13 percent of the personal income tax receipts and 9 percent of the total public sector deficit. (For details, see OECD, *Economic Surveys: Turkey 1991/1992*, pp. 65-70.)

Mortgage interest payments are not among the deductible items in deriving taxable income. Social security taxes, payroll taxes, manpower taxes, and the insurance premiums paid to the various extra-budget retirement funds are among the deductible items. As of 1986, capital gains from the sale of stocks held a year or longer are exempt from the income tax. As of 1988, interest earnings are only subject to a 10 percent withholding tax. Dividends are not subject to personal income tax, implying that double taxation of distributed corporate earnings is avoided. Finally, a portion of rental incomes and earnings from the sale of plays, films, books, etc. have been exempted since the early 1980s. (For details, see Erginay, 1990, pp. 263-71.) The amounts exempted have been adjusted for inflation over time. There is no estimate of the "tax expenditures" associated with these deductions and exemptions.

II. Corporate Tax

As mentioned earlier, the Corporate Tax Law was passed in 1949 and went into affect in 1950. Following the tax reform of 1949, the most important changes in the Corporate Tax Law took place in the 1980s. One objective of these changes was to increase the public revenues from the corporate tax. Table 14 shows that in spite of fluctuations, the share of public revenues from the corporate tax in the 1980s averaged about 11 percent, which was more than twice its share in the 1970s. The share of public revenues from the corporate tax was never over 6 percent a year in the 1970s, and had declined to less than 4 percent in 1979. (OECD, *Economic Surveys: Turkey 1981*, tables in various issues.) Other objectives of the changes in the corporate tax were to stimulate private investment in export related activities and in less developed regions of the country.

Corporate Tax has always been a flat-rate tax. At the time of the 1980 *coup*, the aggregate rate (inclusive of the withholding tax) was 43 percent of the corporate profits. With the consolidation of some levies, the rate was increased to 50 percent in 1981. By 1984, the preferential tax treatment of the SEEs was abolished, and the tax rate was lowered to 40 percent in order to provide (supply-side) incentive to growth. This reduction in the tax rate accounts for the declining share of the corporate tax in total revenues. In response to pressing revenue needs, however, the legislature again increased the corporate tax rate to 46 percent in 1986, reversing the trend in the share of corporate tax in total revenues.

The "advance payment" feature of the corporate tax is meant to reduce inflationary losses in public revenues. Corporations can carry their losses forward for five years but the losses cannot be indexed for inflation. However, as of 1987, corporations in Turkey have been allowed to use the wholesale price index to fully adjust their depreciation base for inflation. While the interest which the corporations receive is subject to a 10 percent withholding tax, all their interest payments, and as much as one-fifth of their export revenues, can be deducted from their tax base. The changes in the Corporate Tax Law in 1990 have made the tax code even more favor-

able for corporations. Corporate incomes from real estate sales and proceeds of sales in the stock market by corporations of their own shares are
tax exempt, provided the proceeds from all such sales are included in the
capital base of the corporation. The corporate tax rate stood at 49 percent
as of 1991 but the effective rate was much less due to various exemptions
and deductions. The Corporate Tax Law also divides Turkey into
"development" zones based on income per capita. The nominal tax rate
on manufacturing corporations that invest in less developed zones is only
20 percent. (For more details, see OECD, *Economic Surveys: Turkey*, various
issues; and Erginay, 1990, pp. 221-238.)

One important administrative reform measure taken in the 1980s, in
order to enforce compliance with the Corporate Tax, was that the tax
administrators were given powers to temporarily shut down businesses
for nonpayment of corporate taxes.

2. Taxes on Goods and Services: VAT

A very important fiscal development in the 1980s was the introduction of
the Value Added Tax (VAT). Authorities started studying its feasibility in
the early 1970s; they examined the different VATs in the EEC countries
and, in 1976, even conducted a pilot project involving 100 industrial concerns in Izmir, the third largest province in Turkey. (OECD, *Economic Surveys: Turkey, 1991/92*, p.114.)

VAT replaced a number of inefficient, indirect taxes, including the
business tax, the communication and advertisement tax, the production
tax on some monopoly products, the sugar consumption tax, the transportation tax, and the retail sales tax. One reason for the introduction of VAT
was its revenue generating potential. Tables 13 and 14 show that the taxes
which were replaced by VAT, each generated an average of 1.6 percent of
the annual revenues of the central government between 1981 and 1983.
VAT, on the other hand, generated more than 12 percent of the revenues
of the central government in 1984, its first year. As Tables 13 and 14 show,
VAT quickly has become the second important source of tax revenue for
the government. VAT's average annual share in total consolidated revenues has been over 16 percent since 1985.

Another reason for the introduction of VAT was Turkey's continuing
efforts to join the EEC; the officials possibly wanted to demonstrate that
they were determined to restructure the economy and could implement a
VAT. As discussed by Uluatam (1991, pp. 314-318) and Erginay (1990, pp.
263-271), the base of VAT in Turkey excludes business expenditures for

investment purposes; thus, the Turkish VAT has been designed as a "consumption-type" VAT.

When VAT was introduced, the officials also took measures to tighten the accounting and bookkeeping requirements. For the first time ever in Turkey, the retailers were required to switch to electronic cash registers by mid-1985. This was done to ensure better compliance with the tax code, reduce cheating, and facilitate inspection and auditing. In order to secure better compliance with the tax laws, the agents of the Tax Department have been known to visit the business establishments at random, sometimes posing as shoppers or window-shoppers; they also interview shoppers leaving the stores in order to ensure proper recording of taxable transactions.

Initially, the VAT Law provided preferential treatment to small retailers and small firms which dominate the rural areas in Turkey. Small firms were allowed to file quarterly rather than monthly returns. Small retailers did not have to file returns at all; their VAT liabilities were collected indirectly.[32] All these efforts were made to encourage compliance by small retailers and sole-proprietorships by reducing the cost of compliance for such establishments. By the mid-1980s, however, most of the preferential treatments were abolished due to revenues lost to both inflation and also cheating. In order to reduce cheating and tax evasion even further, "tamper-proof" registers will be required in the 1990s.

Like other taxes, the brief history of VAT is distinguished by the number and nature of legislative actions. Initially, the general rate was 10 percent, imposed on goods and services in agricultural, industrial, commercial, and various service-related activities. Concerns with the inflationary impact of growth in aggregate demand prompted the authorities to raise the rate to 12 percent in December, 1986. In response to complaints on the impact of VAT on production costs and VAT's regressivity, the rate was lowered to 10 percent in 1988. In December, 1990, because of increasing public sector deficits and the need for additional revenues, the rate was raised back to 12 percent.[33] In 1986, firms engaged in oil exploration were excluded from VAT. Given Turkey's dependence on imported oil, this is meant to encourage domestic oil exploration. Other current exemptions from VAT are: financial transactions intended to encourage the development of financial markets; exports; imported investment goods; gold; and the materials used in the construction of owner-occupied housing. This last exemption is meant to encourage home-ownership by middle and low-income classes; the exemption is extended only to houses that satisfy a legislated size limit, based on the amount of heated floor space.

3. Foreign Trade Taxes

In the 1980s, Turkey abandoned import quotas in favor of tariffs. In 1984, tariffs on capital goods were lowered; those on consumption goods and agricultural products in general were increased. Over time, some other trade levies were abolished altogether; others (such as stamp duty on imports) were first raised, then abandoned, and then reinstated. As a result of the tax reforms in the 1980s, foreign trade taxes have become simpler than they were in the 1970s. The most significant development in the 1980s was the extension of VAT on virtually all imports, except investment goods, in 1985. Most of the proceeds from VAT on imports are earmarked for the extra-budget funds and, therefore, are not included in Tables 13 and 14. Still, Table 14 shows that taxes on foreign trade have constituted an average of about 14 percent of the consolidated budget revenues in the 1980s, the same as in the 1970s. (*IMF. Government Finance Statistics Yearbook*, various issues.)

4. Other Sources of Revenue

Table 14 shows that the remaining taxes are not important sources of revenue. The tax reform of the early 1980s eliminated or replaced a number of taxes besides those cited earlier. The reasons ranged from reducing red tape and bureaucratic involvement in the economy to simplifying the tax system to raising more revenues. One tax that was eliminated was the Fiscal Balance Tax on corporations; its rate was 3 percent on corporate profits and revenues when abolished in May 1981. In January, 1982, the real estate purchase tax was abolished. It was replaced by a real estate duty, imposed on both parties to real estate transactions, at the rate of 4 percent. This is the main reason for the increase in the share in total revenues of the "Stamp Duty/Fees" item after 1982.

V. WAGES, SEEs, PRICE SUPPORT PROGRAMS, MONETARY POLICY, AND INFLATION

The policies of the 1980s resulted in significant changes in the economy. Tables 1 and 7 show some of these changes. For instance, Table 1 indicates that agriculture and manufacturing each had accounted for 22 percent of the GDP in 1979-1980. By 1990, the share of agriculture declined to 15 percent while the share of the manufacturing sector alone increased to 26 percent; the combined share of manufacturing and "Other Industrial" sectors reached 33 percent of GDP in 1990. Table 7 shows that total real GDP increased by more than 50 percent between 1979 and 1988; in spite of a decline in 1980, real GDP per capita (in US dollars) increased by almost 23 percent over the same period.

An assessment of the policies of the 1980s reveals certain shortcomings. One such failure was inflation. Table 5 shows that the rate of inflation was never below 30 percent in the 1980s and exceeded 60 percent by the end of the decade. One reason for the increase in the rate of inflation was the wage policy followed in the 1980s. In the early 1980s, the officials advocated keeping wage increases in both the public and the private sectors in check; this was perceived to be a key element in the fight against inflation. During most of the 1980s, governments succeeded in doing so because of the 1980 ban on most union activities, including the right to strike.[34] The result was a steady loss in the purchasing power of the wage-and-salaried classes during the period 1981-87, when inflation averaged over 35 percent a year, as shown in Table 5. After 1988, large wage increases were given to the public sector employees; that also had a "demonstration effect" on the private sector. Even though, Özal's party (MP) had won the 1987 elections, the results indicated that public support for its economic policies was weakening. The reversal in the wage policy was a response to the election results, and because of concern for the impact of inflation on income distribution and political stability. The wage increases since then have more than compensated for the earlier losses in purchasing power, and far exceeded the increases in worker productivity throughout the economy. The inflationary implications of this for the private sector of the economy are obvious. Given the labor's share in government expenditures, the impact on the public sector has been increased deficits.[35] Thus, the problem with the wage policy was "denying the workforce at least parity with inflation, consistently and for as long. Otherwise, granting huge (and sudden) annual raises at the end of the decade was a 'solution' to the labor and equity issues which simply compounded the problem." (Uyar, 1993, pp.17-8.)

A second failure of the 1980s policies was the inability of the Turkish authorities to follow up on their promises regarding the State Economic Enterprises (SEEs). The SEEs had filled a vacuum in the economy in the early years of the Republic but had become hotbeds of nepotism in time, "used by successive governments to repay political debts." (Ramazanoglu, 1985b, p.232.) Most SEEs produced low-quality, high-cost items whose prices were kept artificially low. This pricing policy especially for "staples," such as, tea, sugar, cigarettes, etc., was an easy concession most governments could make to "equity." It also meant that most SEEs ran operating deficits which contributed to inflationary forces. The stabilization programs of the 1980s acknowledged the need to make the SEEs self-supporting by streamlining their operations, trimming their payrolls, decontrolling their prices, and opening them to competition. The goal ultimately was to sell them to the private sector. In order to make privatization easier, the Parliament passed a decree reorganizing the SEEs in 1983. Initially there was an improvement in the overall finances of most SEEs and by the mid-1980s most of the funds they received from the Central Bank were for investment purposes. However, after the 1987 elections, the pace of reforms slowed down. The prices of most SEEs products again were administratively set below cost; the price-cost adjustments often were delayed and lagged behind inflation. The efforts to trim the SEEs workforce and payrolls lost their urgency. The resulting increase in the operating deficits of the SEEs meant increased reliance for funds from the Central Bank. Tables 8 and 11 show that on occasion the deficits of the SEEs even exceeded that of the central government. The SEEs deficits as a percentage of the GNP in 1990-91 were the highest they had been in a decade. The privatization of only a few of the SEEs were completed by the end of the 1980s. Today there are still about 30 nonfinancial SEEs which control over 350 establishments, plants, and operations in Turkey. (A detailed discussion of the continuing economic importance of the SEEs is in OECD, *Economic Surveys: Turkey 1991/1992*, pp. 88-91.) The SEEs which have been privatized were the most efficient and profitable ones; historically they had operating surpluses while most of the rest of the SEEs had operating deficits. Therefore, one accounting impact of the privatization of the more successful SEEs has been an apparent increase in the net deficits of the remaining SEEs taken together.

A third failure of the 1980s policies was the continuation of agricultural price supports and credits. The Turkish authorities have traditionally granted price supports to agricultural producers, and sold the agricultural products to consumers at prices below the cost of purchase. As discussed earlier, one objective of the 1980 stabilization package was to reduce the extent of supports and credits to agriculture and open this sector to competition. Indeed, during the period 1980-83, agricultural price supports were kept in check; however, they were eased before the 1983 elections and since then they have resumed their traditional role. In 1987, the agricultural supports were extended to the dairy farmers for the first time. The same year, government introduced new incentives for farmers, in the form of subsidized interest rates. Agricultural support programs in Turkey always have been redistributive in intent, and inflationary in practice. (For details, see Ergüder, 1980, Ch.6, and Ulusan, 1980, Ch.5.) No matter what form the supports assume, "... the burden of financing agricultural support purchases lies mainly on the Central Bank. Although (some are called) 'credits,' particularly those obtained by discounting Treasury guaranteed bonds, they really are not, since they never seem to be paid back. Let it suffice to say at this point that agricultural support policy in Turkey is financed mainly by printing money." (Ulusan, 1980, p. 127.)

Finally, one has to understand the nature of "monetary policy" in Turkey in order to put in context Turkey's experience with inflation. In spite of measures taken in the late 1980s to give it more independence, the Turkish Central Bank still is not autonomous. It is not even the sole "monetary authority." In Turkey, monetary policy is determined and implemented jointly by the Treasury, the State Planning Organization, and the Central Bank, and "(t)he Central Bank is obliged by law to finance up to 15% of the budget (appropriations), and also permitted to print money to cover the deficits of state enterprises." (Reynolds, 1992, p. A10.) The SEEs have no incentive to contain costs and be self-sufficient. In the late 1980s, the government limited the SEEs access to the Bank, and forced them to borrow to cover some of their operating deficits. This will prove to be a futile exercise, however, if the Bank is eventually called on to pay those debts.

Even with complete autonomy, it is doubtful that the Central Bank could control the monetary aggregates, particularly M2. The reason is that the financial markets in Turkey are not fully developed. Under these conditions, monetary policy's impact in checking inflation depends on two factors: a) the size of the deficit, and b) the extent to which the deficit is monetized. In 1989 and 1990, the Central Bank and the Treasury agreed to finance the deficit mainly through domestic borrowing. Such agreements are, however, nonbinding; the Treasury has the authority to abrogate unilaterally and ask the Central Bank to monetize the deficit to the extent allowed by law. For instance, the agreement was not renewed in 1991 and, partially due to the Gulf Crisis, the Treasury's borrowing from the Bank in the first quarter of 1991 alone was 155 percent higher than a year earlier. (See OECD, *Economic Surveys: Turkey, 1991/92*, pp.45-60 and 113.)

The lack of autonomy for the Central Bank makes it difficult to properly distinguish monetary policy from fiscal policy in Turkey. The governments' attempts to exercise fiscal restraint are abandoned easily because "monetary policy" provides such a convenient way out in the short run. The institutional setup enables the government to rely extensively on the Central Bank.

VI. CONCLUDING OBSERVATIONS

Preliminary figures show that the inflation rate in Turkey was over 70 percent in the early 1990s (see Table 5). It continues to be the most serious problem facing the country. Another issue likely to re-emerge as a social-political problem is unemployment. Europe can no longer be counted on to ease the pressure of unemployment in Turkey. There is no reason to believe migration from rural areas to urban centers in Turkey will slow down in the near future either. Given the nature of the industrialization process, most of the immigrants will not be absorbed by the manufacturing sector. Instead, some will continue to strive at the periphery of the services sector; others will join the ranks of the unemployed.

The new government, which assumed power in November, 1991, is a coalition of diverse groups. The main partner in the coalition is Süleyman Demirel's True Path Party (TPP), which replaced the Justice Party (JP) after the latter was disbanded and outlawed following the 1980 *coup*. The 1991 change in government indicated public disappointment and dissatisfaction with the policies of Özal's Motherland Party (MP). Yet, and in spite of stated differences, the principal figures and parties constitute a continuum in Turkish politics and economic affairs. After all, Süleyman Demirel and his governments were behind the 1970 and 1980 stabilization packages. Özal himself was involved with both packages in different roles, and his 1984 stabilization program was an effort to consolidate the 1980 package. Following Özal's death in 1993, the Turkish Parliament elected Demirel to succeed Özal as the President of Turkey. Tansu Ciller, who replaced Demirel as the head of the TPP and the prime minister, is a long time Demirel protege; prior to becoming the prime minister, she was responsible for implementing Demirel's economic programs.

The nature of this coalition places on the government a unique responsibility as well. The TPP's coalition partner is a resurrected offshoot of an old nemesis, the Republican People's Party. Given their differences over the years, the fact that these two parties could agree on a platform and form a government is quite telling and cause for cautious optimism. Yet one cannot help but wonder whether and when such supra-party commitments might give way to political struggles between the coalition partners as the next general elections approach.

The Central Bank of Turkey has to be organized as an autonomous unit. This will compel the government to exercise fiscal restraint, and force the SEEs to exercise fiscal prudence. Decontrolling the SEEs' prices will entail economic hardships in the short run and may cause social unrest. Yet people have shown their resiliency and strength in adjusting to the drastic changes of the 1980s. The agreement between the Central Bank and the Treasury has limited the monetization of the deficit since the late 1980s. Even though the agreement was not renewed in 1991, such agreements should continue even as the government undertakes the legal and the institutional reforms needed for economic stability.

ENDNOTES

1. This is a revised and updated version of "Public Finances in Turkey in the 1980s," *Journal of Economics and Administrative Studies (JEAS)*, Vol.6 (1-2), 1992. The author thanks Ziya Önis, the Editor of JEAS, for permission to use parts of that article.

2. This is not an exhaustive review of the economic and political developments of almost six decades. For details, see Hershlag (1968), Keyder (1989), Ramazanoglu (1985b), and Barkey (1990).

3. Özbudun (1980, p.69) contends that only during the election squabbles of the mid- to late-1970s, the differences between growth and development were first acknowledged and discussed explicitly.

4. For discussions of etatism, its nature, policy implications, and impact, see Hershlag (1968; 1988), Ramazanoglu (1985b), and Barkey (1990, pp.43-51).

5. There are differing views about the circumstances surrounding the emergence of etatism, the philosophy underlying it, the nature of the fiscal-monetary tools used to implement it, and even the timing of economic planning in Turkey. Hershlag (1988, p.6) places the beginnings of planning in the 1930s, and states "Turkey was, apart from Soviet Russia, the first country which adopted and implemented the concept of mandatory central planning, with the focus, as in Russia, on industrialization." Others view these events, and the beginnings of planning, differently. See Conway (1987, pp. 37-45), Keyder (1989), Ramazanoglu (1985a; 1985b).

6. For analyses of the policies followed, see Anand et *al.* (1990), Keyder (1989), Ramazanoglu (1985a), Schick and Tonak (1989), Senses (1985), and particularly Barkey (1990).

7. Turkey did not participate in World War II, but her economy was mobilized to support her armed forces. Tax reform would have kept the pent-up consumer demand in check. Instead, the tools used were borrowing, depletion of foreign currency and gold reserves, and money creation. For details, see Conway (1987, pp. 37-45), Hershlag (1968), Keyder (1989), Odekon (1988), Ramazanoglu (1985b), and Senses (1985).

8. Asar (tithe), an agricultural income tax, was plagued with administrative abuse and had become a symbol of Ottoman injustice. So, it was abolished in 1925 for political reasons. Another reason for its abolition was to encourage agricultural production. Hershlag (1968, p. 45) mentions that when it was abolished in 1925, Asar was generating about 29 percent of the annual public revenues. Authorities tried taxing agricultural incomes indirectly through a Land Tax and Animals Tax instead; but these never generated the tax revenue that Asar did. For details, see Durdag, 1973, pp. 166-171.

9. The real GNP increased at an average rate of over ten percent during the period 1949-53. The rate of mechanization in the agricultural sector during this period was unprecedented. Additionally, the size of the cultivated area was increased, and the weather conditions were most favorable. So, Turkey was able to take advantage of the increased world demand for agricultural products during the Korean War years. The end of the War plus two consecutive years of bad harvests due to adverse weather, proved to be devastating to the Turkish economy. Their impact dominated the economy in the rest of the 1950s. In Fiscal Year 1956-7, the deficit of the central government was 19 times greater than what it was only six years earlier. Over the same period, the nominal domestic debt increased by a factor of 2.4, the external debt by a factor of 6.5. (Hershlag, 1988, pp. 19-22.)

10. Based on both annual sales *and* scale of operations, "small" farmers were exempted from the tax. For details, see Erginay (1990, pp.130-3), Özbudun (1980, p.62), and Durdag (1973, pp.166-174).

11. For example, they postponed the taxation of agriculture until 1964. Even then, the exemption standards were so liberal that agriculture remained a rather insignificant source of state revenues until after 1980. See Erginay (1990, pp.130-3), and Durdag (1973, pp.166-174).

12. The 1982 Constitution replaced the 1961 Constitution but retained the promotion of social welfare as an objective of the government.

13. Until the early 1980s, the interest rates were set by administrative fiat. Since these rates were unchanged between 1960 and 1970, they did not reflect accurately the actual returns to investment or the cost of borrowing. For details of the 1970 package, see Barkey (1990, pp.154-7) and OECD (*Economic Surveys: Turkey 1970*, pp.23-7).

14. This was an incremental value tax, levied on the change in the value of real property since the last time it was sold.

15. The structural change becomes even more striking when we compare 1980 with, for example, the early 1950s. During the years 1949-51, employment in the agricultural sector averaged about 79 percent of the civilian labor force and the agricultural sector generated an average of 51 percent of the GDP (Dervis-Robinson, 1980, p.88).

16. Economic problems experienced by the developed European countries also contributed to the worsening of unemployment. Large numbers of Turkish workers who were laid off in Europe began returning to Turkey in the mid to late 1970s.

17. Subsequently, the Lira was devalued twice each in 1973, 1974, 1977, three times each in 1976 and 1979, and five times in 1975.

18. These remittances were increasing even as increasing numbers of Turkish workers laid-off in Europe were returning to Turkey.

19. Turkey's problems at the end of the 1970s have been analyzed extensively by a number of authors; see Hershlag (1988, pp.38-41), Keyder (1989), Ramazanoglu (1985a), Schick-Tonak (1989), Senses (1985), and Barkey (1990, Ch. 8).

20. There was no such external support for the 1970 package. The impetus for this new external support was the severity of the problems in

1980 (relative to 1970) and the events in neighboring Iran. For detailed analyses of the stabilization package and of the period, see Barkey (1990, Ch.8), Baysan-Blitzer (1990), Celasun (1990), Ekinci (1990), Ramazanoglu (1985a; 1985b), and OECD (*Economic Surveys: Turkey, 1980, 1981, 1982*).

21. The parliamentary squabbles were aimed at scuttling the stabilization package. The non-governing parties knew that the JP could translate the successes of the package into a dominant parliamentary majority, thus, denying them a chance to assume power for years to come. See Barkey (1990, pp. 176-8).

22. Some of the developments were at the expense of basic freedoms, such as, the right to strike.

23. Fortunes were made and lost in short order. During the period 1983-86, there was an official retrenchment and re-regulation, aimed at bringing order into the financial markets. (See Inselbag-Gultekin, 1988.) For the first time in 1985, a banking law was passed imposing uniform accounting standards on banks; since 1987, banks have been required to be audited by external auditors. After the crash, the monetary authorities resumed setting the interest rates on deposits. Until 1986, the real return on most types of deposits were positive; but from 1986 to 1990, most were negative again, adding to the inflationary pressures. (OECD, *Economic Surveys: Turkey 1990*, pp. 91 and 104.)

24. The MP also won the 1987 elections but lost in 1991. Özal, though, became the President in the mid-1980s. In spite of extended powers under the 1982 Constitution, Presidency in Turkey remains a ceremonial post. So, Özal's influence as President until his death in 1993 was due as much to his personality as to anything else.

25. For details, see Barkey(1990, Ch.8), Baysan-Blitzer (1990), Celasun (1990), Ekinci (1990), Ramazanoglu (1985a and 1985b), and OECD (*Economic Surveys: Turkey, 1983 and 1984*), among others.

26. See Uyar (1993) for a summary of the wage policies in the 1980s. By the end of the decade, the real wage gains in both the private and the public sectors more than made up for the earlier losses in purchasing power, and far exceeded the productivity increases.

27. The "extra-budget funds" are designed to provide low-income housing, promote exports, subsidize certain investments (in export oriented industries, or in underdeveloped regions of the country), promote small businesses, and provide certain types of agricultural price
supports, etc. Some of the funds were established to promote "social
welfare." Turkey has always had such funds but after 1984 the number of specifically designated funds has increased so that presently
there are over 100 of them. As the term "extra-budget" implies, such
funds were meant to be "off-budget" in order to keep them outside
the regular budgetary deliberations and partisan squabbles. (OECD,
Economic Surveys: Turkey, 1991/1992, pp. 45-6.)

28. Karluk (1994, p.50) mentions that the Budget Law has been changed
again so that 63 of these extra-budget funds are no longer "extra-
budget" as of 1993. As a result, their transactions will be included in
the consolidated budget statements from 1993 on. This change will
limit further the comparability of budget statements for different
years.

29. The appeal system was also changed making it more difficult to reduce real tax liabilities by lengthy and repeated appeals in inflationary
times. Penalties and fines for various tax violators were sharply increased. A system of bonuses and premiums was established to secure better law enforcement by tax inspectors. For details, see OECD,
Economic Surveys: Turkey 1991/1992, pp. 82-6.

30. Erginay (1990, p. 172) mentions that significant changes were made in
tax provisions regarding agriculture in the early 1980s: the scope of
exemptions were narrowed, and a withholding tax was imposed on
all sales by farmers. "Another important change concerns deductions
for expenditures. Previously a minimum of 70 percent of sales receipts
was considered as expenditures; the new law fixes the maximum limit
at 70 percent." (OECD, *Economic Surveys: Turkey 1981,* p.44.)

31. Under the law, the rebate claims filed by the taxpayers were checked
against the invoices submitted by the taxpayers. Thus, the individuals
who wanted to receive a rebate on their income taxes had to request
receipts and invoices from the merchants, thereby, forcing the merchants to record the transactions. The VAT's base included essentially
the same transactions and commodities which were eligible for rebates.

32. The "indirect" collection process worked as follows. The retailers which were exempt from filing returns, still collected the regular 10 percent VAT on their *retail sales*; they in turn were required to pay a tax of 12 percent on their *wholesale purchases*. The 12 percent tax they paid to the wholesalers was reported on the tax returns of the wholesalers. The retailers and sole-proprietorships were exempted from all bookkeeping and filing requirements and, instead, were allowed to keep the difference between their tax collections and payments. (OECD, *Economic Surveys: Turkey, 1991/92,* pp.75-7.)

33. Some items are taxed at different rates. Alcoholic and nonalcoholic beverages, and tobacco products have a supplemental VAT. "Luxury" goods were taxed at 15 percent initially; as of 1991, the rate was 20 percent. In January, 1988, automobiles and electrical appliances were separated from general VAT and taxed at 15 percent. VAT on newspapers, books, pharmaceuticals was increased from 5 to 8 percent in 1988, but it was reduced to 5 in a few months. Foodstuffs were included under VAT for the first time in 1988; the rate was increased from 3 to 6 percent in December, 1990, and again to 8 percent in June 1991. See the Annexes (called "Calendar of main economic events") in OECD, *Economic Surveys: Turkey* (various issues).

34. The Supreme Arbitration Board and the Wage Negotiations Coordination Board played important roles in controlling the wages. For details, see Kopits (1987).

35. Annual real wage gains averaged 30-35 percent. (For an examination of the developments, see OECD, *Economic Surveys: Turkey 1991,* pp.26-8, and OECD, *Economic Surveys: Turkey 1991/1992,* pp.24-7). The point is simply that the wage policy in the public sector *contributed* to inflationary pressures, *not* that it was more important than the factors (such as, monetization of the deficits, agricultural price supports, the problems of the SEEs, etc.) discussed in the rest of the paper.

124   Bülent Uyar

REFERENCES

Akturk, N., (1990), "Kamu Finansmani ve Borc Yonetimi," in *Journal of Economics and Administrative Studies* 4,2: pp. 245-260.

Akyuz, Y., (1990), "Financial System and Policies in Turkey in the 1980s," in *In The Political Economy of Turkey: Debt, Adjustment and Sustainability*, ed., T. Aricanli and D. Rodrik, 98-131, New York, St. Martin's Press.

Anand, R., A. Chhibber, and S. van Wijnbergen, (1990), "External Balance and Growth in Turkey: Can They be Reconciled?" in *Political Economy of Turkey: Debt, Adjustment and Sustainability*, eds., T. Aricanli and D. Rodrik, pp. 157-182, New York, St. Martin's Press.

Barkey, H.J., (1990), *The State and the Industrialization Crisis in Turkey*, Westview Press, Boulder, CO.

Baysan, T. and C. Blitzer, (1990), "Turkey's Trade Liberalization in the 1980s and Prospects for its Sustainability." in *Political Economy of Turkey: Debt, Adjustment and Sustainability*, eds. T. Aricanli and D. Rodrik, 9-36, New York: St. Martin's Press.

Bulutoglu, K., (1967), *Türk Vergi Sistemi* (Second ed.) Istanbul: Fakülteler Matbaasi.

Celasun, M., (1990), "Fiscal Aspects of Adjustment in the 1980s," in *The Political Economy of Turkey: Debt. Adjustment and Sustainability*, eds., T. Aricanli and D. Rodrik, 37-59. New York: St. Martin's Press.

Conway, P.J., (1987), *Economic Shocks and Structural Adjustments: Turkey After 1973*, New York: North Holland.

Conway, P., (1988), "The Impact of Recent Trade Liberalization Policies in Turkey," *In Liberalization and The Turkish Economy*, eds., T.F. Nas and M. Odekon, 47-68, New York: Greenwood Press.

Dervis, K. and S. Robinson, (1980), "The Structure of Income Inequality in Turkey (1950-1973)," in *The Political Economy of Income Distribution in Turkey*, eds., E. Özbudun and A. Ulusan, 83-122, New York: Holme and Meier Publishers, Inc.

Durdag, M., (1973), *Some Problems of Development Financing: A Case Study of the Turkish First Five-Year Plan 1963-1967*, D. Reidel Publishing Co., Holland.

Ekinci, N.K., (1990), "Macroeconomic Developments in Turkey: 1980-1988," *METU Studies in Development*, 17,1-2, 1990: 73-114.

Erginay, A., (1990), *Vergi Hukuku* (Tax Law) 14th ed. Ankara, Turkey: Savas Yayinlari.

Ergüder, Ü., (1980), "Politics of Agricultural Price Policy in Turkey" in *The Political Economy of Income Distribution in Turkey*, eds., E. Özbudun and A. Ulusan, 169-195, New York: Holme and Meier Publishers, Inc.

Fry, M.J., (1988), "Money Supply Responds to Exogenous Shocks in Turkey," in *Liberalization and The Turkish Economy*, eds., T.F. Nas and M. Odekon, 85-114, New York: Greenwood Press.

Hershlag, Z.Y., (1988), *The Contemporary Turkish Economy*, New York: Routledge.

Hershlag, Z.Y., (1968), *Turkey: The Challenge of Growth*, Leiden: E.J. Brill.

Inselbag, I. and G. and N. Bülent, (1988), "Financial Markets in Turkey," in *Liberalization and The Turkish Economy*, eds., T.F. Nas and M. Odekon, 129-140, New York: Greenwood Press.

International Monetary Fund (IMF). *Government Finance Statistics Yearbook*, Washington, D.C. (various issues).

IMF (1991), *International Financial Statistics, 1991,* Washington,   DC.

Karluk, R.S., (1994), *Türkiye Ekonomisi*, Eskisehir, Turkey.

Keyder, C., (1989), "Economic Development and Crisis: 1950-80," in *Turkey in Transition: New Perspectives*, eds., I.C. Schick and E.A. Tonak, 293-208, New York: Oxford Press.

Kopits, G., (1987), "Turkey's Adjustment Experience, 1980-85," *Finance and Development*, (September 1987): 8-11.

Mumcuoglu, M., (1980), "Political Activities of Trade Unions and Income Distribution," in *The Political Economy of Income Distribution in Turkey*, eds., E. Özbudun and A. Ulusan, 279-408, New York: Holme and Meier Publishers, Inc.

Odekon, M., (1988), "Liberalization and the Turkish Economy: A Comparative Analysis," in *Liberalisation and The Turkish Economy*, eds., T.F. Nas and M. Odekon, 29-46, New York: Greenwood Press.

OECD (Organization for Economic Co-operation and Development). *Economic Surveys: Turkey Paris, 1970, 1978, 1980, 1982, 1983, 1984, 1985, 1986, 1987, 1988, 1990, 1991, 1991/1992.*

OECD (1991), *Historical Statistics, 1960-1989*, Paris.

OECD (1992), *National Accounts: Main Aggregates, 1960-1990*, Vol 1, Paris.

OECD *Revenue Statistics of OECD Member Countries*, Paris, (Various issues).

Özbudun, E., (1980), "Income Distribution as an Issue in Turkish Politics," in *The Political Economy of Income Distribution in Turkey*, eds., E. Özbudun and A. Ulusan, 55-82, New York: Holme and Meier Publishers, Inc.

Özmucur, S. and M. Çinar, (1978), "Türkiye'de Gelir Vergisi Alinabilirligi ve Tahsilati, 1974," *METU Studies in Development*, Vol. 21 (Fall), pp.130-141.

Ramazanoglu, H., (1985a), "The Politics of Industrialization in a Closed Economy and the IMF Intervention of 1979," in *Turkey in the World Capitalist System: A Study of Industrialization, Power and Class*, ed. Huseyin Ramazanoglu, 80-97, Brookfield, Vermont: Gower.

Ramazanoglu, H., (1985b), "The State, The Military and The Development of Capitalism in an Open Economy," in *Turkey in the World Capitalist System: A Study of Industrialization, Power and Class*, ed., Huseyin Ramazanoglu, 227-247, Brookfield, Vermont: Gower.

Reynolds, A., (1992), "Turkey's Growth Does Not Require Pain," *Wall Street Journal*, (January 17), p. A10.

Schick, I.C. and E.A. Tonak, (1989), "The International Dimension: Trade, Aid, and Debt," in *Turkey in Transition: New Perspectives*, eds., I.C. Schick and E.A. Tonak, 333-364, New York: Oxford Press.

Senses, F., (1988), "An Overview of Recent Turkish Experience with Economic Stabilization and Liberalization," in *Liberalization and The Turkish Economy*, eds., T.F. Nas and M. Odekon, 9-28, New York: Greenwood Press.

Senses, F., (1985), "Short-Term Stabilization Policies in a Developing Economy: The Turkish Experience in 1980 in Long-Term Perspective," in *Turkey in the World Capitalist System: A Study of Industrialization, Power and Class*, ed., H. Ramazanoglu, 130-10. Brookfield, Vermont: Gower.

Uluatam, Ö., (1991), *Kamu Maliyesi* (4th ed.), Ankara, Turkey: Savas Yayinlari.

Ulusan, A., (1980), "Public Policy Toward Agriculture and Its Redistributive Implications," in *The Political Economy of Income Distribution in Turkey*, eds., E. Özbudun and A. Ulusan, 125-167, New York: Holme and Meier Publishers, Inc.

United Nations (UN, 1991), *National Accounts Statistics: Analysis of Main Aggregates*, 1988-1989. New York.

Uyar, B., (1992), "Public Finances in Turkey in the 1980s," *Journal of Economics and Administrative Studies*, 6, 1-2, pp. 1-40.

Uyar, B., (1993), "Reforms, Economic Stability, and Coups: The Case of Turkey," (Submitted to the *Journal of Economic Studies*.)

World Bank (1990), *World Tables, 1989-90 Edition*, The John Hopkins University Press, Baltimore.

CHAPTER FIVE

A REVIEW OF GOVERNMENT EXPENDITURES AND TAXATION TRENDS IN CANADA

Sohrab Abizadeh

I. INTRODUCTION

A widely discussed topic in public finance is the growth of government expenditures, particulary the increased share of such expenditures in gross domestic product (GDP). The interest in the size of government expenditures has intensified since the Great Depression of the 1930s. This topic has received special attention in recent years in Canada due to a relatively high level of deficit and overall debt. A related issue is the sources of government revenues since reduction in deficits would have to come from either increased revenues, decreased expenditures, or both.

In the case of less developed coutries (LDCs), tax revenues are needed to develop the infrastructure necessary for economic development while providing incentives in the private sector for increased investment and output. On the other hand, most more developed countries (MDCs) are in need of higher tax revenues to finance their rising expenditures on social programs and correcting for market failure and externalities.

Much of recent applied and theoretical work on taxation has focused on the task of constructing tax systems suited to the particular economic or social conditions of various countries. It is argued that, in MDCs such as Canada, social awareness and the emergence of mass communication, coupled with direct public participation in the political process of decision making, have imposed some restrictions on the ability of governments to further increase their reliance on traditional taxes such as personal and corporate income taxation. Along with the persistent deficits a higher level of tax revenue for the Canadian government has become very critical. This was the impetus behind the introduction of the now famous goods and services tax (GST) on January 1, 1991 by the Canadian government.

This chapter begins with a brief historical analysis of taxation and expenditures and then takes a closer look at the anatomy of government expenditures and taxation in Canada. An analysis of the existing sources of expenditures and tax revenues will follow. We will discuss the specific reasons and causes of the growth of government in Canada. The existing Canadian political structure requires an examination of expenditures and taxation at all levels of government, provincial, local, as well as federal. When necessary such information will be provided throughout the text.

II. HISTORY

The Canadian Constitution Act of 1867, formerly referred to as the British North American Act (BNA), empowers the federal government of Canada to raise tax revenues by any mode while restricting the provincial governments to raising funds only by means of direct taxation within the province (Canadian Tax Foundation, 1990, p.10:1)[1]. In 1867, however, the limited role of the federal government in the Canadian economy meant that the principal sources of revenue were custom duties and excise taxes, both being means of indirect taxation. As such, the federal government controlled the most lucrative source of raising revenue[2]. Although it was first felt that political factors would make it difficult to levy direct taxes at either the federal or provincial level, all levels of governments soon found ways to impose such taxes. For example, provincial personal income taxes were levied as early as 1876 (by British Columbia) and the first corporation income tax, was imposed by the government of Prince Edward Island in 1894. By 1941 all nine provincial governments had their corporation income taxes in place and all but two were levying personal income taxes.[3]

At the time of confederation (1867), some municipal governments had already implemented their own income taxes. The federal government entered the field of personal and corporate taxation in 1917 as a temporary wartime measure.[4] Immediately after the war the federal government began levying a sales tax. However, the tax base sharing arrangements among the three levels of government became controversial and has been since in the Canadian politics. This conflict has led to a few agreements signed between Ottawa and provinces since the first world war.[5] Out of the ashes of the Wartime Tax Agreements, whereupon provinces turned over all personal and corporate income taxes to the federal government, rose a series of negotiated tax agreements between Ottawa and the provinces known collectively as the Tax Rental Agreements (TRA). These arrangements took place during 1947-51, 1952-56, and 1957-61. The arrangment for the first two periods were similar to the war years. The 1957-61 agreement, however, became the forerunner of the present system. A different system was negotiated for the 1962-66 period under the Tax Collection Agreement (TRA), a system which continues to be in effect today. Under this system, the federal government would collect taxes enacted by the provinces and withdraw its own taxes to leave tax room for the provinces. The provinces are allowed to impose their own rates provided that their tax base conforms with federal legislation (See Moore, et al., 1966 and Perry, 1990).

The Canadian tax system has seen three major reforms since the end of the second world war. The first reform was in 1949 when the Wartime Tax Agreement was replaced by the Tax Rental Agreements. The second tax reform came in 1971 after the Report of the Royal Commission on Taxation (1966) was released. Finally, a series of changes beginning in 1985 resulted in the third stage of tax reforms in Canada (See Perry, 1989, for detail).

III. TOTAL GOVERNMENT EXPENDITURES IN PERSPECTIVE

The Canadian economy is characterized by a heavy reliance on government to provide social services. More than 32 percent of the total federal expenditures is spent on social services and programs. This figure is about 22 percent of total consolidated government expenditures at all levels. As Strick (1992, p.35) points out "During the last two decades, the most costly government functions at each level of government have been related to social services, particularly health care, welfare, and education...." Canadians in general cherish their social programs and refer to the universality of those programs as a "secret thrust." The importance of these programs cannot be emphasized enough since elections are lost and won on this single issue in Canada. During the 1993 federal campaign, Kim Campbell, the leader of the Progressive Conservative Party of Canada, declined to deal with the issue of social programs. In her view, issues related to social programs were too important to be dealt with during the election. This position, taken by Kim Campbell, proved to be a turning point in the campaign which worked against her. The Liberal Party, on the other hand, kept insisting that social programs cannot be cut and universality of those programs already in place will be preserved. This party concentrated on the issues of job creation and reducing unemployment, issues which proved to work in the party's favor in winning the election.[6]

Despite preoccupation with social programs, the issue of deficit and how to control it has received renewed attention from politicians. During its eight years in office, the former Conservative government repeatedly stressed its desire to reduce government expenditures, and thus lower the federal budget deficits.[7] Yet despite these apparent emphasis and attempts made to reduce total expenditures, including the cost of social programs, deficits and expenditures continue to rise. In fact federal government expenditures as a percentage of GDP was 20.3 in 1981 (before the Conservative government came to power) and rose to 23.9 in 1993 when it left office. Meanwhile deficits, on a national account basis, rose from $23.5 billion in 1982/83 fiscal year to $27.8 billion in 1991/92 fiscal year. At the same time total expenditures on social programs rose from $29.0 billion in 1982-83 to $57.0 billion in 1993-94.

At this stage, it is useful to closely examine expenditure activities among the three levels of government in Canada. Table 1 shows the total government expenditures as a percentage of GDP for selected years since 1950. It also indicates that the share of government expenditures at the federal level, including grants to other levels of government, increased from 12.4 percent in 1950 to 23.4 percent in 1992. Total government expenditures at all levels, as a percentage of GDP, increased by more than 100 percent during the same period. This reflects an increase from 21.3 percent in 1950 to 55.3 percent in 1992 in the overall government expenditures-GDP ratio. Most of this increase is attributed to the relatively sharp rise in government expenditures at the provincial level, which rose from a low of 6.4 percent to a relatively high figure of 24.6 percent in 42 years—a four fold nominal increase. Some of this increase can be attributed to changes in federal policy regarding the level and kinds of transfer payments made to the provinces, and to changes in the tax policies, as provinces renegotiated their role in the federation vis à vis the central government (For details, see Boadway, 1980). As for the local governments, the growth of their expenditures has followed a more or less stable pattern. This is expected since municipalities are created by the provinces, exist at their pleasure, and are granted rights to the real property tax for the sole purpose of financing local projects and (partly) education.

Overall, during the 1950-1992 period, increased provincial government expenditures accounted for approximately 40 percent of the total growth in public expenditures whereas local and federal government expenditures have been responsible for 25 and 10 percent respectively of the increase during the same period. These figures point towards a shift in the provincial government responsibilities in Canada; provincial governments are forced to become more responsible for providing public goods and services. Regardless of division of responsibility more than 50percent of all income created in Canada in 1992 originated with government—the public sector—not in the private sector. This has serious implications for public policy and changes in resource allocation when such changes become necessary or desirable. In other words, the Canadian economy, because of the size of public sector, is very sensitive to economic decisions of the government.

Table 1 Total Government Expenditures Expressed as a Percentage of Gross Domestic Product (Selected calendar years).

Year	Federal[a]	Provincial[a]	Local[a]	Total[b]
1950	12.4	6.4	4.8	21.3
1955	16.4	6.2	5.7	25.6
1960	17.1	9.0	7.2	28.8
1965	14.9	11.0	7.8	28.7
1970	17.2	15.9	9.0	34.9
1975	20.8	18.4	8.5	39.9
1980	19.8	19.3	8.1	40.3
1985	24.0	21.5	8.0	46.8
1989	21.5	20.2	7.6	44.0
1992	23.4	24.6	8.8	51.3

Source: The National Finances (1993) Table 3.14.
[a] Includes intergovernmental grants from payer government
[b] Excludes grants

A. ANATOMY OF THE GOVERNMENT EXPENDITURES IN CANADA

So far, we have given an overview of government expenditures at the three levels. In this section a more detailed examination of the major components of the consolidated budget of these levels of governments will be undertaken.[8] Table 2 and charts 1-3 are presented to facilitate this task.

Table 2 Consolidated Government Expenditures all levels[a] (billions of dollars).

Type of Expenditures	1978 Absolute	1983 Absolute	1983 % rate of Growth Since 1978	1988 Absolute	1988 % rate of Growth Since 1983	1991 * Absolute	1991 * % rate of Growth Since 1988
Social Services	22.55	47.07	108	63.08	34	67.13	6
Debt Charges	10.01	24.71	146	43.87	77	62.68	43
Health	12.04	24.15	100	35.22	45	41.57	18
Education	14.95	25.01	67	31.77	27	38.77	22
Protection	8.38	15.25	82	21.40	40	23.56	10
Resource Conservation	5.83	14.10	142	14.09	0	12.79	-9
Transportation and communications	8.58	11.38	32	13.10	15	15.12	16

Table 2 (continued)

Recreation and Culture	2.46	4.13	67	5.32	29	6.62	24
Environment	2.69	3.73	39	5.67	52	6.88	21
Foreign Affairs and International Assistance	0.95	1.74	83	3.36	93	3.49	4
Regional Planning	0.86	1.02	18	1.70	66	1.60	-6
Other Expenditures	11.08	22.23	100	26.31	18	31.27	19
Total consolidated Expenditures	**100.39**	**194.54**	**94**	**264.89**	**36**	**309.50**	**17**

Source: The National Finances (1990 and 1993) Table 4.2

a   Fiscal year ending nearest to December 31, 1978 to 1988
*   Fiscal Year ending nearest to March 31

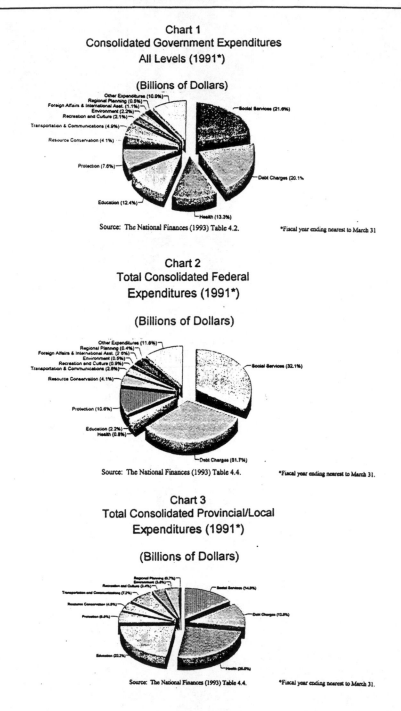

Chart 1
Consolidated Government Expenditures
All Levels (1991*)

(Billions of Dollars)

Source: The National Finances (1993) Table 4.2.   *Fiscal year ending nearest to March 31

Chart 2
Total Consolidated Federal
Expenditures (1991*)

(Billions of Dollars)

Source: The National Finances (1993) Table 4.4.   *Fiscal year ending nearest to March 31.

Chart 3
Total Consolidated Provincial/Local
Expenditures (1991*)

(Billions of Dollars)

Source: The National Finances (1993) Table 4.4.   *Fiscal year ending nearest to March 31.

Table 2 gives figures for the absolute consolidated government expenditures for four selected years. It also provides the corresponding rate of growth of expenditures for these years. This Table breaks the overall expenditures into twelve major categories. Table 2 shows a decline in the rate of growth of the majority of the twelve expenditure categories. Table 2 indicates a sharp decline in the rate of growth of total consolidated budget from 1983 to 1991 as compared to the same rate for the 1978-83 period, despite a more than tripling of the absolute expenditures between 1978 and 1991.

Chart 1 breaks down the consolidated government expenditures for 1991 into twelve major categories and shows each category as a percentage of total expenditures. Charts 2 and 3 give similar breakdowns for the federal and provincial/local governments.

Government expenditures are normally divided into two broad categories: exhaustive and non-exhaustive. Exhaustive expenditures include expenditures on goods and services and the factors of production (including capital). The allocation of resources will be altered based on the exhaustive expenditure decisions made by the government. Exhaustive expenditures, represent a government demand for real goods and services. Non-exhaustive expenditures are transfer payments to individuals and business firms. Although they constitute a large portion of overall government expenditures, they do not have a direct impact on the total amount of resources available to the private sector. How the recipients of transfer income decide to spend, and whether to spend or save, will affect the allocation of resources.

In Canada, the largest portion of non-exhaustive expenditures are for social services. Non-exhaustive expenditures experienced a declining growth rate between 1983-1991 as opposed to the 1978-83 period (Table 2). The sharp increase in social services expenditures during 1978-1988 represented the government's desire to improve the quality and quantity of the existing social programs in Canada. The Liberal government began this trend in the 1970's and the momentum continued even when the Conservatives came to power in 1984. Subsequently, the trend has subsided.

As a percentage of the consolidated budget, expenditures on social services is about 22 percent of the total (Chart 1). About 32 percent of federal expenditures (Chart 2) and about 15 percent of provincial/local (Chart 3) expenditures were allocated to social services in 1991. These figures imply that the majority of Canadians wish to see a continuation of their welfare state whereby the government, particularly the federal government, is responsible for establishing and maintaining a safety net to protect those in need and those who may be victims of unfavourable economic circumstances. Among those programs are family allowances (or baby bonus, most recently replaced by Child Benefit Program), unemployment insurance, income security programs and the Canada Pension Plan. Most social programs fall under the jurisdiction of the federal government. The federal transfers on welfare has come under the Canada Assistance Plan (CAP) since its inception in 1966 and has had a surprisingly untroubled history. This plan replaced the previous federal conditional grant programs under the Old Age Assistance Act, Blind Persons Act, Disabled Persons Act, and the Unemployment Assistance Act. In general, CAP pays 50 percent of the amount of provincial expenditures eligible for assistance and does maintain some flexible conditions.

Debt charges, which largely consist of government interest payments on its debt, rose significantly during 1978-83 due, in large part, to the prevailing high nominal rate of interest. The high rate of growth in debt charges continued into the 1988 period. However this rate declined substantially with the easing of interest rates during the mid eighties and early nineties. Debt charges constitute a relatively higher percentage of federal government expenditures (32 percent, Chart 2) than those of the provinces (12 percent, Chart 3). The lower debt charges for the provinces is due to two reasons. First there exists a wide spectrum of budgetary circumstances for the provinces in Canada, mainly due to their size. Second, Canadian provinces range from very poor (e.g. Newfoundland) to very rich (e.g. Ontario). Some of the poorer provinces have a very high debt load whereas richer provinces, often the larger provinces, have a relatively low debt load.

Federal grants for health care in Canada were consolidated into a single program when the Hospital Insurance and Diagnostic Services Act of 1957 was passed. This program provided for federal sharing of most operating and maintenance costs of patient care in hospitals and gave the provinces some discretion as to the range of out-patient services to be covered. This plan was replaced in 1966 by the Medical Care Act that offered medicare assistance to any province provided it met the four basic criteria of: 1) comprehensiveness of scope; 2) universal coverage; 3) public administration; and 4) portability of benefits. Similar to education, this plan called for federal grants to constitute a 50 percent share of the costs. The program lasted until 1977 when again, along with education, health care came under the Established Programs Financing (EPF) Act. The most recent change in the field of health care has been the passing of the Canada Health Act of 1984 which, among other things, penalizes provinces that allow extra-billing with reduced payments. It also defines part of what can be covered under provincial programs and imposes restrictions concerning doctors' fees. As such, the program has been criticized by some for reducing provincial autonomy and returning Canada to the era of conditional federal grants for health.

Government expenditures on health increased by 100 percent during the 1978-83 period. This rate of growth dropped to only 18 percent between 1988 and 1991 (Table 2)[9]. Health care, according to the Canadian Constitution, is a provincial responsibility. The role of the federal government is limited to providing financial support to the provinces through different transfer payment programs in order to ensure that more or less identical health services are provided to all Canadians. This arrangement has led to a relatively larger expenditure on health by provincial governments (25 percent of total expenditures in 1991) relative to the federal expenditures on health (only about 1 percent of total federal expenditures in 1991).

The same holds true for expenditures on education. Provinces are constitutionally responsible for the provision of education to their population and the role of the federal government is limited to providing financial assistance to the provinces for post-secondary education, bilingualism and retraining of the unemployed Canadians for newly developed jobs and skills. Accordingly, the provincial share of expenditure on education (22 percent) is relatively much greater than that of the federal government (2percent). Expenditures on education followed a similar pattern to health expenditures with the rate of growth dropping from 67 percent to 22 percent during the period under study (For details, see Boadway and Flatters, 1991).

Education transfers have been a source of contention in Canada dating back to 1951 when the federal government implemented a program of direct grants to universities. Quebec objected to such a program, fearing it would, according to Bird (1987, p. 10) "replace a system of fiscal autonomy of the Provinces, in the field of taxation, by a system of grants that would allow the Dominion Government to exercise over them a financial tutelage control." In 1960 these grants were terminated for Quebec and in their place the federal corporate income tax abatement was increased by one percentage point for that province. In 1964 this opting-out provision was extended to all provinces but only Quebec continued to take advantage of the offer.

The next major change came in 1966 when the federal government replaced its grants to universities with a provision which reduced its personal income tax by 4 percent and corporate tax by 1 percent to allow the provinces to raise their taxes accordingly. Additional cash payments were given to provinces to ensure that the federal contribution for post secondary education equalled a certain percentage of total provincial expenditures for this purpose. The final arrangement in 1967 set the federal share of eligible expenses at 50 percent. This system remained in place until 1977 when post secondary education grants were incorporated into the Established Programs Financing (EPF) Act. The responsiblity for education rest with the individual provinces. Federal governments participation in education is through transfer payments. In recent years, the federal government has frozen transfer payments for education to the provinces. Public support for higher education across Canada is declining. This has forced the provincial governments to significantly reduce their support of higher education in most jurisdictions in Canada.

Protection expenditures include spending by the Solicitor General's department, the department of justice and the various agencies under its jurisdiction. In addition, it includes expenditures related to the protection and development of business activities. For example, the Petroleum Monitoring Agency, established in 1980 and responsible for monitoring the reinvestment behavior of the oil industry, falls into this expenditure category. Due to its broader mandate, the federal government spends relatively more on this activity than the provincial governments.

Spending on resource conservation includes expenditures directed to programs which lead to the conservation and development of renewable and nonrenewable energy resources and similar activities. Federal and provincial governments naturally cooperate in this area and both spend approximately the same proportion of their total expenditures on these activities. Expenditures on resource conservation grew by 142 percent from 1978 to 1983. However, the rate of growth was almost unchanged during the second period under study and fell to -9 percent between 1988 and 1991, a fact which seems inconsistent with the current emphasis on resource conservation objectives in general and nonrenewable resource conservation in particular. The ending of the oil boom during the late 1970s and early 1980s can partly explain the decline in these rates.

The overwhelming public support for environmental concern caused the rate of growth of federal expenditures in this area to increase between 1978 and 1988. In addition to a relative increase in the rates of growth experienced in the two categories of regional planning and foreign affairs and international assistance, expenditure on the environment is the only one which shows an increased growth rate until 1988 and a subsequent sharp decline. The Department of Environment is responsible for most of the expenditures in this area and the role of the provinces varies to a considerable degree. Since 1988, spending on environmental programs have slowed down (Table 2). For instance, rate of growth of environment expenditures dropped to 21 percent between 1988 and 1991. In light of the current interest and involvement expressed by the public, the relatively low percentage of government expenditures allocated to the environment is likely to increase at both the provincial and the federal level in the future.

Transportation and communications expenditures experienced a modest increase over the 1978-1991 period. The same holds true of expenditures on recreation and culture. At the federal level, transportation and communications expenditures include the activities of the Canadian Radio Television and Telecommunications Commission (CRTC) and costs related to air, land and water transportation which include two or more provincial/local levels. The three levels of governments are also responsible for construction and maintenance of most roads and highways in their respective jurisdictions.

Expenditures related to foreign affairs and international assistance are primarily based on current internal economic conditions and political circumstances. For example, if the Canadian economy is experiencing a prosperous year, along with a low rate of unemployment, these expenditures could be increased and *vice versa*. Expenditures related to regional planning primarily fall under the federal jurisdiction. One component of these expenditures is regional development expenditures in the province of Quebec. Decisions regarding these spendings are largely based on political issues and circumstances, i.e., no economic reason is given in support of such decisions. This explains the relatively significant fluctuation in this category of expenditures.

Trends in government expenditures are critical in a sense that they reflect the direction of policy orientations that the government in power pursues. For example, the relatively slower rate of growth of government expenditures during the 1983-91 period reflects the federal government desire to reduce its deficit.

Figure 1 summarizes the trend in the federal, provincial and local government expenditures including grants since 1926, expressed as a percentage of GDP. In Figure 1, time (1926-1992 period) is measured along the horizontal axis and government expenditures expressed as a percentage of GDP along the vertical axis. The sharp rise in federal spending (shown in figure 1) during the 1940s is due to government participation in the Second World War. After 1948, while this spending continued to grow at the federal level, its rate of increase was more moderate and followed the pre-war pattern. Additionally, although the growth rate of spending fell, its absolute level was much higher than the pre-war level. This phenomenon is consistent with the replacement hypothesis discussed in

Chapter I. It is interesting to note the wide gap between the two spending ratios for the federal and provincial governments between 1950 and 1970 when the gap was back to its pre-1939 level. Expenditures on health and welfare and education, which are a provincial responsiblity, were increasing during the 1950-1970 period and the federal government was continually transferring tax points to the provinces and making special grants so that the provinces could finance their expenditures.

Figure 1
Trends in Growth of Gov't Expenditures

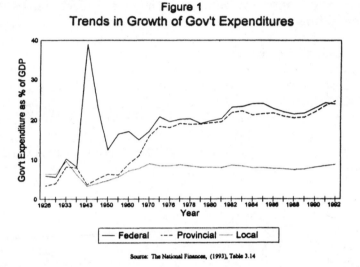

Source: The National Finances, (1993), Table 3.14

Figure 1 indicates a fairly stable trend for local government expenditures. This illustrates the point made earlier that municipal governments are, constitutionally, created by the provinces who in turn delegate to the municipal governments any taxing power they can have. As a result they have limited revenue sources and hence little capacity to arbitrary increase their expenditures.

B. CAUSES OF GOVERNMENT EXPENDITURES GROWTH IN CANADA

General statements related to the growth of government need some modifications when we examine countries at different levels of socio-economic and political development (Abizadeh and Gray 1985). For example, it is argued that during the early stages of development and change, a relatively higher level of government expenditures is required to foster the primary objectives of economic development. At early stages of development there is a great need for government expenditure in the areas of education and health and those expenditures which would improve the economy's infrastructure such as roads and transportation and communication. However, once an economy reaches its developed (or highly developed) stage, as is the case with Canada, expenditures on education, health and transportation would not be considered a luxury but as a necessity. In economic terms the demand for these goods now levels off since the income elasticity of demand for necessities is less than unity. In other words, there is a limit to how many hospital beds, how many schools, and how many kilometres of super highways which a stable population (a characteristic of highly developed countries) would demand, although consideration should be given to improved quality of these services and possibly higher expenditures in these areas. As we saw in Table 2, the rate of growth of government expenditures on health, education, and transportation has declined in recent years in Canada. It does not follow that the quality or quantity of services provided has deteriorated. All it suggests is that, once the basic infrastructure is in place, the need for increased expenditures in such areas would stabilize. The logical question is why, despite such considerations, does the absolute level of government expenditures and its relative share of GDP continue to grow. Part of the answer is that with high economic development and growth different social and economic problems emerge. For example, sociologists point out that economic growth and urbanization lead to a higher crime rate, a social problem that often requires governments action and thus increased expenditures. On the economic side, an outcome of industrialization is the emergence of externalities such as environmental deterioration and pollution. This requires more government involvement and interference in the market in order to reduce the negative impact of such developments on the society as a whole. Witness the sharp rate of growth of expenditures experienced in the area of environment as reported in Table 2. (See Abizadeh, 1988).

Researchers further suggest that political circumstances may also affect the level of government expenditures in a country. It has been observed that the political stance of the leader of the party in power will have a role to play in determining the level of government expenditures and that the more "liberal" the leader of the party in power the larger the size of government expenditures and *vice versa*. (See Abizadeh and Yousefi, 1988). Abizadeh and Gray (1993) examined the growth of government expenditures in Canadian provinces over the past three decades and concluded that the expenditure policies of provincial governments are independent of the political stance of the of the political parties in power. In essence, the growth of provincial spending has been stimulated by the demand for social services including education and health and thus derived by federal transfer payment programs. Thus, in a federal system like Canada, it is the policies of the central government that most influence the overall government expenditures and the economy as a whole. That the majority of the provinces in Canada (at least six out of ten) are too small in size to exert any meaningful influence on the national scene, politically or economically by themselves, may be a partial explanation of the federal role.

Table 3 Total Government Revenue Expressed as a
Percentage of Gross Domestic Product (Selected Calender Years)

Year	Federal	Provincial[a]	Local[a]	Total[b]
1950	15.8	6.4	4.2	24.2
1955	17.1	6.3	4.7	25.5
1960	16.5	8.4	6.5	27.1
1965	15.8	11.0	7.0	29.0
1970	17.4	15.6	8.4	35.7
1975	18.5	17.4	8.0	37.4
1980	16.3	19.1	7.8	37.5
1985	17.4	20.6	7.8	40.7
1989	18.3	20.4	7.7	41.5
1992	20.1	21.3	9.3	44.9

Source: The National Finances, (1993) Table 3.12.
[a] Includes intergovernmental grants to the receiving government
[b] Excludes grants

IV. TOTAL TAX REVENUES IN PERSPECTIVE

Before giving a detailed discussion of different sources of taxes in Canada, it is useful to look at the relative growth and relative share of different taxes at the three levels of government, federal, provincial and local, in Canada.

Table 3 indicates that the total federal government revenue as a percentage of GDP only increased from 15.8 percent in 1950 to 20.1 percent in 1992. At the same time, total government revenue as a percentage of GDP for the three levels of governments (last column in Table 3) increased from 24.2 percent in 1950 to 44.9 percent in 1992. Similar to total government expenditures, the total government revenue as a percentage of GDP continued to increase during the period under study. Comparing the last columns of Tables 1 and 3 one can detect a few notable differences. In 1950 total tax revenue as a percentage of GDP was 24.2 percent whereas the same figure for total expenditure was 21.3 percent. Over time, despite continued increase in the relative share of total tax revenue in GDP, the relative growth in tax revenues fell short of the increased expenditure. Compare these relative shares for 1992, 51.3 and 44.9 percent of the GDP for total expenditures and total tax revenues, respectively. The obvious outcome of these differences is the growth of government deficits which prevailed during the 1980s.

Most of the overall increase in tax revenues can be attributed to the sharp rise in government revenues at the provincial level. The share of these taxes in GDP went from a low of 6.4 to a relatively high figure of 21.3 percent in 42 years — a more than three fold increase. The relative rise of tax revenues at the provincial level is similar to the pattern of expenditures for this level of government. Comparing relative share of taxes and expenditures in GDP in Tables 3 and 1, it becomes clear that the rise in government revenue, more or less, kept pace with the growth of government expenditures at this level. As for the local governments, the growth of their revenues followed a more or less stable pattern as has the growth of their expenditures. This further indicates the fiscal dependency of the local government on the provinces. Federal and provincial grants and transfers make up a large portion of total revenues of these governments (See Boadway, 1980).

Overall, during the 1950-1991 period, total federal revenue as a percentage of GDP increased from 15.8 in 1950 to 20.1 in 1991. Compare this with the increase in revenues for provincial governments, from a low of 6.4 to 21.3 percent of the GDP — a more than three fold increase. Once again, as pointed out earlier, the provincial governments' contribution to the growth of the public sector in Canada far exceeds that of their federal counterpart.

A. ANATOMY OF THE GOVERNMENT REVENUE IN CANADA

So far we have examined the general level of government revenues at the three levels of government. In this section we will examine in detail the major components of government revenues at the three levels of government.

Table 4. Consolidated Government Revenue, all level[a]
(Billions of Dollars)

Type of Revenue	1978 Absolute	1983 Absolute	1983 % rate of Growth Since 1978	1988 Absolute	1988 % rate of Growth Since 1983	1991 Absolute	1991 % of Growth Since 1988
Personal Income Tax	25.02	48.10	92	77.84	62	100.41	29
Corporation Income Tax	8.80	10.28	17	18.02	75	18.30	2
Property and Related Taxes	8.10	14.04	73	19.48	39	23.05	18
General Sales Taxes	9.25	15.72	69	32.89	109	35.82	9
Fuel, Alcohol and Tobacco	4.10	7.03	71	12.15	73	12.10	-
Customs duties	2.75	3.38	23	4.68	38	4.15	-11
Health and Social Insurance Levies	8.77	17.93	104	27.73	55	22.07	-20
Total taxes[b]	69.54	122.26	76	200.00	63	228.90	14
Other sources of revenue (Total)	20.4	135.71	75	35.92	0.6	45.63	27
Total consolidated revenue[b]	89.94	158.17	76	235.91	49	274.54	16

Source: The National Finances (1993) Table 4.1

a   Fiscal year ending nearest to December 31, 1978 to 1988

b   May not add due to omission of minor revenue sources and rounding.

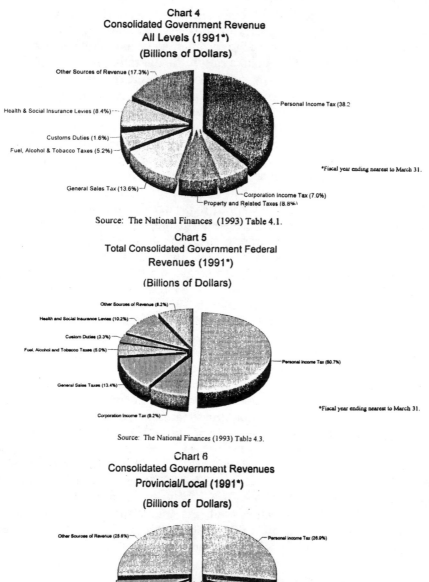

Chart 4
Consolidated Government Revenue
All Levels (1991*)
(Billions of Dollars)

Other Sources of Revenue (17.3%)

Health & Social Insurance Levies (8.4%)

Customs Duties (1.6%)

Fuel, Alcohol & Tobacco Taxes (5.2%)

General Sales Tax (13.6%)

Personal Income Tax (38.2

*Fiscal year ending nearest to March 31.

Corporation Income Tax (7.0%)

Property and Related Taxes (8.8%)

Source: The National Finances (1993) Table 4.1.

Chart 5
Total Consolidated Government Federal
Revenues (1991*)

(Billions of Dollars)

Other Sources of Revenue (8.2%)

Health and Social Insurance Levies (10.2%)

Custom Duties (3.3%)

Fuel, Alcohol and Tobacco Taxes (5.0%)

General Sales Taxes (13.4%)

Personal Income Tax (50.7%)

*Fiscal year ending nearest to March 31.

Corporation Income Tax (9.2%)

Source: The National Finances (1993) Table 4.3.

Chart 6
Consolidated Government Revenues
Provincial/Local (1991*)

(Billions of Dollars)

Other Sources of Revenue (25.6%)

Health and Social Insurance Levies (6.8%)

Fuel, Alcohol, and Tobacco Taxes (5.3%)

General Sales Taxes (13.6%)

Personal Income Tax (26.9%)

Corporation Income Tax (5.0%)

Property and Related Taxes (16.6%)

*Fiscal year ending nearest to March 31.

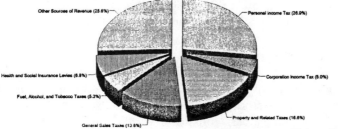

Source: The National Finances (1993) Table 4.3.

Table 4 gives figures for the absolute consolidated government revenues at all levels of government for four selected years. It also shows the
rate of growth of consolidated government revenue between 1978, 1983,
1988, and 1991. This Table breaks down the overall revenue sources into
two broad categories: tax revenue and other sources of revenue. Other
sources of revenue includes items such as natural resource revenues, return on investment, etc. The total tax revenue is in turn broken down into
seven major categories. Chart 4 gives a breakdown of consolidated
sources of government revenues in Canada at all three levels of government for 1991. Charts 5 and 6 give similar breakdowns for the federal and
provincial/local governments.

Turning now to Table 4, it can be observed that the rate of growth of
consolidated total revenue in Canada experienced a decline between 1983-
1991. Between 1978 and 1983, personal income taxes showed the highest
rate of growth (92 percent) among all major sources of tax revenue other
than health and social insurance levies. Between 1983 and 1988, general
sales taxes showed the highest rate of growth (109 percent) followed by
corporation income taxes.[10] However, personal income tax showed the
highest percentage of increase between 1988-1991 and the sharp increase
in personal income tax from 1978 to 1983 is quite noticeable.

During this period, the Canadian economy, like most other countries
of the western world, was suffering from stagflation and growing budget
deficits. The sharp increase in personal taxes was seen as a remedy to cool
off the inflationary pressures in the economy while providing governments with additional revenues to reduce their deficits. Clearly, the rising
popularity of a supply-side economics necessitated a relatively less reliance on corporate income taxes, as shown by the low rate of growth of
this type of tax revenue during the 1978-1983 and 1988-1991 periods
(Table 4). After the recession of the early 1980s, the overall growth of tax
revenues dropped from 76 percent (1978-1983) to 63 percent (1983-88) and
further to 16 percent. As shown in Chart 4, the breakdown of total consolidated government revenue confirms that Canada relies heavily on
personal income taxes as one of the major sources of government revenue
(38.2 percent of total consolidated revenue in 1991 came from personal
income taxes).

When total federal government revenue is broken down into its component parts (Chart 5), the relatively heavy reliance on personal income
tax becomes more evident. By far the largest portion of total federal government revenue comes from personal income tax sources (50.7 percent).
The corporation income taxes constitute a relatively low percentage of
federal government total revenue (9.2 percent), while property taxes are

nonexistent at the federal level. General sales taxes constitute 13.4 percent of total federal government revenue. Until January 1991, the federal government had in place a sales tax system which applied the tax at different rates on different manufactured products. This tax was known as Manufacture's Sales Tax (MST) (see Gilles, 1985). On January 1991 this tax was replaced with the new Goods and Services Tax (GST).[11] Fuel, alcohol and tobacco taxes constitute a very small portion of total federal government revenue (5 percent). The share of these revenues in the provincial budgets is also insignificant. The same is true for the provincial governments (5.3 percent). Custom duties, which used to be a major source of tax revenue at the federal level in Canada before and during the two world wars, have lost their importance in the recent past and only constitute 3.3 percent of total revenues. This is consistent with the hypothesis that international trade taxes, including custom duties, continue to lose their relative importance in the revenue structure of growing economies (Abizadeh and Yousefi, 1985). Health and social services levies experienced the highest rate of growth from 1978 to 83 (104 percent), and along with the federal sales tax they form the second largest component of the total federal government revenue. Despite the relatively low rate of growth that these taxes experienced during the 1983-88 period, based on recent legislations introduced at the federal level, it is expected that the share of these taxes will continue to rise in Canada.[12]

The major item included in other sources of revenue is natural resource revenues and return on investment. These sources of income rank low in the list of revenues received by the federal government compared with its provincial counterparts. The reason is that most of the royalties on oil and natural gas are levied and collected by the provincial governments.

Personal income tax continues to play a dominant role in the provincial budgets, as it does in the federal budget. It constitutes 27 percent of total provincial/local revenue, the largest source of tax revenue. Corporation income tax is the smallest contributor to the provincial revenue source. Due to regional competition that prevails between Canadian provinces in trying to attract investment and capital, these governments usually do not want to discourage investors by increasing their reliance of corporation income taxes.

The reason for the relatively high share of property and related taxes (16.6 percent) in the provincial/local government budget is that more than 90 percent of the property taxes collected in Canada are primarily a municipal (local) tax.[13] In fact, property taxes plus other property-based taxes constitute the single most important source of local government revenue.

These taxes account for somewhere between 35 to 45 percent of the total government revenue at the municipal level.

While provincial governments generate the largest percentage of their tax revenues from personal income tax (26.9 percent), they rely heavily on the provincial sales tax (PST). The PST applies to sales by retailers at rates and ranges from 6 to 12 percent.[14] At the same time, a relatively small portion of the provincial/local tax revenue (5.3 percent) comes from taxes on motor fuel, alcohol and tobacco taxes. Thess taxes have been gaining in importance in recent years due to health and environmental concerns.[15]

While health and social insurance levies constitute 6.8 percent of the total revenue at the provincial/local level, their relative importance fall short of that of the federal government levies. As mentioned above, the reason for the relatively high percentage of total revenue received by the provincial governments from other sources has to do with the royalties levied by these governments on oil and gas and minerals. This is particularly true in the case of oil rich provinces such as Alberta and Saskatchewan. For example, in the 1989-90 fiscal year the government of Alberta received $3.13 billion in natural resource revenue, which was 24 percent of its total revenue. In contrast, Ontario, which is not an oil producing province, eared $0.32 billion from the same source, only 0.7 percent of its total revenue.

Figure 2 summarizes the trend in the federal, provincial and local government revenues, including grants (since 1926) expressed as a percentage of GDP. In Figure 2, time (1926-1992 period) is measured along the horizontal axis and total revenues expressed as a percentage of GDP along the vertical axis. The need to finance the second world war is clearly reflected by the sharp increase in the growth of government revenues at the federal level during the 1940s. This trend was followed by a sharp decline after the war ended and subsequently followed a relatively stable pattern. In contrast, the trend for provincial taxes shows a continuous and relatively sharp increase since the end of the second world war. This trend is an indication of increased involvement of provincial governments in the provision of social services including health and education. Since transfers from the federal government to the provinces constitute a major source of revenue for them, increased transfers along with continued deligation of tax points (resulting in higher tax revenues for the provincial government) to the provinces by the federal government and making special grants to finance social expenditures, are partly responsible for this notable increase.

Figure 2
Trends in Growth of Gov't Revenues

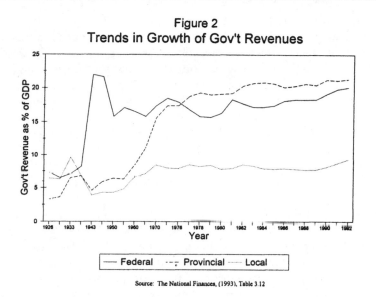

Source: The National Finances, (1993), Table 3.12

In examining the trend of local government revenues in Figure 2, the dotted line indicates a relatively stable ratio. This, once again, illustrates the point made earlier that the responsibilities of municipal governments are constitutionally limited and their taxing power based on the generosity of the provinces. As a result they have limited revenue sources and hence little room to expand or diversify those sources. This trend is very similar to that observed for local government expenditure pattern examined in Figure 1.

B. RECENT DEVELOPMENTS IN THE CANADIAN TAX SYSTEM

In a highly developed country such as Canada, tax changes occur on a continuous basis to respond to the rapidly changing economic, social, and political circumstances. Tax reforms, however, involve major restructuring of the tax system based on detailed and extensive analysis of existing structure and its comparison with available alternative tax measures. Although it is difficult to clearly define what constitutes tax reform as opposed to "tax changes," Canada has experienced three major tax changes since the second world war, major enough to be called tax reforms. The first of such reforms came when the Wartime Tax Agreements were changed in 1949 to pave the way for the introduction of new social programs such as Family Allowance (baby bonus). This relatively minor reform was followed by a major tax reform in 1971. The 1971 tax reform was based on the elaborate studies done by the Royal Commission on Taxation known as Carter Commission (appointed in 1962). The finding of this commission appeared in a six volumes (1966) publication which led to a comprehensive proposed tax reform in 1971 and was adopted in 1972. Since 1972 several minor and major tax changes have been implemented. The latest tax reform process began by changes proposed in the March 1985 budget. This was followed by the government's white paper on Tax Reform (Department of Finance 1987). This report proposed a two-phase tax reform for Canada. Phase I of this reform, which put its main thrust into broadening the base of taxation and reducing the tax rate, went into effect in the spring of 1987.

Prior to the 1987 tax reform, there were ten tax brackets and ten different marginal tax rates applied to each bracket. These income brackets were indexed and each taxable income bracket was deflated by an inflation factor for each taxation year. Comparison of Tables 5 and 6 shows that this reform led to a reduction of the federal personal taxable income brackets and their corresponding marginal tax rates from ten to three. In addition, since 1988, most personal deductions were replaced by tax credits, either refundable or non-refundable. The main goal behind this change was to improve equity in the tax system. The application of this credit system allows individuals to add up an "amount" based on the items subject to a tax credit and then apply the lowest marginal tax rate (17 percent), in most cases, to calculate the credit. For example, an amount is specified as basic personal amount for each taxpayer. The tax credit is 17 percent of this amount.

Phase I also made drastic changes in corporate tax by tightening up tax loopholes and reducing tax rates and increasing tax credits.

Phase II, however, involved the process of tax reform which led to the introduction of the Goods and Services Tax (GST) in January 1991. The GST is essentially a value added tax. The government began by proposing a tax rate of 9 percent which was later reduced to 7 percent. This tax is collected by suppliers of commodities and is levied on a broad base. The base covers services which were not subject to tax under the old federal sales tax (MST) referred to earlier.

The introduction of GST in Canada should come as no surprise. Research has shown that once a country reaches the "highly developed stage" it becomes possible and at the same time attractive to introduce one or another form of sales taxes for the purpose of raising additional revenues.[16] It would have been impossible and at the same time impractical for a country such as Canada to stay away from this general trend.

There are four main reasons for the general acceptance and popularity of these taxes in more advanced countries. First, a highly developed country is endowed with the necessary social, political and economic infrastructure which easily lend themselves to the implementation and administration of such a relatively complicated and sophisticated tax measure. A successful implementation of any sales tax scheme is dependant upon the ability of the society and the economy to comply with it. Second, there is a limit to the amount of direct taxes, such as personal and corporation income taxes, that can be collected by any government at a given point in time. This is specifically true for Canada that is labelled as a "small open economy."

Third, there is a very strong political element involved in the introduction of sales taxes. Other taxes such as personal income taxes are perfectly visible. Any marginal change in their rates will be reflected directly on our paychecks. However, sales taxes can be hidden from the public and buried in the price paid by the consumers on goods and services. In other words, direct tax increases have a high political cost whereas such costs would be minimal in the case of indirect taxes. Although generally true, this argument only holds in cases where both systems of direct and indirect taxes are already in place and the government is interested in marginal tax increases.

Table 5 Federal Taxable Income Brackets Subject to Indexing and Tax Rates, 1984 to 1987

	Inflation Factor			
Rate, %	1984: 5%	1985: 4%	1986: 0.8%	1987: 1.1%
	taxable income bracket			
6	First $1,238	First $1,295	First $1,305	First $1,320
16	1,239 — 2,476	1,296 — 2,590	1,306 — 2,611	1,321 — 2,639
17	2,477 — 4,952	2,591 — 5,180	2,612 — 5,221	2,640 — 5,279
18	4,953 — 7,428	5,181 — 7,770	5,222 — 7,832	5,280 — 7,918
19	7,429 — 12,380	7,771 — 12,950	7,833 — 13,054	7,919 — 13,197
20	12,381 — 17,332	12,951 — 18,130	13,055 — 18,275	13,198 — 18,476
23	17,333 — 22,284	18,131 — 23,310	18,276 — 23,496	18,477 — 23,755
25	22,285 — 34,664	23,311 — 36,260	23,497 — 36,550	23,756 — 36,952
30	34,665 — 59,424	36,261 — 62,160	36,551 — 62,657	36,953 — 63,347
34	59,425 +	62,161 +	62,658 +	63,348 +

Source: The National Finances, 1987-88, Table 7.5.

Table 6 Federal Taxable Income Brackets, 1993[a]

Taxable income bracket	Federal marginal tax rate
	percent
Up to $29,590	17
$29,591-to $59,180	26
$59,181 and over	29

[a] Brackets has been indexed by the increase in the consumer price index in excess of 3 percent, beginning in 1989 to present.

This was not the case with the GST in Canada. This is a new and major tax grab which does not go unnoticed by anyone who works and lives in Canada. In particular, the GST, with the 7 percent rate, is so broad and major that its impact on the economy can be abrupt and brusque. The Canadian voters directly feel its burden and will react accordingly in the political arena. If the political cost of introducing such a measure is so obvious why did the government of Canada decide to go ahead with it in the first place? This question leads us to the fourth reason for the popularity of sales taxes in highly developed countries. Canada, as well as many other major industrialized nations, is suffering from an unacceptably high level of deficit. Most economists agree that the current deficit and the accumulated debt are too high. Since sales taxes are so broadly based (in fact if no exemptions are applied, sales taxes are tax on GDP) they provide an alternative and indeed attractive source of revenue for the government. Once in place, it would be fairly easy for the government to change its rate by a very small percentage and increase the required revenue[17].

Although GST, when introduced by the former Conservative government, was extremely unpopular, the public has more or less accepted it as an economic reality. During the 1993 federal election, the Liberal Party announced its intention to replace the GST. This was not a well thought-out economic decision. After the election, the Liberal government began the process of looking into possible replacements for the GST, a task given to a parliamentary committee. It is no secret that this committee is having a hard time finding a suitable and economically viable substitute for the GST. It is the view of the author that the government, instead of replacing the GST, will suggest minor cosmetic changes to save face in light of the election promise that it has made.

ENDNOTES

1. Note that current distinction between direct and indirect taxes is rather unclear in the literature. This lack of clarity has been a source of discontent among provincial and federal governments and has caused significant debate between the two levels of government.

2. This is consistent with the hypothesis that the lower the rate of growth and economic achievements, the higher the governments will rely on international trade related taxes. For empirical support, see Abizadeh and Yousefi (1985).

3. Newfoundland joined the confederation in 1949, thus bringing the number of provinces in Canada to ten.

4. The discussion on the history of taxation is drawn heavily from Abizadeh and Hudson (1983).

5. Canadian provinces have always expressed a certain amount of discontent with the arrangements made between Ottawa and provinces regarding their respective tax jurisdictions. For more detail on this, see Abizadeh and Hudson (1983).

6. It is interesting to note that the Liberal government, immediately after the election, began looking into different ways of reducing government expenditures in all areas including social programs.

7. It is argued that the previous government was obsessed with deficit reduction and lowering the government expenditures. For an interesting account on this see Hartle (1988, pp.xiii-xiv).

8. Consolidated budget is the overall budget of all three levels of governments. It is important to deal with government expenditures in this context since the macro economic variables, such as the rate of inflation, respond to the consolidated budget expenditures rather than just one level of government expenditure. This takes account of the interrelationships among all levels of expenditure.

9. This decline is mainly due to the fact that the income elasticity of demand for such services may have declined after it peaked in the 70s and early 80s.

10. Sales taxes are generally imposed at the provincial level and they play an important role in the budget of the provincial governments.

11. For background see Department of Finance (1987). Also see, Sapona (1990) for analysis of GST. Later a brief discussion of new tax changes in Canada will be given.

12. Best example is Bill C-21 (1989) which proposed amendments to the Unemployment Act. For detail see Canadian Tax Foundation (1990), p. 8:14.

13. Only Prince Edward Island and New Brunswick impose province-wide property taxes. All other provinces impose property taxes only in the "unorganized region" of the province. See Canadian Tax Foundation (1990), p. 11:1. Also note that local governments rely heavily on transfers from other governments and enterprises. In 1988 transfers accounted for 47 percent of total gross revenue of these governments.

14. Alberta is the only province in Canada which does not have a provincial sales tax in place.

15. Most recently,(spring of 1994), the federal government reduced the tax on tobacco products to discourage smuggling which was proving to be a major problem particularly in the province of Quebec.

16. For support see, Abizadeh (1976) pp. 112-119. Also witness the surge of value added taxes (VAT) in Western Europe and other developed countries (see Tait, 1988 for evidence).

17. Department of Finance (1989) provides detailed information on the GST.

REFERENCES

Abizadeh, S., (1976), *Tax Components and the Degree of Economics Development*, An Unpublished Ph.D. Thesis, Oregon State University, Corvallis, Oregon, U.S.A.

Abizadeh, S. and R. Hudson, (1983), "Trends in The Federal-Provincial Tax Collection Agreements: The Case of Alberta," *Canadian Tax Journal*, 38:653-664.

Abizadeh S. and J. Gray, (1985), "Wagner's Law; A Pooled Time-Series, Cross-Section Comparison," *National Tax Journal*, 38:209-218.

Abizadeh, S. and M. Yousefi, (1985), "International Trade Taxes and Economic Development: An Empirical Analysis," *International Review of Economics and Business*, 32:735-749.

Abizadeh, S., (1988), "Economic Development and Income Elasticity of Demand for `Government'," *Social Indicators Research*, 20:15-43.

Abizadeh, S., and M. Yousefi, (1988), "Growth of Government Expenditure: The Case of Canada," *Public Finance Quarterly*, 16:78-100.

Abizadeh, S., and J. Gray, (1993), "Provincial Government Expenditures in Canada: A Empirical Analysis," *International Review of Applied Economics*, 7:69-90.

Bird, R. (1987), "Federal-Provincial Fiscal Transfers in Canada: Retrospects and Prospect," *Canadian Tax Journal*, 35:118-33.

Bird, R., (1971), "Wagner's "Law" of Expanding State Activity," *Public Finance*, 26:1-26.

Boadway, R.W. and F. Flaters, (1991), "Federal Provincial Relations Revisited: Some Consequences of Recent Constitutional and Policy Developments," in M. McMillan (ed)(1991), pp. 87-128.

Boadway, R. W., (1980), *Intergovernmental Transfers in Canada*, Toronto: Canadian Tax Foundation.

Canadian Tax Foundation, (1990), *Provincial and Municipal Finances 1989*, Toronto: Canadian Tax Foundation.

Canadian Tax Foundation, (1990), *The National Finances*, Toronto: Canadian Tax Foundation.

Canadian Tax Foundation, (1993), *The National Finances*, Toronto: Canadian Tax Foundation.

Department of Finance, (1987), *Supplementary Information Relating to Tax Reform Measures*, Tabled in the House of Commons by the Honourable Michael H. Wilson.

Department of Finance, (1989), *Goods and Service Tax Technical Papers*, Issued by the Honourable Michael H. Wilson (August).

Gilles, M., (1985), "Federal Sales Taxation: A Survey of Six Decades of Experience, Critiques, and Reform Proposals," *Canadian Tax Journal*, 33:68-98.

Hartle, D.G., (1988), *The Expenditure Budget Process of the Government of Canada: A Public Choice-Rent-Seeking Perspective*, Toronto: Canadian Tax Foundation.

McMillan, M., (ed), *Provincial Public Finance: Plandits, Problems, and Prospects*, Toronto: Canadian Tax Foundation.

Moore, M.A., J.H. Perry, and D.I. Beach, (1966), *The Financing of Canadian Confederation: The First Hundred Years*, Canadian Tax Paper no. 43, Toronto: Canadian Tax Foundation.

Perry, H.J., (1990), *Taxation in Canada*, (5th ed.), Canadian Tax Paper no. 89, Toronto: Canadian Tax Foundation.

Perry, H.J., (1989), *A Fiscal History of Canada—The Postwar Years*, Canadian Tax Papers no. 85, Toronto: Canadian Tax Foundation.

Royal Commission on Taxation, (1966), *Report of the Royal Commission on Taxation* (Vols I-IV), Ottawa, Queen's Printer and Controller of Stationary.

Sapona, I., (1990), "Canada: Goods and Services Tax," *Bulletin For International Fiscal Documentation*, 44:489-498.

Strick, J.C., (1992), *Canadian Public Finance*, (4th ed.), Toronto: Holt, Rinehart and Winston of Canada Ltd.

Tait, A.A., (1988), *Value Added Tax: International Practice and Problems*, Washington, D.C.: International Monetary Fund.

CHAPTER SIX

AN ANALYSIS OF PUBLIC EXPENDITURES AND TAXATION IN SOUTH KOREA

Mahmood Yousefi and Sohrab Abizadeh

I. INTRODUCTION

Scholars and policy makers marvel at the success of South Korea, an emerging industrialized nation. In one generation this country has been transformed from a nation of war torn poverty to an industrial giant. This fact renders an examination of public expenditures and taxation in South Korea a worthwhile exercise. The objective of this chapter is twofold: a) to examine the impact of industrialization on government spending in South Korea, and b) to provide an analysis of taxation trends in Korea. We will begin with a brief historical review of the South Korean economy in Section II. In Sections III and IV, we will analyze South Korean government expenditures and taxes. The chapter will end with a summary in Section V.

II. A REVIEW OF ECONOMIC CONDITIONS

A. A BRIEF ECONOMIC HISTORY

South Korea, a country of 38,000 sq. miles (or 98,400 sq. km) with a demilitarized zone of 487 sq. miles (or 779.2 sq. km.), is rapidly becoming a modern industrialized state. Its people have known hunger, disease, bitter poverty, political chaos, military destruction and suffering, and the tramp of invader's hoof. They have known, too, art, literature, the powerful philosophies of Buddha and Confucius. They have loved since time immemorial, music, the dance, poetry, the flavor of makkoli rice wine (Korea, Overseas Information Service, 1985, p. 5.)

South Korea was ravaged by the second world war. The war's end brought the division of the country into north and south and concluded forty-five years of Japanese colonization. Korea was ravaged again by the bloody war of 1950. In the 1950s and early 1960s poverty was widespread, complicated by severe overcrowding. Manufacturing made up less than 10 percent of all output. Exports made up 3.5 percent of GNP and per capita income in 1961 was $80 (Alam, 1989, p. 24). After the armistice and the inauguration of the U.S. economic assistance, the Korean economy became aid-dependent. In the 1950s, the U.S. assistance of $208 million enabled Korea to finance all of its current account deficits (Das, 1992, p.21).

As recently as 1960 Korea was a typical low income LDC, characterized by an abundance of unskilled and underemployed labor. The economy was stagnant and saving and investment were at low levels. Although the structure of the economy was essentially agrarian, land distribution was highly skewed. According to Amsden (1989, p.38), 3 percent of all farm households owned two thirds of all the land in 1930 and because of the land reform, instituted in early 1960s, the portion of landless fell to less than 7 percent.

After the armistice, the U.S. policy in Korea centered on stability as a precursor to growth. The year 1961 saw the rise of General Park Chung Hee, a leader of the *coup d' etat*. The ascendancy of Park Chung Hee to power set the stage for a period of sustained economic growth and social development. This growth took place without debilitating effects known to occur in growing LDCs. For instance, "Inflation which has plagued many LDCs, was kept under control "(Das, 1992, p. 2). By 1970, Korea had established itself as a NIC (newly industrializing country) and its per capita income had surpassed North Korea and the Philippines (Song, 1990, p. 1). Korea maintained its rapid rate of growth throughout the 1970s despite the oil crisis, and by late 1970s it had overtaken Malaysia and Cuba in terms of economic well-being (p.1).

Park Chung Hee remained in office until his assassination in 1979. While President, he represented the Democratic Republic Party. The 1979 *coup* paved the way for a democratic transition of Power and the eventual election of Roh Tae Woo in 1988. Korea continued to prosper amid these political changes. By mid-1980s, it had overtaken countries such as Mexico and Argentina in terms of per capita income (p. 1). "By the time of the 1988 Summer Olympics Korea had become known as one of the highest income developing countries..." (p.1). By late 1980s, South Korea's GNP was $239.5 billion and its per capita income had risen to $5,569. The literacy rate that hovered around 30 percent in the mid 1950 had reached 95 percent level by 1990.

As Korea's economy grew, the government was able to pay attention to education, social services, and income distribution. Since the importance of education is recognized, it receives the highest priorities of the Korean people. Two-third of the cost of education in the early years of industrialization was privately funded. The distingusihed heritage of YANGBAN, the scholar class, is still a characteristic of the system. The system is tough and many make great sacrifices to give their children the chance to make into one of the more eminent schools, Seoul, Yonsel, Koryo, Hanyang and Pohang. Korean students are enticed to technical careers by offers of special scholarships, exemption from military service and promise of employment opportunities after graduation.

Real spending on social services has increased over the period 1960-90. However, these programs do not match the scope of the social programs of the more developed countries. While social welfare is complementary to economic growth, South Korea's programs have been pragmatic in nature. There is increasing pressure by various groups who demand more and better social programs. Today 2.8 million or 7.7 percent live at the poverty level. Welfare programs include rice rationing, free medical service and hospital cost coverage, those who can afford payments pay 50 percent of their own medical costs. For the poorest segment of the society these services are free but it is highly debated whether benefits provided are adequate. For the middle class, social programs include a contributory social insurance scheme (pension and medical).

Koreans are particularly sensitive to the issue of income distribution. At present 75 percent of the population is urbanized. In the 1970s it was feared that rapid economic growth and urbanization would contribute to the development of two social cultures, an urban one which is modern and industrial, and a rural one characterized by backwardness and antiquity. To prevent this duality, a comprehensive rural development plan was initiated to bring modern facilities such as roads, irrigation, water facilities, and power to the countryside. The government provided capital and training while villagers provided labor. The result was local revenue generation and a cooperative effort to promote community improvement.

B. ECONOMIC PLANNING AND POLICY

South Korea began its official economic development strategy in 1961 by creating the Economic Planning Board (EPB). This institution was set up with the explicit purpose of formulating allocative decisions in the industrial sector of the economy. Clear objectives, a competent staff, and effective channels of communication were the hallmark of the EPB. Later, in 1971, the Korean Development Institute (KDI) was founded to support the initiative of the EPB. The mandate of KDI was to provide technical assistance to the EPB and assist it in drawing up detailed economic plans designed to meet the EPB's overall objectives (See Petri, 1986, pp. 69-70).

Since its founding, the EPB has played a crucial role in formulating and implementing Korea's five-year economic plans. The objectives of successive five-year plans have varied in accordance with the rising national income, changes in the country's economic structure, and changes in economic priorities. Song (1990, p. 129) posits that an examination of these objective should be viewed in the context of the government's major functions which are: a) to create the economic and legal framework, b) to promote equity, c) to promote macroeconomic stability, and d) to promote economic efficiency.

Many people, inside and outside of Korea, believe that the achievement of a high growth rate has been the consequence of planning by a small group of elites and excessive government intervention in the market. There is some validity to this argument since the most important characteristic of the decision-making machinery involved in formulating and implementing economic plans and policies in Korea is that it is headed by the President and as such is a nationwide apparatus (p. 139). It is also true that the planning apparatus has been basically managed by military leaders committed to economic development. This type of management usually lends itself to a top-down decision-making process. Though efficient in a sense of avoiding the give and take of a democratic process, this style of decision-making has its own disadvantages. Recognizing this problem, "The Chun Doo Hwan government ... proclaimed its intention to ... decentralize the economic decision-making process in Korea" (p. 140)

As already discussed, the Korean government launched a planned approach to economic development in 1962 and actively intervened in business activity. Beginning with this period, accelerated growth became a common feature of the Korean economy. This growth, however, unleashed a series of structural changes. For instance, the share of domestic output "originating in agriculture dropped from 45 percent of total product in 1960-62 to less than 30 percent in 1970-72". At the same time the share of industrial output rose from 17 to 35 percent (Kuznets, 1977. P. 87). These changes brought about a corresponding shift in the composition of the labor force. According to Kuzents, economic changes became possible because of the underlying long-term and short-term elements. Decolonization set into motion long before the 1960s was one such long-term institutional change. Short-term elements dealt with such policy changes as the Park government's emphasis on economic development and a stabilization program with the fiscal reform of 1963-64.

Governments remain strong in industrialized nations, not through tyranny but, through achieving pragmatic goals that meet the needs and expectations of the polity. Alam (1989, p. 30) observed that "Several scholars are of the view that rule of men, not law, is an important guiding principle embedded in Korean bureaucratic tradition." The regimes of Park and Chun pursued effective policy to realize clear national objectives. While abuse of human rights was rampant, these regimes succeeded in improving the economic status of the poorest segment of the society. The Korean regime took initiatives in uncertain economic times when other nations suffered from world recession. In the 1970s, policies of currency devaluation were matched with careful fiscal and monetary measures to maintain export markets and an average growth rate of 9 percent. In the beginning of the Park regime, the government showed its commitment to economic development by normalizing relations with Japan in spite of domestic public opposition. This enabled the Koreans to gain access to Japanese capital, raw materials, and industrial technology. Instead of favoring small cottage businesses, the Korean choice was to favor the formation of large, vertically integrated, industrial conglomerates, modelled after the Japanese ZAIBATSU, the CHAEBOL. These are usually controlled by a single family that set up a promising new business without relying on other firms for parts or service.

In early 1960s, the Korean currency was devalued, from 50 won per dollar in January 1960 to 130 won per dollar in February 1961. The devaluation, subsidies to exports, and the liberalization of the exchange rate regime did not curb inflationary pressures. These pressures led to the deterioration of the balance of payments which, in turn, set the stage for the reemergence of the multiple exchange rates and import restrictions (see Balassa, 1990). After the August election of 1964, far reaching reforms were introduced which involved "the devaluation of the official exchange rate from 130 to 247 won to the U.S. dollar, the unification of exchange rates, import liberalization, and increased incentives to exports, represent-

ing the adoption of an outward-oriented development strategy" (P. 4).
Exporters were authorized to import their inputs duty free and were
given "generous wastage allowances for the importation of raw materials" (P. 5).

In 1964, the Koreans Trade Promotion Corporation (KTPC) was
founded to promote Korean exports and conduct market research abroad.
Since that time Korea has been known for its aggressive pursuit of new
markets and its ability to react to changes in world economic conditions.
This strategy is accomplished through a partnership of private and public
sectors. The public sector takes the controlling hand in the partnership,
guiding and nurturing new industries and shaping the productive future
of the nation. The private sector is actively involved in this process and
businesses play an advisory role in formulating policy. In addition to
KTPC, the government established export targets for individual firms. As
Balassa (p. 5) points out "export targets had largely a psychological value
as did the honors bestowed on large exporters."

The economic liberalization of the mid-1960s was designed to assist
the development of manufacturing technologies. The devaluation, tax
credits and subsidies targeting improved productivity and the ease of restrictions on imports brought about more international contact and competition. Alam (1989) viewed these policies as a replacement of import
substitution strategy (inward-looking) of development by an export oriented approach (outward-looking). This strategy paid dividends as
growth rate hovered around 9.5 percent during 1960-70. Domestic saving
rate rose from 3.7 percent to 15.7 percent and foreign saving rate, used to
finance domestic investment, fell from 80 percent to 33 percent. (See
Alam, pp. 23-50; Das, 1992, pp. 21-55; and Song, 1990, pp. 135-146).

The 1970s brought a move away from labor-intensive manufacturing
goods to capital-intensive industries. Recognizing that Korea would not
be able to maintain its comparative advantage in labor-intensive goods for
long, attempts were made to promote the production of ferrous and non-
ferrous metals, chemicals, petrochemicals, ship-building, automobiles,
and heavy machinery. Attempts were also made to increase productivity
in capital-intensive industries through the allocation of domestic credit
and access to foreign credit. The importance of reduction in the cost of
credit to industries through preferential interest rates were noteworthy.
Balassa observed the importance of fiscal measures "in the form of exemption from corporate income taxes and accelerated depreciation provisions...[to lowering] the cost of capital to industries in question"
(Balassa, 1990, p. 6).

In the late 1970s several factors contributed to the rise of imports. Among these were the high intensity of fixed investment and machinery, and the deterioration of Korean industry's competitiveness. Although the devaluation of the won - 656 won per dollar by late 1980 - led to increases in exports, Korea was not able to match the performance of Hong Kong, Taiwan, and Singapore (p. 7). Following the policy changes adopted in the aftermath of President Park's assassination, the Fifth Five-Year Economic Plan (1982-86) "called for a full-fledged outward-oriented development strategy" (p. 7). Therefore, export promotion became a national obsession and the policy of setting export targets for firms was strengthened. These targets were based on the recommendation of "export advisors" that specialized in the financial and production aspects of the process. Companies continued to consult with the government to meet their exporting goals and the governments took an extremely active role in the coordination of export capacity on a national scale.

The economic strategy of the 1980s stressed the importance of light and high technology industries. Increased pressure to liberalize trade, however, placed stress on the financial and traditional export sectors. At present, the country is under external pressure to protect intellectual property rights to meet increased demand for royalties, and to ease restriction on technology transfers. Economic planners intend to devote 5 percent of GDP to R & D expenditures by the year 2001. Businesses will receive financial and tax incentives for their R & D investment. The government has already implemented policies targeting R & D by: a) applying a system of tax credits to R & D investments; b) exempting imported R & D equipment from tariffs; c) offering venture capital funding; and d) revising the nation's procurement policy to attract the private sector to longer-term R & D efforts. (For details, see Perry, 1991, pp. 63-64).

III. TRENDS IN GOVERNMENT EXPENDITURES

A. GENERAL ANALYSIS

Has government spending fueled Korea's economic growth? Has there been a change in government spending over time? We address the second question first. Table 1 provides information on economic classification of government expenditures by functions. One such function is the Economic Services category which accounted for 42 percent of total spending.

Table 1 Break-down of Expenditures by Function Consolidated Central Government (Billions of Won)

Type of Expenditures	1960[a]		1965[a]		1970[a]		1975[a]	
	Absolute	% of Total	Absolute	% of Total	Absolute	% of Total	Absolute	% of Total
Defence	14.8	35.1	29.5	29.2	98.9	19.0	425.1	20.0
Education	6.5	15.0	15.0	14.9	74.4	14.1	227.5	11.0
Health	0.6	1.4	1.3	1.2	6.4	1.2	15.6	0.8
Social Security and Welfare	2.0	4.5	5.3	5.2	27.9	5.3	89.1	4.3
Housing and Community Amenities	1.8[b]	4.1	1.3	1.3	8.4	1.6	112.0	5.5
Economic Services	8.3	19.4	30.2	29.8	186.5	35.4	855.5	42.0
General Public Services	6.1	14.0	12.6	12.5	53.1	11.6	209.1	10.2
Others	2.8	6.5	4.4	4.4	62.1	11.8	126.7	6.2
Total Expenditure	42.6	100	99.6	100	455.6	100	1835.7	100

Type of Expenditures	1980		1985		1990	
	Absolute	% of Total	Absolute	% of Total	Absolute	% of Total
Defence	2253.3	34.3	3957.0	30	6773.0	25.8
Education	1122.3	17.1	2459.0	18	5158.0	19.6
Health	80.4	1.2	192.0	1.4	579.0	2.2
Social Security and Welfare	416.5	6.3	754.0	5.6	2541.0	9.6
Housing and Community Amenities	123.4	1.9	283.0	2.1	836.0	3.2
Economic Services	1022.7	15.6	2333.0	17.5	4468.0	17.0
General Public Services	657.2	10.0	1401.0	10.5	2627.0	10.0
Others	887.2	13.5	1957.0	14.6	3484.0	13.2
Total Expenditures	6562.0	100	13336.0	100	26278.0	100

Sources: Buhl, et.al. (1986), 1960-75
International Monetary Fund, *Government Finance Statistics Yearbook*, various issues for 1980-90.
Notes: a)   Figures on Housing and Community Services are residual data and inclusive of interest payments for 1960-75

This category is inclusive of spending on agriculture and non-mineral services; fuel and power; mining, manufacturing, and construction; transport, storage, and communication; roads and waterways; and other economic services.

Several observations regarding government expenditures are in order. First, both consumption and investment spending rose during 1953-86 period, in later years there was a shift away from investment spending to consumption spending (Lee, 1990, p. 263). Since the country's infrastructure was devastated during the war, in the immediate post-war period the share of investment in government expenditures was large. Non-defense expenditures rose between 1953-64 in order to assist the reconstruction efforts. The consumption spending before 1966 was low because of the poor tax performance.[1] Further, "...the Korean War left the country saddled with a swollen army and bureaucracy that were more than large enough to meet Korea's needs for many years" (Kuznets, 1977,P.64).

Second, the three largest spending categories are in defense, education, and economic services as evident from Table 1. While the share of administrative spending has declined over time, that of welfare spending has risen.

Finally, an important feature of government spending in Korea is the relative share of central government in total expenditures. It "spends more than four times as much as the combined local governments do" (Lee, 1990, p. 263). This arises, largely, from the nature of government structure and transfers from the central government to other levels of government. According to many observers (e.g. Jisoon Lee) the government functions are highly centralized in Korea.[2]

Regarding the first question posed earlier, the contribution of government spending to Korea's economic growth appears to be controversial. Jisoon Lee (p. 277) states that the share of investment spending (economic services) "in total government spending is judged to be very large by international standard." Although "government spending has been unfavorable to economic growth in general," Lee posits that public investment spending has been a major contributing factor to Korea's economic growth. Lee attributes 10 percent of economic growth to the accumulation of public capital. Paul Evans (1990) lays out a simple neoclassical model of the Korean economy and applies data to it. He concludes "that the marginal product of government purchases exceeds one, that the Korean tax system is highly distorting, and that Ricardren equivalence holds" (p. 298).

This view is not shared by all observers of the Korean economy. Das (1992), for instance, contends while the "visible hand" of the government has played a significant role in the Republic of Korea, this intervention has been enlightened and flexible in nature. He posits that in Korea, Taiwan, and Singapore while "the governments were actively, consistently and coherently interventionist, the market character of these economies remain intact, the initiatives rested with the enterprise with profits being its basic motive" (p. 146).[3] Das holds that tax rates have been very low and generally supportive of industrial and economic growth. Additionally, as the economy has matured, the government has adopted a new industrial policy. For instance, financial support has been withdrawn from CHAEBOL, but extended to small and medium size firms.

Lee (1990) discusses, in detail, the cyclical changes in government spending. During 1953-61 spending rose substantially to reconstruct the basic apparatus of government. It declined during 1963 and 1964 in response to concerns with stabilizing the economy. The second and third cycles of spending occurred during 1964-73 and 1973-86.

Despite periodic fluctuations in government expenditures, Korea's public spending shows a rapid growth which began during the modernization process. Bahl, et al. (1986) report that the average annual growth rate was 9 percent in real terms. This is consistent with the growth of spending suggested by Jisoon Lee (1990). This growth rate was higher than the average annual growth rate of GNP which was 7.6 percent during 1953-1986. In relative terms, the share of government spending in GNP "grew from 10.9 percent in 1953 to 20.2 percent in 1986." (p. 263).

According to Das (1987), public subsidies reached their peak in 1985 when they constituted 5.3 percent of GNP. This low level is because until recently the government was not primarily concerned with the provision of social services except education. "More than half of the social development outlay was earmarked for education, and was treated as investment in human capital formation" (P.103). Other categories of welfare spending such as health, housing, social security, and urban development received little attention until recently.

B. GROWTH AND INEQUALITY

After the Korean war, physical capital was virtually destroyed, and agriculture was the mainstay of economic activity. But agriculture itself was unmechanized and subject to the vagaries of nature. At the same time, the population's main concern was the basic human needs. Thus, "Foreign aid provided the margin of survival for many Koreans" (Song, 1990, p. 167). As the economy improved, awareness of relative income and wealth also emerged.

What was the role of the government in regard to equity? Opinions differ on this issue. For instance, Choo (1980, p. 326) states that the priority of distributive measures "have been low in the past, since planners have been preoccupied with investment and defence requirement." The actions of the government in the 1950s seem consistent with the philosophy of "develop now and distribute later." In the 1950s, the government's main objective was to rehabilitate the war ravaged economy, particularly the country's agricultural foundation. Additionally, incomes were distributed in a surprisingly even fashion. Song (1990) suggests that until 1963, there was virtually no change in income distribution.

After 1963, the government began to address the distributional issues. The overall improvement in the economy gave rise to an increase in consumption standards which had welfare consequences. Such improvements for many people who "were either illiterate or poorly schooled, inadequately fed, ...[in] poor health combined with short-life expectancy" was a welcome event (Kuznets, 1977, p. 92). A series of illiteracy campaigns which had been inaugurated in the 1950s began to bear fruit by improving the overall well-being of the Koreans. "By mid-1960s, 7.8 percent of GNP was being allocated to education, of which two-thirds or more was private expenditure" (p. 93).

Rapid economic growth created structural transformation of the economy which we alluded to earlier. One consequence of this transformation was rapid urbanization and an absolute decline in the population of rural areas. Industrialization along with urbanization enhanced regional income disparities. In response to overurbanization and concentration of people in large cities, " the government started the *Saemul Undong*, or New Village Movement, in 1971" (Song, 1990, p. 169). The purpose of this scheme was to improve the living conditions of people in the rural areas and encourage them to stay in those areas. Accordingly, beginning in the mid-1970s, each year 10 percent of total national investment was allocated to rural areas. To temper inequality arising from overurbanization and inequality related to rising wages and wealth, the government placed limit on the overexpansion of large cities. This policy, however, worsened income disparity as land prices rose.

Are growth and equity congruent? Simon Kuznet's U-curve suggests that the answer is affirmative during the middle phase of economic development. That is, inequality tends to worsen during the take-off stage as the economy grows rapidly. Equity conditions tend to improve once economic development is achieved and people are able to enjoy high living standards. Is the evidence on Korea consistent with Kuznet's U-curve? Views on equity and growth in Korea seem to be divided. Adelman and Robinson (1978), for instance, conclude "that the time path of the size distribution of income is exceedingly stable" (p. 17). In other words, Korea did not experience the income distribution implied by Kuznet's U-curve. Adelman and Robinson attribute this phenomenon to a development strategy which was export-centered and labor-and skill-intensive. Such a "strategy can improve the distribution of income when, as in Korea, the ownership of human capital is widespread and land is reasonably equally distributed" (p.17). This view is shared by Leightner (1992). He concludes that his analysis confirms the pro-equality argument for Korea between 1963-1980. Leightner maintains that a marginal redistribution of income from corporations to households would have produced greater growth.

Yoo (1990, P. 373) is, however, skeptical of the congruency of growth and equity in Korea. He maintains that even though Korea has been hailed as a prime example of this congruency, it "has not harmonized equity with growth.... [and] equity has deteriorated with growth" (p. 388). Song (1990) posits that while Korea is known to have achieved a high degree of equity for structural reasons, the manner with which equity is measured is questionable. Song suggests that the use of the usual yardsticks of GNP and GNP per capita as measures of income equality is fraught with difficulties. Using wealth concentration, Yoo identifies three principal factors which may have contributed to "the pattern of income and welfare inequalities in Korea:... the government interest rate policy (or inflation rate) and the trend of urbanization as well as business concentration" (p. 388).

Song also casts doubt on measurement of income equality in Korea. He identifies two reasons for his doubt. First, measuring income equality in forms of GNP is difficult when the population is highly mobile and changing. Second, people have a tendency to underreport their income, particularly when income is obtained from illegal activities and abuse of power. His overall assessment of the income distribution in Korea is that it: a) improved from 1965 to 1970; b) deteriorated between 1970 and 1980; and c) seems to have improved since 1980. (For details, see Song, p. 172).

Despite the equity problems identified above, Song contends that many scholars consider the Korean income distribution as one of the best among the nations of the developing world. He identifies land reform, the Korean war, cultural homogeneity, equal educational opportunities, equity oriented policies, and the extended family system as factors which have influenced equity in Korea.

C. DEFENSE SPENDING

Table 1 shows that all expenditure categories experienced a significant rise over time. Defense spending seems to dominate all other expenditure categories, notwithstanding its recent decline. In 1980, defense spending consumed 34.3 percent of total central government expenditures. By 1990, this share had fallen to 25.8 percent. For the years 1986 and 1987 (not shown in Table 1), this share was 28.3 and 26.1 percent. The pattern of defense spending in Korea seem to be a function of government concern with military security and social order.

These concerns are rooted in the Korean War and the political chaos of the 1950s. Syngman Rhee assumed the presidency of the Republic of Korea on August 15, 1948, the day after the republic was proclaimed. He barely had any "time to put his political house in order before North Korea launched its attack on South Korea in June 1950" (Lee, 1992, P. 31). The North Korean army overwhelmed the ill-equipped and much inferior military forces of South Korea. Had it not been for the swift American decision to commit forces and resources the South Korean army would have been crushed.

The war left indelible marks on the Korean Psyche, engendering a strong resolve to build the South Korean armed forces. This required the country to devote considerable resources to defense spending. During 1953-65, for instance, "Korea's defense spending share of GNP averaged 7.13 percent" (Bahl, et al., 1986, P.39). In contrast, the average share of defense spending in GNP for forty-four countries of similar economic status was 3.62 percent. Under Rhee and Park, South Korea "remained largely dependent on the U.S. to deter another North Korean invasion and to provide the needed equipment and training by the armed forces" (Katz, 1992, P. 276). Defense spending is supposed to subside under the democratic regime of President Kim Young Sam. This regime is, however, stymied in its derive to liberalize Korea's trade and financial markets because of "the crisis over North Korea's nuclear program, which has pushed South Korea into geopolitical prominence just as it is fading from the world stage as an emerging industrial power" (Glain, 1994, p. A1).

The need for social order and stability was a second factor for a rising military expenditures in the aftermath of the Korean war. The period 1948-60 was marked by political chaos; there was an absence of law and order, continued factional wrangling, and Syngman Rhee's manipulation of the political process and his blatant use of force to establish himself as the sole authority in South Korea. The departure of Rhee from the political scene in 1958 exacerbated the political chaos. The political vacuum generated by Rhee's resignation and the preoccupation of the Liberal Party leaders with political survival set the stage for the student revolution and the subsequent *coup d'etat* by the military junta. "The junta under Park Hee quickly consolidated its power, removed those it considered corrupt and unqualified from government and military positions" (Lee, 1992, P. 38). After the *coup*, the role of the military was embedded in politics and the economy. Since dissatisfaction with ineffective and corrupt regime was the motivating factor for the May 1961 *coup d'etat*, the Park regime felt that the survival of the nation depended on the reestablishment of social and economic stability. To this end, opposition was not tolerated and often "political opposition was confused with communist subversion. The communist threat at times provided justification for authoritarian regimes to maintain power and to suppress public criticism or demand for democracy" (Katz, 1992, p. 303).

The role of the military in political and economic arena has diminished since the installation of Roh Tae Woo government. The election of Kim Young Sam as President cemented democratic principles which had been undermined by previous regimes. Currently, the armed forces is comprised of 650,000 active-duty personnel in the army, air force, and navy. It has a reserve force of 1-2 million and service in these components are compulsory for a period of thirty to thirty-six months.

D. EDUCATION

Education spending has been largely on the rise in Korea since the 1950s. As Table 1 shows the share of government spending devoted to education rose from 14 percent in 1975 to 19.6 percent in 1990. The importance of education is embedded in Korea's confucian heritage. The distinguished heritage of YANGBAN, the scholar class, is still an element of the Korean social system. This explains the country's long history of providing formal education.

The American style of education in Korea began with the presence of the U.S. military forces. Accordingly, the modern system emphasized "six years of primary school, six years of secondary school... and four years of higher education" (Seekins, 1992, p. 114). The impetus for this new system was a nationwide effort to raise literacy rate among Koreans. This effort received momentum by "the time of liberation in 1945 and [was] based on infrastructure developed during the Japanese colonial period" (Cho and Breazeale, 1991, p. 567). The goal was to make primary school universally available at the public expense. This goal was not achievable until the mid-1950s since much of educational infrastructure was destroyed during the Korean War. Cho and Breazeale point out that "By 1952 about 60 percent of classrooms had been damaged or badly damaged... and more than 80 percent of equipment, books, and furniture were lost..." (p. 575). The implementation of universal primary education became possible in 1954. This process was completed by 1959. By this time 96 percent of school-age children had entered primary schools (p. 568).

In the 1950s and beyond, particularly during the administrations of Syngman Rhee and Park Chung Hee, educational decisions came under the control of the Ministry of Education. Currently, this ministry is "responsible for administration, allocation of resources, setting enrollment quotas, certification of schools and teachers... and other basic policy decisions" (Seekins, 1992, p. 115).

National attempts to improve educational opportunities have been very successful in Korea. This success is evident in enrollment at all levels (primary, secondary, and higher) of education. Although six years of school is compulsory for school-age children, "percentages of age-groups of children and young people enrolled in primary, secondary, and tertiary level schools are comparable to those in Japan and other industrialized countries" (p. 118). Recently, the government has decided to make the middle-school compulsory on an incremental basis; beginning in rural areas and expanding it to urban areas. Cho and Breazeale contend that "enrollment at the high-school level... is expected to exceed 86 percent by the turn of the century" (Cho and Breazeale, 1991, p. 577). In the late 1980s, the proportion of college age students attending college "was second only to the United States" (Seekins, 1992, p. 118).

Educational success has not been only quantitative in nature. The Koreans have made qualitative improvements in their educational system as well. This is evident by the gradual and progressive decline in the students per-teacher ratio. In 1945 the students per-teacher averaged 69.2 in elementary school. This ratio had fallen to 38.3 by 1985.

Many observes believe that a rapid progress in modernization and growth is largely attributable to Korea's educated population. In addition, easy access to education has helped improve the income distribution by reducing wage and salary differentials (Das, 1992, p. 103). Bhal, et al. (1986) posit that the income elasticity of demand for education is high. "This means that the government sector could afford to underspend for human capital development knowing that the private sector would pick up the difference through tuition and so forth" (p. 221). Jeong (1977, p. 301), on the other hand argues that there has been an overinvestment in human capital formation in Korea. For 1960-71, he found the ratio of stock of human capital to physical capital to be 124.79. He contends the opposite is true for the developed countries. Park's analysis leads him to the conclusion "that social marginal rates of return on investment in education are relatively lower than the rates of return on physical capital" (p. 301).

IV. TAXES

A glance at the ratio of tax revenue to GNP in Korea reveals a rising trend, particularly since the passage of tax administration reform in 1966. Generally, the effectiveness of tax machinery influences the ratio of tax revenue to GNP. In LDCs low levels of income limit sources and coverage of taxes. Additionally, the effectiveness of tax administration is constrained by the inadequacy of skilled personnel to enforce tax laws. Lax enforcement of tax laws and fraud would add to the foregoing complications.

These conditions characterized Korea's tax system until the mid-1960s. For instance, between 1960 to 1964, the ratio of internal taxes to GNP fell from 8 percent to 4.2 percent. Chong Kee Park (1991, p.248) attributes this to the inflationary pressures of the early 1960s and "structural defects of the tax system that prevented [it] from responding to increases in prices and money income". Another contributing factor was the system of tax exemptions, much of economic growth took place in industries that enjoyed substantial tax benefits. Despite the exemptions, the Korean tax system did not contribute to the development of the country. According to Bahl, et al. (1986, p. 45), the tax system did not either stimulate private investment nor did it mobilize adequate revenues for the government sector.[4]

The decline in the share of tax revenues to GNP arose from low priority given to the tax administration by the Park government. Being primarily concerned with economic growth, the regime gave top priority to expenditures. The situation changed in 1966 as President Park Chung Hee recognized that weak tax administration was a source of public discontent. To ameliorate this discontent, he "took a personal interest in the improvement of tax enforcement, and appointed one of his close associates in the 1961 military coup as Commissioner of National Tax Administration" (Choi and Kwack, 1991, p. 252).

Two other factors contributed to a new sense of awareness about the importance of tax revenues and broader tax base. First, the country needed resources for investment capital. Second, the U.S. assistance to Korea declined (Das, 1992, p. 99). The need to mobilize domestic resources prompted the regime to implement tax reforms. Korea also received assistance from IMF, the World Bank, and the U.S. Agency for International Development for this purpose. Tax reforms culminated in policy measures the main features of which were: a) improving the administration of existing taxes; b) improving the system of tax compliance since compliance was lax and there were no penalties for tax evasion; and c) curtailing official failure to enforce fair and equitable tax assessments.

These measures led to the "establishment of the Office of the National Tax Administration (ONTA) in 1966, which is considered to be a watershed in Korean fiscal history" (p. 99). Subsequently, the country's tax administration was revamped, its tax system was modernized, and the government began to pay attention to increasing tax efforts. Despite many difficulties facing ONTA, it compiled a remarkable record. Initially, it concentrated on a fraud investigation and internal audits. Abuse by tax officials, a widespread concern against the government, was dramatically reduced (Park, 1991). Das (1992) believes that a principal "element in strengthening the tax administration was successfully insulating it from political interference" (p. 102). Concomitant with these changes, more attention was paid to direct taxes, particularly income and corporate taxes. The improved efficiency and administrative competence resulted in a substantial rise in the central government's direct and indirect tax revenues. This view is corroborated by Park who maintains that administrative improvements, rather than tax laws, were the essential reason for a rapidly rising tax revenues. He points out that as an example, "The unprecedented tax revenue goal of 70 billion won for 1966...was exceeded by 11 million won" (Park, p. 265).

In the budget front, there was a shift from deficit to a surplus position after 1964. This made a major contribution to the growth of domestic savings. "Given the low level of income and the difficulties involved in bringing about a rapid increase in private savings, the fiscal sector assumed a major share of the task of meeting the national domestic savings requirement during the 1966-68 period" (Park, p. 267).

A. TAX REVENUES AND TAX STRUCTURE

Total revenues accrued to the central government in 1992 was 42,756 billion won. This total was comprised of 37,652 billion won of taxes and 5,104 billion won of non-tax and capital revenues. Tax revenues doubled between 1960 and 1980 and rose by 440 percent between 1982 and 1992. The central government's total revenues in 1992 were approximately 428 percent higher than what they were in 1982. Out of all revenues 88 percent were generated by various taxes. The remaining portion of revenues came from non-tax sources and capital revenues. (See Table 2).

The central government plays a dominant role in tax revenues generated; about 85 percent of all revenues in Korea are raised by the central government. The share of local governments in revenues is small since "They have limited access to tax sources" (Das, 1992, p. 97). These political entities are not empowered to impose tax because of the nature of political process in Korea which is highly centralized. Local governments raise revenues through sources such as horse race tax, city planning tax, property tax, automobile tax, etc. The central government provides local governments with grants to make up the difference between their revenues and expenditures.

Table 2: Revenue and Grants, Consolidated Central Government, 1992

	Total (billions of Won)	Percent of Total Revenue
1. Total Revenue	42,756	100.0
2. Tax Revenue	37,652	88.1
a) Internal Taxes		
i. Income	8,250	
ii. Corporate income	5,728	
iii. Estate, inheritance and gift taxes	367	
iv. Social Security contributions	2,202	
v. Taxes on goods and services	14,920	
vi. Other taxes	1,299	
b) International Trade Taxes	3,503	
3. Nontax revenue	4,159	9.73
4. Capital revenue	945	2.21

Source: International Monetary Fund (1990), *Government Finance Statistics Yearbook*, 17:328.

Revenue (Billions of Won)

Type of Revenue	1960 Absolute	1960 % of Total	1965 Absolute	1965 % of Total	1970 Absolute	1970 % of Total	1975 Absolute	1975 % of Total
Individual Taxes	2.1	7.7	11.7	20.0	44.6	12.1	137.7	9.8
Corporation Taxes	0.9	3.3	5.7	9.7	75.5	20.5	134.5	9.6
Social Security	-	-	-	-	3.-	0.8	13.4	0.9
Property Taxes	0.7	2.6	3.2	5.5	11.3	3.2	52.5	3.7
Goods & Services Tax	1.0	3.7	4.4	7.6	171.5	46.5	718.0	51.1
International Trade Taxes	5.2	19.1	12.6	21.6	50.9	13.8	201.9	14.3
Other Taxes	-	-	0.4	0.7	1.7	0.5	12.8	0.9
Non-tax Revenue	-		-		41.4	11.2	130.2	9.2
Total Tax Revenue	27.2	(a)	58.2	(a)	369.0	100.0[b]	1406.2	100.0[b]
Total Revenue	-	-	78.2		471.3	-	1563.6	-

Type of Revenue	1980 Absolute	1980 % of Total	1985 Absolute	1985 % of Total	1990 Absolute	1990 % of Total
Individual Taxes	766.0	13.0	1845.0	15.2	4099.0	17.6
Corporation Taxes	737.8	12.5	1626.0	13.4	4818.0	20.7
Social Security	72.9	1.2	207.0	1.7	1286.0	5.5
Property Taxes	36.5	0.6	80.0	0.6	759.0	3.2
Goods & Services Tax	3092.6	52.4	5934.0	49.0	8794.0	37.8
International Trade Taxes	1013.6	17.2	1950.0	16.1	2778.0	11.9
Other Taxes	33.9	0.6	459.0	3.8	728.0	3.1
Non-tax Revenue	839.9	14.2	1634.0	13.5	2989.0	12.8
Total Tax Revenue	3896.9	100.0[b]	12104.0	100.0[b]	23262.0	100.0[b]
Total Revenue	6833.2	-	13923.0	-	26618.0	-

Source: International Monetary Fund, *Government Finance Statistics Yearbook*, various issues for 1970-90. United Nations, *Statistical Yearbook*, various issues and Bahl *et al.*, (1986) for 1960-1965.

Notes: a) Do not add up to 100 due to missing data.
        b) Without the percentage of non-tax revenues added in.

The central government's tax revenues are comprised of international trade taxes, defense tax (abolished in 1991), education tax, monopoly profit tax, and internal tax. Internal taxes include individual income taxes; corporate income taxes; estate, inheritance and gift taxes; social security contributions; taxes on goods and service; and other taxes (e.g. stamp taxes). The goods and services taxes is inclusive of general sales taxes, value added taxes, and taxes on specific services. International trade taxes are essentially comprised of import or customs duties. Table 2 highlights major sources of revenue for the central government.

The non-tax revenue item (Table 2) is inclusive of entrepreneurial and property income, revenues obtained from nonfinancial enterprises, and income derived from public financial institutions and other property. Capital revenues pertain to income from the sale of fixed capital and assets, sales of stocks, sales of land and intangible assets.

As discussed in Chapter 2, a feature of industrialization process is a rise in the share of income and corporate taxes in total revenues as the economy develops. In tandem, the share of international trade taxes in total revenues fall. This is true in Korea. Customs duties and monopoly profit taxes have declined since the 1960s while personal and corporate income taxes have risen. As shown in Table 2, the share of individual income taxes in total revenues was 19.29 percent in 1992. Ten years earlier, individual income taxes totaled 1,229.7 billion won; about 12 percent of 9,983.2 billion won of total revenues. Corporate income taxes in 1992 were 13.39 percent of total revenues. In 1982, these taxes accounted for 11.3 percent of total revenues. While the share of individual income and corporate taxes in total revenues increased between 1982 and 1992, the share of international trade taxes fell from 13.18 percent to 8.19 percent. This is indicative of two phenomena: a) less reliance on foreign trade taxes, and b) a move toward a freer trade environment.[5]

Table 3 presents a more detailed account of taxes in South Korea for selected years along with their respective rates of growth.

B. INCOME TAX

The Korean tax system has been the subject of continuous reform since the early 1950s and the personal income tax is no exception. During the Korean War government spending rose by 270 percent and the government was forced to adopt new taxes to meet the rising expenditure needs. In response to these needs, the Temporary Tax Incremental Law was adopted in December of 1950. This "Law resulted in drastic rate increases for all existing taxes" (Bahl, et al., 1986, p. 47). In 1951, the passage of the Extraordinary Tax Law superseded all existing tax laws. This new measure resulted in a substantial rise of the effective tax rate on income, corporate income, liquor, commodity, etc. "The personal income tax became a schedular tax with progressive rates applying to wages and salaries, real estate income, and business income" (p.47).

In 1954, with the armistice in place and reconstruction being the sole preoccupation, a major tax reform repealed the Temporary Tax Increment Law and the Extraordinary Tax Law. The tax laws were reformed again in 1956. "The reform...included several major changes in personal income tax: incentive measures for promoting self-compliance and voluntary payment; increased tax exemption levels; increased progression in the rate structure..." (p. 48). In 1958 a surtax, the education tax, was levied to the personal income tax.

In 1961, the new military government began working on restructuring tax reform and adopted measures to improve tax administration. (For details, see Bahl, et al., 1986, p. 49). One aspect of the restructuring was raising the number of personal income tax brackets from three to four in 1963. As already mentioned, the year 1966 witnessed the establishment of the ONTA, a watershed in Korean fiscal history. The ONTA introduced a new "green return" system (the term green pertaining to the color of the forms) in an attempt to encourage individuals and businesses "to file tax returns on self-assessment basis rather than under government supervision" (P. 50). The introduction of the "green return" system was a first step away from having tax officials prepare tax returns for individuals. When the government embarked on its second Five-Year Development plan (1967-71), another tax reform was enacted. The purpose of the reform was to provide financial support for the economic plan. (See Park, 1991, pp. 256-258 and Bahl, et al., 1986, p. 51 for a discussion of objectives).

Major changes affecting personal income taxes included: a) a rise in the number of tax brackets from five to seven (see Table 4); b) an increase in the tax exemption level; and c) a move toward a global personal income system. The introduction of a partial globalization system was a major feature of the 1967 tax reform. The partial globalization of the existing "schedular" system was designed to remedy some of the defects of the existing system of tax rates. Under the schedular system rate structures, exemptions and deductions varied considerably depending on the type of income. For instance, tax rates varied among five schedules (sources) of income: wages and salaries, business income, real estate income, dividends and interest, and other income (Chong, 1991, p. 256). In 1974, a new tax reform replaced the schedular system with a global system, "One in

which virtually all personal income previously included in the five different schedules would be taxes under a global system" (Bahl, *et al.*, 1986, p.
52). The basic reason for this change was the defects and the complexity of
the schedular system. The new system also tried to reduce the tax burden
on families. It increased the maximum level of deductions and reduced
tax rates on most ranges of taxable income. In 1975 the Defense Tax Law
was passed. The purpose of this Law was to provide the armed forces
with financial resources needed for its modernization. Thus, "a surtax at
rates ranging from .1 percent to 30 percent was applied to customs duties,
personal income tax, corporate tax,...

Table 4. Changes in the Statutory Tax Rate Before
and After the Tax Reform of 1967

Before the Reform		After the Reform	
Monthly Income	Rate (%)	Monthly Income	Rate (%)
20,000 won or less	7	15,000 won or less	7
In excess of 20,000 won	15	In excess of 15,000 won	9
In excess of 40,000 won	25	In excess of 20,000 won	16
In excess of 60,000 won	35	In excess of 30,000 won	18
In excess of 80,000 won	40	In excess of 40,000 won	30
		In excess of 60,000 won	40
		In excess of 80,000 won	50

Adopted: from Park (1991), p. 259

The surtax, adopted as a temporary measure in 1975, was expected to
expire in 1980" (p. 53).

The current personal income tax is comprised of five brackets (See
Table 5). Personal income tax and tax rates vary between residents and
nonresidents. The tax treatment of expatriates working in Korea is also
somewhat different than that of residents.

The rates shown in Table 5 apply to an individual's taxable income
(after deducting all exemptions and basic deductions). Residents whose
wages and salaries do not exceed 36,000,000 won per year are allowed a
tax credit of 20 percent (of the income tax) per year. This credit cannot

Table 5 Income Tax Rates: Personal Income Tax Base

Tax Base Over (in Won)	Tax Base Not Over	Tax on Lower Amount (in Won)	Percentage on Excess
0	4,000,000	-	5
4,000,000	10,000,000	200,000	16
10,000,000	25,000,000	1,160,000	27
25,000,000	50,000,000	5,210,000	38
50,000,000		14,710,000	50

Source: Wright (1992, P. K-17).

exceed 500,000 won. Individuals who receive income from sources outside Korea are also entitled to a 20 percent tax credit. Expatriates employed in Korea are allowed to exclude service allowances (e.g., cost-of-living allowance, education allowance, etc.) within 20 percent of one's base salary. If overseas service allowance is unidentifiable, 1/6 of total salary (including taxable allowance) may be deductible as an overseas service allowance (Wright, 1992, p. 18).

C. CORPORATE INCOME TAX

As discussed in chapter 2, corporate income accounts for a small share of national income in early stages of economic development. To begin with, the manufactuirng sector of the economy in which corporations dominate is very small. Second, the corporate form of business is a negligible segment of the economy. These conditions characterized Korea in the 1950s and 1960s.

Since early 1960s the Korean economy has undergone widespread structural changes. The share of manufacturing output in the country's total output has risen. At the same time, the share of corporate income in GNP has risen. In tandem, corporate income taxes have risen as well. Corporate income's share in GNP was 1 percent in the mid-1950s and had risen to 5 percent by 1976 (Bahl et al., 1986, pp. 74-75). In 1972, corporate income taxes of 54.8 billion won accounted for 9 percent of all revenues (481 billion won) raised by the central government. In 1992, corporate income taxes had risen to 5,728 billion won, almost 13 percent of total revenues of 42,756 billion won.

Although the original justification for corporate taxes was revenue need, the equity consideration has assumed an important role in recent years. The reason is that corporate shareholders tend to have a higher income and a higher taxable capacity than do wage and salary earners. Administratively, it is easier to impose taxes on corporations since they are easily identifiable, keep fairly adequate records, "and cannot easily escape taxable liabilities by frequent changes of location" (p.74).

As discussed in the previous section, tax reforms have been a common feature of the Korean fiscal landscape and corporate income taxes have witnessed reforms as well. The Temporary Tax Increment Law and the Extraordinary Tax Law alluded to earlier raised the effective rate of corporate taxes. Additionally, the corporate income tax became progressive in 1951. Bahl et al. (1986, p. 48) point out that the corporate income tax system in the 1950s was criticized for "its inequities, its adverse effects on business expansion because of the extremely high rates applied to business income..." The 1961 tax reform lowered corporate tax rates to encourage proper record keeping practices. It also reduced the rate on corporate profits set aside for investment in plant and equipment. Finally, it made special tax incentive provisions for export industries (p. 49).

The 1961 tax reform classified corporations into closely held family type and "open" corporations. In 1962, the same statutory rate applicable to both was adopted. The statutory tax rate applying to corporate income was 35 percent during 1959-62. This rate was lowered to 20 percent for both classes of corporations in 1962 (Park, 1991, p. 259). The statutory rate was raised to 25 percent in 1963 for firms whose taxable income exceeded one million won. This was again raised to 30 percent in 1964. In 1965, a new package of tax incentives was adopted "to encourage export industries, and the Foreign Capital Inducement Law was amended in the following year to augment special tax concessions to foreign investors" (Bahl et al., 1986, p. 50). The 1966 tax reform lowered the statutory rate on firms with income of less than one million won and raised it for firms with incomes of over five million won. In 1967, the local government surtax raised the rate in each bracket by 10 percent (pp. 74-75). By 1967, the statutory tax rate was 22 percent, 33 percent, and 38.5 percent respectively on the incomes of one million won, 1-5 million won, and above five million won.

An important feature of the 1967 tax reform was the "introduction of discriminatory rates for closely held family corporations; for which tax rates were from 5 to 10 percent higher than for 'open' corporations" (Park, 1991, p. 259). The discriminatory tax rate structure was an inducement to transform closely held corporations into open corporations. In reality, this tax reform served as an incentive for tax abuse and did not lend itself to a perceptible rise in the number of open corporations. Because of the abuse and insignificant change in the pattern of corporate ownership, the discriminatory tax rate was later abandoned.

The Defense Tax Law of 1975 imposed a surtax, ranging from .1 to 30 percent, on several sources of income including corporate income. This surtax was repealed effective January 1, 1991 (Wright, 1992, K-15). Another practice abolished was the discriminatory tax rate structure on different classes of corporations. The 1990 tax revision adopted a single tax rate for all corporations and rates no longer vary in acordance with the type of corporation. The new rate is 20 percent for a tax base of 100 million won. For corporate incomes exceeding 100 million won, a rate of 34 is levied (p. K-15). Additionally local governments levy a 7.5 percent surtax on the corporate tax.

D. VALUE-ADDED TAX

The introduction of a value-added tax (VAT) in 1976 overhauled the Korean tax structure. This was another attempt, besides the establishment of the ONTA, to modernize and develop the country's tax system. The introduction of VAT replaced "eight of the eleven existing taxes--business, commodity tax, textile product tax, petroleum product tax, electricity and gas tax, transportation tax, admission tax, and entertainment and restaurant tax" (Bahl, et al., 1986, p.53). Liquor tax, stamp tax, and telephone tax were not replaced by a VAT. These taxes account for a small share of total revenues. During 1976-77, liquor tax accounted for 5 percent of total revenues accrued to the central government whereas the combined total of stamp tax and telephone tax raised 1.5 percent of total revenues.[6]

An objective of the VAT system was to avoid duplication and overlapping auditing practices under a complicated system of indirect raxes. Each indirect tax had its own rate structure, tax base,and administrative procedure. Replacing this system with a VAT has introduced administrative ease and efficiency. Additionally, VAT would be "an important instrument against tax evasion by means of the reciprocal controls exercised by taxpayers themselves" (Park, 1991, p. 273). Another objective of VAT was to promote exports and capital formation. "A corporation that exports its whole product will obtain refunds of tax paid on its purchases" (Wright, 1992, p. K-21).

This tax went into effect on July 1, 1977 and it was supposed to have a single rate of 13 percent. In order to minimize the inflationary effects of a high rate, a temporary tax of 10 percent was adopted which is still in existence. At the outset, the government was allowed to adjust the normal rate (13 percent) by as much as 3 percent as economic conditions warranted. This was changed in 1988 when "the National Assembly... [fixed] the VAT rate at 10 percent, removing the discretionary power of the government..." (Park, 1991, p. 276).

The structure and administration of the Korean VAT is similar to those of the European Community. It is a consumption type VAT and is collected by invoice method. Ultimately, the cost of administration and the degree of compliance depend on the existence of a modern distribution system, good record keeping by businesses, "and on the share of business activity carried out by small establishments. The lack of systematic record keeping in many parts of the Korean economy would make adminisntration difficult and evasion easy even under the best of circumstances" (p. 297). Since small businesses cannot cope with the requirements of keeping adequate records, they are considered special taxpayers for VAT purposes. Special taxpayers are businesses whose annual sales are less than 6 million won. These businesses are taxed at a rate of 3.5 percent of their annual sales (p. 280). Although special taxpayers file 76-78 percent of all VAT returns, the general taxpayers are the important source of revenue. They pay 94-96 percent of total VAT, whereas special taxpayers pay 5-6 percent of VAT collected (p. 280).

The government originally stressed that the purpose of VAT was not to increase tax revenues. It was purportedly implemented to reduce the negative impact of the previous gross turnover taxes. Value-added tax revenues have risen over time, and since its inception VAT has become a major source of government revenue. In 1992, it yielded 10,382 billion won, about 28 percent of national taxes. This is approximately as much revenue as the sum of corporate income and personal income taxes.

The impact of VAT on prices depends on whether it is a new additional tax or a substitute revenue source. Additionally, the impact is a function of monetary policy being accommodating or otherwise. Thus far, no solid evidence has emerged about the inflationary effects of the Korean VAT. Under the previous indirect tax system investment was taxed. Since investment is not taxed under VAT, there is a tendency for the cost of capital to fall. There is some support for this claim "which shows that the switch to VAT provided industries such as manufacturing and electricity and gas with substantial benefits" (Park, 1991, p. 287).

The impact of VAT on international trade depends on the treatment of export commodities and imports. The Korean VAT system exempts exports from taxes and imports are subject to tax. By and large, the business community views the new VAT as "more favorable to exports than the old indirect taxes" (p. 289). Finally, the most controversial aspect of the VAT is its incidence and effect on the distribution of tax burdens. Generally, this tax implies a higher burden for lower income people than other income groups. For this reason "The regressivity of VAT continues to be a topic of heated debate" (p. 291). Nonetheless, evidence about the rise of regressivity is mixed.

V. FISCAL INCENTIVES

In the 1950s and early 1960s fiscal incentives did not influence economic growth. The extent of the industrial sector was limited and the administration of the tax system was not fully developed. By 1966 and the establishment of the ONTA, the fiscal environment had changed considerably.

The reason was that supply-side economics became a salient feature of the Korean fiscal system long before this concept gained popularity elsewhere.(See Goo, 1990, pp. 260-270). Thus, government spending was kept relatively low and the government relied extensively on indirect consumption tax to spur saving and investment. These policies and inattention accorded welfare spending created incentives for saving and investment. To foster economic growth, the Korean government introduced a series of tax incentives. Choi and Kwack (1990) identify eleven types of tax incentive systems, three major ones being: 1) tax incentives for export promotion; 2) tax incentives for key industries; and 3) tax incentives for small and medium firms.

A. TAX INCENTIVES FOR EXPORT PROMOTION

The incentive system for exports began in 1960 with a 30 percent corporate tax exemption on income earned from exports. It also allowed a 20 percent tax exemption to income derived "from the sale of goods and services to foreign military forces based in Korea and from foreign currency income from tourism" (p. 248). In the following year, a uniform exemption rate of 50 percent was adopted to apply to all foreign exchange earning activities.

In 1973, the above system was replaced "by two tax-free reserve systems: reserves for losses in the export business and reserves for overseas market development" (p. 248). In 1977, reserves for price fluctuations was added to the list of tax incentives for export promotion. Throughout the 1960s and 1970s exporters were assured that, despite inflation, the real return on their investment would be protected (Das, 1992, p. 105). As a whole, the 1970s set of incentives for export promotion had three outstanding features: a) they were diverse; b) they had the flexibility of adjustment; and c) their main goal was to affect the sectoral allocation of investable resources (p. 105).

B. TAX INCENTIVES FOR KEY INDUSTRIES

Since 1949, the Korean government has provided a tax holiday for heavy industries such as machinery, shipbuilding, petrochemicals, basic metal, and chemical fertilizers. The tax reform of 1967 substituted an investment tax credit system for the tax-holiday incentive. In the early 1970s, the incentives for heavy industries were reinforced. A major tax reform in 1974 unified all major incentives "under the title of 'special tax treatment for key industries' in the Tax Exemption and Reduction Control Law..." (Choi and Kwack, 1990, p. 249). This set of incentives allowed for a 6 percent tax credit under corporate tax law, a 40-80 percent investment tax credit, and a 10 percent temporary investment tax credit (Das, 1992, p. 107). The unified system allowed qualified firms in the selected heavy industries to choose one set of incentives from three optional sets: tax holiday, investment credit, and special depreciation. The tax holiday option was allowed "for five years, plus 100 percent tax exemption for three years and a 50 percent exemption for the ensuing two years" (p. 107). The investment tax credit allowed a credit of 8 percent for machinery and equipment. The tax credit allowed was 10 percent if industries in question used domestic capital goods. The special depreciation option allowed a 100 percent depreciation allowance (p. 107).

In 1981, the tax reform reversed some of the tax provisions in existence. It "abolished the tax-holiday option altogether and limited eligibility for the investment tax credit option to the machinery and electronic industries" (Choi and Kwack, 1990, p. 249). Some industries were eliminated from the beneficiary list and for many the 100 percent special depreciation became the only available option. This reform was amended in 1982 and again in 1983.

C. TAX INCENTIVES FOR SMALL AND MEDIUM FIRMS

Functional tax incentive, incentives for a class of firms, is preferred to the industry-specific system of tax incentives. This system satisfies the "specificity rule" of government intervention; i.e., it is closer to the source of distortion and, thus, in a better position to correct market failure. Two examples of functional tax incentives adopted by the Korean government are: tax incentives for small and medium firms (SMFs) and tax incentives for R & D.

Until late 1960s, tax incentives designed to help SMFs were nominal. In 1968, the government granted a 30 percent depreciation to SMFs operating in mining and manufacturing for their capital investment. "The special depreciation rate was raised to 50 percent by the tax reform implemented in 1977" (p. 252) The tax incentives granted SMFs include: a) tax-free reserves for investment loss, b) no taxes for capital gains, and c) separate taxation on dividend income at a 10 percent rate" (p. 253).

The revision of the Tax Exemption and Reduction Control Law (TERCL) which went into effect in 1982, extended the investment reserve system to SMFs. In recent years, the government has been trying to promote the development of SMFs. This is designed to foster competition and is in sharp contrast to the policies of the 1960s and 1970s in which conglomerates were dominant forces in production and employment. The government's objective is to assist people with entrepreneurial talent and know-how to establish themselves in business (p. 252).

It is worth noting that heavy reliance placed on fiscal incentives to spur economic growth has entailed the unavoidable problem of regressivity of the tax system. Prior to the 1967 tax reform minor emphasis was placed on the equity aspect of taxation. Since then, the government has introduced a series of measures to address the equity issue. (For details, see Lee, 1990, pp. 269-270).

VI. CONCLUSIONS

The evolution of South Korea from a war ravaged LDC to an emerging industrialized state, within 40 years, provides a fascinating example for many contemporary LDCs to emulate. The economic and social progress in Korea have materialized without prolonged episodes of extreme inequality and inflation. An educated and skilled labor force, a strong industrial base, and an adequate infrastructure has enabled the country to become an economic force to be reckoned with.

A country that was ravaged by WWII and the Korean War, Korea was atypical LDC as recently as 1960. By late 1970s, it had overtaken countries such as Malaysia and Cuba in terms of living standards. In mid-1980s, Korea had achieved a higher per capita income than Argentina. By late 1980s, Korea had established itself as an emerging NIC. The election of

Roh Tae Woo as President set the stage for the democratization process that followed.

In this chapter we have tried to examine some of the following questions. What are some of the underlying causes of Korea's remarkable progress? Was the enlightened management of the economy the principal reason? What roles did government expenditure and tax policies play in this process? Was income equality a concern of the Korean economic planners or did they pursue a "grow now and distribute later" policy?

Korea adopted an indicative planning strategy in 1961 and the Economic Planning Board played a crucial role in formulating and implementing the country's five-year economic plans. Throughout the 1960s and 1970s, the Korean approach to planning was characterized by a top-down decision-making process. This approach began to change when the Chun Doo Hwan government recognized the disadvantages of excessive centralization. A combination of factors such as heavy investment in physical infrastructure in the early stages of development, enlightened economic management, trade liberalization, exploitation of the country's comparative advantage, and the assumption of an outward-looking strategy of development seem to have contributed to Korea's high rate of economic growth.

The main features of government spending in Korea have been its cyclical changes and heavy emphasis on defense spending, education, and economic services. Although the share of South Korea's defense spending in GDP has never been much higher than those of the U.S., France, and Britain, it has been much higher than comparable figures for the developing world. The basic reason for this relatively high level of defense spending is rooted in the Korean War and the political chaos of the 1950s. The war left an indelible impact on the Korean psyche and created a strong resolve to build and maintain a strong armed forces. The political climate of the cold war era strengthened that resolve.

Education spending in Korea has been on the rise since the 1950s. In early 1990s, the government was devoting almost 20 percent of its spending to education. The importance of education in Korea is rooted in its confucian heritage. The emphasis on education has paid respectable dividends. The percentage of age-groups of children and young people in all levels of schools is now comparable to that of industrialized countries. Additionally, the proportion of college age students attending college lies behind that of the United States. Korea's approach to human capital development, many believe, is a key to its industrial success.

Official concern with equity issues, *per se*, is a new phenomenon in Korea. For instance, in 1971 the government initiated the *Saemul Undong*, or the New Village Movement, in response to overurbanization, an undesirable aspect of economic transformation. We argued that some observers contend that this initiative worsened income disparity in Korea. Easy access to education has, indirectly, improved the income distribution by reducing wage and salary differentials. Despite the lack of explicit attempts to improve the income distribution, Korea has a better record of equality than many nations of the developing world. Adelman and Robinson (1978) believe that Korea's time path of income distribution is remarkably stable. In fact, Korea seems to have avoided the income distribution implied by Kuznet's U-curve during its developing.

In terms of revenue sources, the Korean tax system shows the familiar pattern experienced by industrialized countries; the relative rise of direct taxes and a relative decline of indirect taxes during the course of its economic development. In the 1950s and early 1960s, the Korean government was not as concerned with taxes as it was with economic growth. This attitude began to change in mid-1960s. The outcome of this attitude change was the establishment of the Office of the National Tax Administration (ONTA) in 1966. As noted earlier, the establishment of ONTA was a watershed in the Korean fiscal history. In addition to investigating fraud and abuse by tax officials, it paid attention to increasing tax efforts. Improved efficiency and administrative competence of ONTA has resulted in a substantial rise in the central government's direct and indirect tax revenues.

Another attempt to modernize and develop the country's tax system was the introduction of a value-added tax (VAT) in 1976. An objective of VAT was to avoid duplication and overlapping auditing practices, a complicated process under the system of indirect taxes. A second objective of VAT was to circumvent tax evasion. Finally, VAT was adopted to promote capital formation and encourage exports. Thus far, VAT has been successful by making contributions to revenue collection. There is no solid evidence indicating that VAT has contributed to inflationary pressures. Some concern is, however, expressed about the regressivity of VAT.

The introduction of fiscal incentives is another feature of Korea's development efforts. Some economists (e.g., Goo, 1990) argue that supply-side economics become a salient feature of the Korean fiscal system long before this concept gained popularity elsewhere. To foster economic growth, the Korean government kept its spending relatively low and introduced a series of tax incentives beginning in 1960. Three of such tax incentives deal with export promotion, tax holiday for heavy industries, and incentive for a class of firms.

An important feature of fiscal system in Korea is the dominant role played by the central government; it collects a disproportionate amount of tax proceeds and it disburses the bulk of these proceeds. This feature stems from the structure of Korea's political process. Political authority is highly centralized in Korea and, thus, provincial and local governments are not generally empowered to impose taxes. We anticipate that some changes, consonant with further democratization of the Korean society, are in the offing. These changes may also entail a closer examination of taxes and expenditures. For instance, spending on social programs may come into more prominence and the regressivity of VAT and fiscal incentives may be addressed.

ENDNOTES

1. This spending is comprised of "employee compensation, purchases of goods and services for current consumption, plus imputed rents and imputed banking services less sale of goods and services" (Kuznets, 1977, P. 62).

2. Appendix I provides the results of an empirical analysis of the government expenditures growth in Korea.

3. Das identifies the followings as unique features of the Korean approach to development:
   a) commitment of the government (particularly President Park's) to economic growth, b) an efficient bureaucracy and c) market conforming nature of intervention.

4. Choi and Kwack (1990) point out that the Korean industrialization period was characterized by a relatively low taxes, a small public sector, conformity to a balanced budget, "liberal use of tax incentives for investments, heavy reliance on indirect taxes, ... relatively little spending for redistributive social services, ..." (P. 260). These authors contend that Korea began practicing supply-side economics before this phenomenon gained popularity in theoretical and policy discussions. As evidence, they cite "the low share of tax and expenditures in GNP, heavy reliance on indirect consumption tax, extensive tax incentives for saving and investments, and less emphasis on welfare spending" (P. 260).

5. Appendix II provides the results of an empirical analysis of the government revenues in Korea.

6. In 1992, 220 billion won of stamp taxes were collected. This accounts for less than .6 percent of national tax revenue of 37,652 billion won. The share of liquor tax in national taxes has fallen as well. In 1992 a total of 1.331 billion won was collected from this source, accounting for 35. of national tax revenues.

REFERENCES

Abizadeh, S. and M. Yousefi, (1994), "An Analysis of Taxation Trends in South Korea." *Seoul Journal of Economics*, 7, No. 2.

Abizadeh, S. and M. Yousefi, (1993), "Industrialization and Government Expenditures: The case of South Korea." Working paper.

Abizadeh, S.and A. Basilevsky, (1990), "Measuring the Size of Government," *Public Finance*, 45:353-377.

Abizadeh, S. and J. Gray, (1985), "Wagner's Law: A Pooled Time-Series, Cross-Section Comparison," *National Tax Journal*, 38:209-218.

Adelman, I. and S. Robinson, (1978), *Income Distribution Policy in Developing Countries: A Case Study of Korea*, Stanford University Press, Stanford.

Alam, S., (1989), *South Korea: Government and Markets in Economic Development Strategies*, Praeger Publishers.

Amsden, A., (1989), *Asia's Next Giant*, Oxford University Press.

An Asia Watch Report, October (1988), *Assessing Reform in South Korea, A Supplement to the Asia Watch Report on Legal Process and Human Rights*, October.

Bahl, R., C. K. Kim, and C. K. Park, (1986), *Public Finances During the Korean Modernization Process*, Harvard University Press, Cambridge.

Balassa, B., (1990), "Korea's Development Strategy," in *Korean Economic Development*, ed., Jene K. Kwon, 3-17, New York, Greenwood Press.

Beck, M., (1979), "Public Sector Growth: A Real Perspective," *Public Finance*, 34:313-343.

Breton, A., (1989), "The Growth of Competitive Governments," *Canadian Journal of Economics*, 22:717-750.

Cho, L. and K. Breazeale, (1991), "The Education System," in *Economic Development in the Republic of Korea: A Policy Perspective*, eds., Lee-Jay Cho and Yoon Hyung Kim, 567-586, Honolulu, The University of Hawaii Press.

Cho, L. and K.Y. Hyung, (1991), *Economic Development in the Republic of Korea: A Policy Perspective*, the University of Hawaii Press, Honolulu.

Choi, K., (1991), "Introduction of the Value-Added Tax (1977)," in *Economic Development in the Republic of Korea: A Policy Perspective*, eds., Lee-Jay Cho and Yoon Hyung Kim, 273-300, Honolulu, The University of Hawaii Press.

Choi, K., and T. Kwack, (1990), "Tax Policy and Resource Allocation in Korea," in *Korean Economics Development*, ed., Jene K. Kwon, 247-262, New York, Greenwood Press.

Chong, K.P., (1991), "The 1966 Tax Administrative Reform, Tax Law Reforms, and Government Saving" in *Economic Development in the Republic of Korea: A Policy Perspective*, eds., Lee-Jay Cho and Yoon Hyung Kim, 247-272, Honolulu, The University of Hawaii Press.

Choo, H.C., (1980), "Economic Growth and Income Distribution," in Park (ed.), (1980), pp. 277-335.

Das, D., (1992), *Korean Economic Dynanaism*, St. Martin's Press, New York.

Dunteman, G., (1989), *Principal Components Analysis*, Sage Publications.

Evans, P., (1990), "The Output Effects of Fiscal Policy in Korea," in *Korean Economic Development*, ed., Jene K. Kwon, 291-299, New York, Greenwood Press.

Glain, S., (March 30, 1994), "South Korean Leader Struggles to Free Up a Regulated Economy," *The Wall Street Journal*, vo.75:A1.

Henning, J.A. and A.D. Tussing, (1974), "Income Elasticity of Demand for Public Expenditures in the United States," *Public Finance*, 29:325-341.

Herber, B.P., (1983), *Modern Public Finance*, Richard F. Irwin, Homewood, Ill.

Jeong, C.Y., (1977), "Rates of Return on Investment in Education," in *Industrial and Social Development Issues*, ed., Chuk Kyo Kim, 257-302, Seoul, Korea Development Institute.

Katz, R.P., (1992), "Development of the Armed Forces," in *South Korea: A Country Study*, eds., Andrea M. Savada and William Shaw, 269-331, Washington, D.C., Library of Congress.

Kim, C.K., ed., (1977), *Industrial and Social Development Issues*, Korea Development Institute, Seoul.

Korea, Overseas Information Service, Ministry of Culture, Seoul Korea, 1985.

Kulessa, M., ed., (1990), *The Newly Industrializing Economies of Asia: Prospects of Co-operation*, Springer-Verlag Berlin, Heidelberg.

Kuznets, P.W. (1977), *Economic Growth and Structure in the Republic of Korea*, Yale University Press, New Haven.

Kwon, J.K., ed., (1990), *Korean Economic Development*, Greenwood Press, New York.

Lee, C., (1992), "Historical Setting," in *South Korea: A Country Study*, eds., Andrea M. Savada and William Shaw, 3-64, Washington, D.C., Library of Congress.

Lee, J., (1990), "Government Spending and Economic Growth," in *Korean Economic Development*, ed., Jene K. Kwon, 263-290, New York, Greenwood Press.

Leighlner, J.E., (1992), "The Compatibility of Growth and Increased Equality: Korea," *Journal of Development Studies*, 29:49-71.

Musgrave, R.A., (1969), *Fiscal Systems*, Yale University Press, New Haven, Conn.

Park, C.K., ed., (1980), *Human Resources and Social Development in Korea*, Korea Development Institute, Seoul, Korea.

Park, C.K., (1980), "The Organization, Financing, and Cost of Health Care," in *Human Resources and Social Development in Korea*, ed., Park Chong Kee, 97-168, Korea Development Institute, Seoul.

Perry, T., (1991), "Asiapower 2000: What's Next," *IEEE Spectrum*, June.

Petri, P.A., (1990), "Korean Trade as Outlier: An Economic Anatomy," in *Korean Economic Development*, ed., Jene K. Kwon, 53-78, New York, Greenwood Press.

Picht, H., (1988), "Government Size and Public Sector Choice," *Kyklos*, 41:436-458.

Rhee, H., (1990), "Korea 2000: Economic and Social Targets and Development Strategies," in Kulessa, (ed.), (1990), pp. 33-44.

Saunders, P. and F. Klau, eds., (1985), *The Role of Public Sector and Consequences of the Growth of Government*, Paris, OECD Publications, 4.

Savada, A.M. and W. Shaw, eds., (1990), *South Korea, a country study*, Library of Congress, Washington, D.C.

Seekins, D.M., (1992), "The Society and Its Environment," in *South Korea: a country study*, eds., Andrea M. Savada and William Shaw, 70-134, Washington, D.C., Library of Congress.

Song, B., (1990), *The Rise of the Korean Economy*, Oxford University Press, Oxford.

Suh, S., (1980), "The Patterns of Poverty" in *Human Resources and Social Development in Korea*, ed., Park Korea Development Institute, Seoul.

Wagner, A. (1970), "Das Gesetz der zunehmenden Staatstätigkeit", in *Finanztheorie* (2nd ed.), ed., Recktonwald, Horst Claus, 241-243, Kiepanheuer Wisch, Köln.

Wright, D., ed., (1992), *International Tax Summaries*, N.Y.: Wiley.

Yoo, J.G., (1990), "Income Distribution in Korea," in *Korean Economic Development*, ed., Jene K. Kwon, 393-407, New York, Greenwood Press.

Yousefi, M. and S. Abizadeh, (1992), "Growth of State Government Expenditures: Empirical Evidence from the United States," *Public Finance*, 47:322-339.

APPENDIX I

The growth of public sector spending continues to be of interest to scholars and practitioners in many countries. (See Breton, 1989, and Picht, 1988). The starting point in many empirical studies of public sector growth is Wagner's law (1970). As summarized by Saunders and Klau (1985, p. 91), Wagner suggested that "the demand for increases in the scope of public sector activity will be a natural consequence of higher living standards which accompany industrialization."

This premise is the impetus for our interest in Korea's scope of public sector activity. This task, however requires a correct measure of government size. While the common measure has been the ratio of government spending to GDP, this measure does not account for different aspects of government spending. Abizadeh and Basilevsky (1990) have developed a technique based on a multivariate principal component factor analysis. This technique combines a large number of variables into a systematically reduced, smaller, conceptually more coherent set of variables. A linear combination of the original variables, a principal component variable, represents the "general government size." Duteman (1989, p. 5) observes that "The potential efficiency gains from such a data-reduction procedure applied to the independent variables are...[reduced] multicollinearity threat [and] conceptual uncertainties regarding index construction."

In order to estimate a general multidimensional variable of government size, we collected data for six variables.(For details, see Abizadeh and Yousefi, 1993). All data used in this analysis were collected from the most current issues of the IMF *International Finance Statistics Yearbook*, the United Nations *Statistical Yearbook*, the United Nations *Demographic Yearbook* and the United Nations *National Account Statistics: Main Aggregates and Detailed Tables*.

Following Abizadeh and Basilevsky, we used a principal component analysis. The results of this analysis revealed that the six variables correlate highly and positively with a factor loading on a single factor for South Korea. Factor scores and the transformed government size index indicated that the size of government doubled between 1970 and 1980. It doubled again between 1980 and 1990.

In order to empirically examine the determinants of growth, we followed Yousefi and Abizadah (1992). An implied assumption of Wagner's law is that the income elasticity of demand for government expenditures is greater than unity for countries experiencing industrialization. This assumption befits Korea. Variable G, the general government size index, affects and is influenced by GDP. In order to avoid simultaneous equation bias we need to regress G on private sector output.(For details, see Henning and Tussing, 1974).

The final regression model to be estimated is given by:

(AI) $\ln G_t = \alpha_0 + \alpha_1 \ln G_{t-1} + \alpha_2 \ln Y_t + \alpha_3 \ln YR_t + \alpha_4 \ln AR_t + \alpha_5 \ln UB_t + \varepsilon$

In equation AI, G_t, Y_t, YR_t, AR_t, and UB_t refer to the actual government expenditures, private sector GDP ($Y_t = GDP - G$), the ratio of full employment GDP (private sector) to Y_t, the share of output in the agriculture sector, and the urbanization ratio. The last term, ε, denotes the random error term. A priori reasoning suggests that α_1, α_2, α_4, and α_5 be positive and α_2 be greater than one. The coefficient of YR_t is expected to vary inversely with the business cycle; rise during a recession and fall otherwise. The regression results are summarized in Table AI.1. This table reveals that all coefficients are statistically significant and have the expected sign, except for the coefficient of the urbanization variables.

Table AI.1 Summary of Regression Analysis: Growth of Government

α_0	α_1	α_2	α_3	α_4	α_5	R^2
9.57	.29*	5.48**	5.48	.29	3.70**	.99
(4.55)	(.18)	(.25)	(.25)	(.26)	(1.35)	

*Significant at the 90 percent level
**Significant at the 95 percent level
Note: Figures in brackets are standard error terms

This is contrary to our hypothesis and may be explained by a recent downward trend in the rate of growth of spending on physical infrastructure.

We also derived the short- and long-run income elasticities of demand for government expenditures via an alternate method.(For details, see

Abizadeh and Yousefi, 1993). The results are summarized in Table AI.2. These results corroborate evidence obtained by Beck (1979), Herber (1983), and Abizadeh and Gray (1985) in different contexts.

Table AI.2 Short-term and Long-term Income Elasticities of Demand
for Government Expenditures
(1970-90) Selected Years

Year	Short-term	Long-term
1970	1.166	1.528
1975	1.167	1.533
1980	1.163	1.516
1985	1.165	1.525
1990	1.165	1.524

APPENDIX II

The tax system in Korea shows the familiar pattern experienced by industrialized countries; the relative rise of direct taxes and the relative decline of indirect taxes during the course of economic development. For instance, during 1975-1990 the share of individual income taxes in total tax revenue rose from 9.8 percent to 17.8 percent (see Table 2). The share of corporate taxes in total revenue rose from 9.6 percent in 1975 to 20.7 percent in 1990. At the same time, the share of property taxes, goods and services tax, and international trade taxes fell.

As discussed earlier, in the 1950s and early 1960s the Korean government was not as much preoccupied with taxes and tax structure as it was with economic growth. This changed with the tax reform of 1966 and subsequent broadening of the tax base. This change was consistent with economic progress. As development takes place government priorities change; resources devoted to physical infrastructure in early periods of development are allocated to social programs. These issues were discussed in chapter 2.

In this appendix, we summarize empirical evidence pertaining to tax structure change which we have reported elsewhere.(See Abizadeh and Yousefi, 1994). Specifically, we are interested in the empirical evidence related to the Korean tax structure change during 1970-1990. Abizadeh and Yousefi linked tax ratio changes to openness (OP), per capita income

(YP), currency-deposit ratio (CU), and the economy's deviations from full employment level of income (YR). This deviation is measured by the ratio of full employment GDP to actual GDP. Thus YR_t measures the degree to which private sector full employment exceeds private sector GDP. At full employemnt, YR_t would be equal 1.0.

Openness is usually defined as the ratio of exports to GDP. It is generally agreed that trade contributes to economic growth which, in turn, diminishes the importance of international trade taxes. The use of CU variable is intended to reflect the extent of modernization of Korea's financial institutions. As the financial system becomes more integrated, the ratio of currency holding to total deposits declines. Per capita income, admittedly an imperfect measure of economic development, reflects the material well-being of a country's population. Finally, the variable YR is intended to reflect the gap between actual and potential GDP.

The regression equation to be estimated is given by:

$$(AII.1) \quad \ln TR_{it} = \ln\alpha + \beta_1 \ln YP_t + \beta_2 \ln CU_t + \beta_3 \ln YR_t + \beta_4 \ln OP_t + \mu$$

In equation (AII.1), the subscript i (= 1,2,...5) denotes the type of tax and t (= 1,2,...21) denotes time period (1970-1990). The dependent variable TR_t refers to five different tax ratios: a) total tax; b) total personal income taxes; c) total corporate income taxes; d) international trade taxes; and e) total sales taxes.(For details, see Abizadeh and Yousefi, 1993). The results of regressions are summarized in Table AII.1.

From Table AII.1 it is clear that the regression model using TR_3 as the dependent variable provides the strongest support for tax structure change hypothesis. That is, growth and development in Korea has implied that more emphasis is being placed on direct taxes (e.g., corporate income taxes). All coefficients are statistically significant and with the exception of β_2 carry the expected sign. An inference to be drawn is that as the Korean tax system has evolved and undergone continuous reform; its tax efforts have matched its tax capacity.

Table AII.1. Summary Regression Analysis for Alternative Tax Ratios
(Corrected for Autocorrelation)

Dependent Variable	Constant (α)	YP_t (β_1)	CU_t (β_2)	YR_t (β_3)	OP_t (β_4)	R_2	D-W st.
TR_1	-3.08	.23** (3.78)	.28* (2.61)	4.86** (2.88)	.02 (.24)	.81	1.91^b
TR_2	-3.50	.32* (2.05)	.37 (1.16)	-7.68^x (1.81)	-.41 (1.67)	.54	1.87^a
TR_3	-4.35	.38** (3.85)	.34 (1.66)	-9.45** (3.55)	-.68** (4.51)	.85	2.35^a
TR_4	-2.10	.30* (2.54)	.62** (3.11)	6.35* (2.15)	.63** (4.22)	.74	1.89^b
TR_5	-1.36	.09 (1.06)	.14 (.90)	4.49 (1.69)	.11 (.92)	41	2.13^b

** Significant at the 99 percent level of confidence.
* Significant at the 95 percent level of confidence.
x Significant at the 90 percent level of confidence.
a. The original Durbin-Watson statistic. No corrections made.
b. Based on the original Durbin-Watson statistics it was not possible to accept the null hypothesis of lack of autocorrelation. The models reported are corrected for autocorrelation.
Note: Figures in parentheses are the t-statistics.

CHAPTER SEVEN

AN ANALYSIS OF GOVERNMENT REVENUES AND EXPENDITURES DURING GHANA'S ECONOMIC RECOVERY PROGRAM

John Kofi Baffoe

I. INTRODUCTION

From the mid-1970s to the early 1990s, Ghana's economic and financial performance was transformed from a continuously deteriorating state to a highly improved steady growth state. This was made possible by the implementation of far-reaching economic and financial reforms, embodied in Ghana's Economic Recovery Program (ERP), launched by the Government of the Provisional National Defence Council (PNDC) in 1983. The ERP was modeled along the lines of the stabilization and structural adjustment programs of the International Monetary Fund (IMF) and the International Bank for Reconstruction and Development (IBRD, or the World Bank). These programs are recommended by the two multilateral financial institutions to member countries experiencing balance of payments problems and a deteriorating domestic economy as a condition for financial assistance.

The ultimate goal of the ERP was to reverse the declining trend in the Ghanaian economy and create a growth oriented, competitive, efficient, and integrated economy (Government of Ghana, 1984). Specific policies were formulated and implemented to achieve these goals. Ghana's ERP has been remarkably successful and is being perceived as an example of an adjustment with growth especially for Sub-Saharan African (SSA) countries faced with similar economic problems (Kapur, *et. al.*, 1991, p.1, Loxley, 1991, p.25; Leechor, 1994, p.153).

Fiscal policy reform was an integral part of Ghana's overall economic strategy. This makes an analysis of the Government's fiscal policy measures under the ERP a worthwhile exercise especially for other SSA countries pursuing similar programs. This chapter therefore attempts to analyse Ghana's fiscal policy measures during its ERP by examining the various reforms in the tax system and government expenditures{ XE "government expenditures" }, and the impact of the reforms on the overall economic growth, investment, fiscal balance, inflation, and government savings. The chapter begins with a brief review of the economic conditions prior to the ERP in Section II. Section III looks at the ERP strategy and its results. Section IV looks at the fiscal policy reforms during the ERP and the impact of the reforms on the Ghanaian economy. The last section, section V, summarizes the major findings, provides some concluding remarks and presents some recommendations.

II. A REVIEW OF ECONOMIC CONDITIONS BEFORE THE ERP

A. AN OVERVIEW

Ghana is situated on the West Coast of Africa, bordered on the west by Côte d'Ivoire, on the east by Togo, and on the north by Burkina Faso. It has a total area of 238,533 sq. km (192,000 sq. miles), and a population of about 15.4 million (Statistical Services, 1992). Essentially, Ghana has an agricultural and mineral based economy oriented towards the production of primary commodities and minerals for export. Cash crops consist primarily of cocoa and cocoa products, which account for about 47 percent of the country's export revenues, and timber products (Statistical Services, 1992, p. 23). Minerals, primarily gold, diamonds, manganese, and bauxite are produced for export, and account for about 19 percent of the export revenues (Statistical Services, 1992, p. 23).

Ghana's industrial base is relatively advanced compared to that of many other African countries. The industrial base was developed in the early post independence period using an import substitution strategy of industralization. The industries include textiles production, oil refinery, and simple consumer goods manufacturing. These industries have high import content, are capital intensive, and are affected by the availability of foreign exchange.

A heavy infrastructural program was launched after independence. The industralization and infrastructural programs were financed mainly from a $481 million (250 million pounds) foreign reserve at the time of independence (Todaro, 1994, p.38; Ofosu-Appiah, 1974). These programs had little revenue generating capacity, and together with falling world cocoa prices and increasing levels of imports for the industralization program caused the country's reserves to be depleted around the mid-1960s. The depletion of the foreign reserves coupled with inappropriate and/or ineffective economic policies to deal with the ensuing economic hardships created some dissatisfaction among Ghanaians. This together with the Government's intention to make Ghana a socialist country led to some political unrests which eventually precipitated in a military *coup* in 1966. The 1966 military *coup* marked the beginning of political and economic struggle in Ghana which culminated in an economic crisis in the early 1980s.[1]

B. THE ECONOMIC CRISIS IN GHANA

The economic crisis in Ghana was multidimensional in nature. There was a continuous decline in Real Gross Domestic Product (RGDP), acute shortages of food and foreign exchange, very high rates of inflation, grossly imbalanced government budgets, a deterioration of the infrastructure including roads, railways, electricity and telecommunications, and a reduction in the capacity utilization of industrial plants. For example, between 1970 and 1983, the average rate of growth in RGDP fell from 10 percent to -4.6 percent, a fall of 14.6 percent. During the same period, real per capita GDP fell by 36 percent (see Table 1). Also, between 1980 and 1983, dollar value of exports fell by 60 percent, that of imports fell by 43 percent, and the current account balance worsened from $29.2 million in 1980 to $174.1 million in 1983 (See Table 1 and Figure 1).

The decline in the value of exports was due to lower outputs of virtually all the major tradable commodities. Cocoa output fell by 62 percent between 1970 and 1983, gold production fell by about 57 percent, bauxite by 79 percent, diamonds by 86 percent, and manganese by 49 percent. Production of logs and sawn timber also declined by 64 percent and 47 percent respectively (see Table 1 and Figures 2 & 3). The decline in exports led to lower foreign exchange earnings. This reduced earnings to-

gether with the lack of external finance constrained imports and resulted
in a steady decline in imports.

Production of major staple food also fell between 1970 and 1983. Output of maize declined by 64 percent, rice by 18 percent, cassava by 30 percent, plantain by 79 percent, and yam by about 5 percent (see Table 1).

Table 1. Trend of Selected Economic Indicators (1970-1983)

Indicator	Year					
	1970	1975	1980	1981	1982	1983
National Product						
Real GDP (mil. of 1975 cedis)	5349	5283	5536	5344	4974	4747
Growth in Real GDP (%)	10	-13.3	0.005	-2.9	-6.5	-4.6
Real Per Capita GDP ('75 cedis)	629	539	499	469	425	389
Balance of Payments						
Value of Exports (mil. of US$)	477	895.4	1213.1	831.8	713.9	477.6
Value of Imports (mil. of US$)	543	922.3	1263.5	1335.6	905.0	724.1
Curr. Account Bal. (mil. of US$)	-68	17.6	-29.2	-420.8	-108.6	-174.1
Output of Major Commodities						
Cocoa ('000 tons)	413	394	258	225	180	157
Gold ('000 kgs)	19.9	16.5	11.0	10.6	10.3	8.6
Diamonds ('000 carats)	2550	2336	1149	836	684	347
Bauxite ('000 tons)	337	325	225	181	64	70
Manganese ('000 tons)	372	415	250	223	160	190
Logs (mil. cub. metres)	1.6	1.3	0.5	0.6	0.4	0.6
Sawn Timber (mil. cub.metres)	0.4	0.4	0.2	0.2	0.2	0.2
Output of staple Food						
Maize ('000 tons)	482	343	382	378	346	172
Rice ('000 tons)	49	71	78	97	36	40
Cassava ('000 tons)	2388	2398	2322	2063	2470	1721
Yam ('000 tons)	909	709	650	591	588	866
Plantain ('000 tons)	1644	1246	734	829	749	342

Table 1 Continued

Central Gov't Finances						
Rev. and Grants (% of GDP)	21.96	15.43	7.65	6.68	6.08	5.56
Total Expend. (% of GDP)	21.5	21.7	19.2	13.13	10.23	8.0
Fiscal Deficit (% of GDP)	0.004	-6.3	-11.5	-6.4	-4.15	-2.44
Recurrent Expend. (% of GDP)	16.7	17.2	16.3	11.85	9.28	7.4
Development Expend. (% of GDP)	4.8	4.5	2.9	1.28	0.95	0.6
Others						
Inflation (%)	9.0	29.8	50.1	117	21.8	123.3
Broad Money Supply (bil. of cedis)	0.43	1.4	7.92	12.03	15.07	20.95
Official Exch. Rate (cedis per US$)	1.02	1.15	2.75	2.75	2.75	20.50
Parallel Exch. Rate (cedis per US$)	1.25	1.98	16.70	21.25	61.61	120.00
Savings Ratio	0.13	0.14	0.05	0.04	0.04	0.03
Investment Ratio	0.14	0.13	0.06	0.05	0.03	0.04
Terms of Trade (1986=100)	105	96	95	62	48	48

Sources: Central Bureau of Statistics/Statistical Services: Quarterly Digest of Statistics (various issues); Economic Survey. Bank of Ghana: Annual Reports, Quarterly Economic Bulletin.

Ghana Cocoa Marketing Board/Cocoa Board, Ministry of Agriculture, Ministry of Finance and Economic Planning. World Bank: World Tables (various issues).

IMF: International Financial Statistics Yearbook (various issues). May Ernesto, (1974), p. 127.

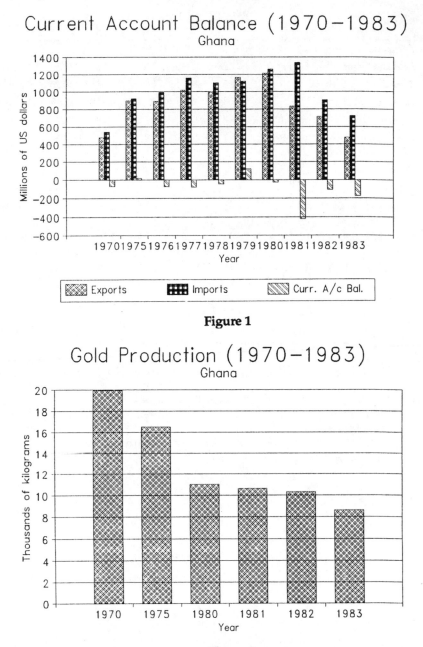

Figure 1

Figure 2

Output of Tradables (1970–1983)
Ghana

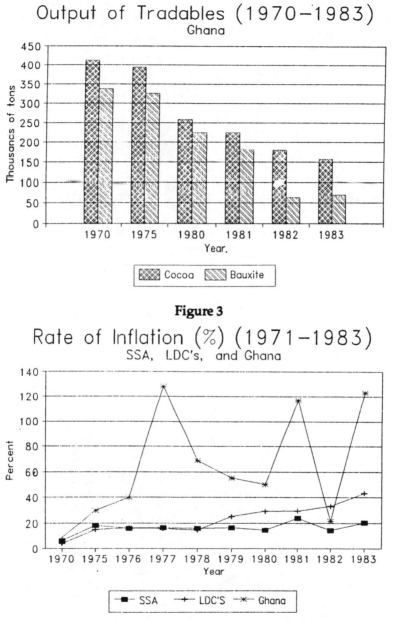

Figure 3

Rate of Inflation (%) (1971–1983)
SSA, LDC's, and Ghana

Figure 4

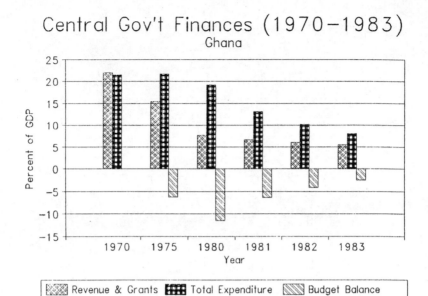

FIGURE 5

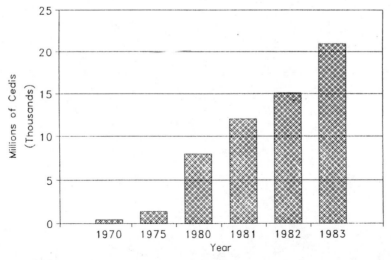

FIGURE 6

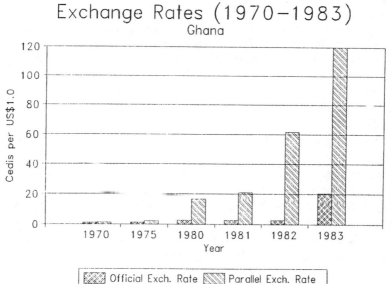

FIGURE 7

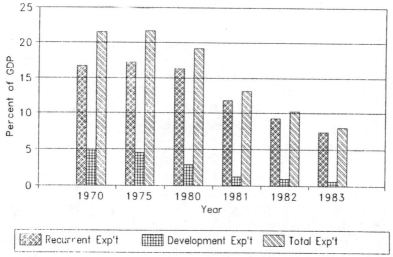

FIGURE 8

Low food production together with constrained imports and a high population growth, caused rising inflationary pressures. Thus, the rate of inflation increased from 9 percent in 1970 to 123 percent in 1983 (see Table 1 and Figure 4). This high inflation rate led to declining real incomes and a drastic reduction in real consumption. Domestic savings and investment virtually collapsed. Domestic savings declined from 0.13 percent of GDP in 1970 to 0.03 percent of GDP in 1983 while domestic investment declined from 0.14 percent of GDP in 1970 to 0.04 percent of GDP in 1983 (see Table 1).

The reduction in cocoa output and exports seriously affected government revenues from cocoa duty. The outcome was severe imbalances in government revenues and expenditures, and large fiscal deficits from 1971 to 1983. Fiscal deficits were 6.3 percent of GDP in 1975, 11.5 percent of GDP in 1980, and 2.44 percent of GDP in 1983 (see Table 1 and Figure 5). These fiscal deficits were financed mainly through borrowings from the domestic banking system which led in excess liquidity and high rates of inflation. Between 1970 and 1983, broad money supply increased by 4805 percent (see Table 1 and Figure 6). Reduction in revenues seriously curtailed government expenditures for recurrent and development purposes. Recurrent expenditures declined from 16.7 percent of GDP in 1970 to 7.4 percent of GDP in 1983, while development expenditure declined from 4.8 percent of GDP in 1970 to 0.6 percent of GDP in 1983 (see Table 1 and Figure 7).

C. THE CAUSES OF THE ECONOMIC CRISIS

The economic crisis in Ghana was caused by domestic as well as external factors. Political instability and economic mismanagement were the main domestic factors while a persistent deterioration in terms of trade was the major external factor.

1. Political Instability

Political instability which led to military *coups* in the 1960s, 1970s, and the 1980s contributed significantly to Ghana's poor economic performance prior to 1983. From the time of independence on March 6, 1957 to the early 1990s Ghana had witnessed the abrupt endings of three democratically elected governments who ruled for a total of fifteen years, and the assumption of power by four military rulers who ruled for a total of twenty-two years. Economic mismanagement, corruption, favoritism, nepotism, patronage by political leaders, dictatorship, and suppression of individuals with different ideological views induced struggle for political power and frequent changes of government. The political instability created uncertainty in Ghana which was not conduscive for investment, especially foreign investment, and was detrimental to economic progress.

2. Deteriorating Terms of Trade and Economic Mismanagement

Between 1970 and 1983, Ghana suffered a 57 percent decline in its terms of trade due to oil price increases and a declining world cocoa price (see Table 1). A deterioration of this magnitude inevitably leads to severe economic problems and governments have to adjust their policies to reflect such external shocks. Successsive governments in Ghana, however, failed to adjust their policies. For example, between 1974 and 1983, despite the deteriorating state of the Ghanaian economy and the high rate of inflation vis à vis Ghana's major trading partners, the official exchange rate was hardly adjusted while the underground or "black" market rate showed a continuous depreciation of the domestic currency (see Table 1 and Figure 8). This resulted in a highly profitable underground market activities. Producers of tradables who used the official channels suffered from the highly overvalued domestic currency. For instance, cocoa producers were adversely affected by this situation. Importers benefited, especially those who imported at the official rate and sold their goods at the black market prices. The outcome was a decline in exports and foreign exchange reserves. This coupled with reduced level of economic activities produced lower tax revenue. These revenues fell from 13.9 percent of GDP in 1975 to 4.6 percent of GDP in 1983. The lower tax revenues forced the government to reduce its expenditures. However, the government continued to experience budget deficits from 1975 to 1983, ranging from 2.44 percent of GDP to 11.5 percent of GDP (see Table 1 and Figure 5).

The performance of Ghana's agricultural sector also deteriorated sharply from the mid-1970s to the early 1980s. The annual growth rate of agricultural output averaged about -1.2 percent between 1970 and 1980, while the average index of food production per capita declined to 82 in 1980 from the base of 100 in 1969 (World Bank, 1983, p.3 and p.27). Various factors contributed to the declining agricultural output. Those factors included deteriorating state of the transport services, particularly vehicles and roads, the unavailability of agricultural inputs (seeds, fertilizers, and skilled labor), low producer prices for industrial crops, and unsatisfactory market conditions. The negative growth in agricultural output along with

an annual growth rate of 2.6 percent between 1970 and 1980 resulted in
food shortages. The problem was compounded by a severe drought in the
early 1980s.

Despite the poor state of the country's finances, the State-Owned Enterprise (SOEs) continued to enjoy special privileges under protective
barriers including financial assistance from the government, the use of
government-owned assets, and special tax treatment. These privileges
contributed significantly to inefficiencies and huge deficits of the public
enterprises. The total deficits in the public enterprises rose from 67 million
cedis[2] in 1973/74 to over 4 billion cedis in 1982, representing about 50 percent of the total government expenditures in 1982 (World Bank, 1983, p.5).

Other government policies exacerbated the already precarious economic conditions. For example, attempts were made to control domestic
consumer prices under a situation of severe shortage of consumer goods,
thus stimulating underground market activities.

3. Consequences of the Economic Crisis

The major consequence of the economic crisis was a substantial reduction
in the living standards of majority of Ghanaians. Many Ghanaians had to
supplement their wages by taking second and third jobs and/or engaging
in petty trading. Underground or black market activities for raising one's
income became rampant. Basic infrastructure fell into a state of disrepair.
Physical conditions in schools, hospitals, health centers, and water supply
facilities deteriorated due to lack of maintenance.

It was against this background that the government of the Provisional
National Defense Council (PNDC) turned to the IMF and The World Bank
for assistance. These institutions established a series of measures including relative price adjustments based on market forces, trade liberalization,
currency devaluation, and reduction in budget deficits, as prequisites for
the receipt of financial assistance. These measures were eventually embodied in Ghana's Three Phase Economic Recovery Program (ERP)
launched in 1983.

III. THE ERP STRATEGY AND RESULTS

The strategy of the ERP was to lay a foundation for sustained growth, and to solve the balance of payments problem. The key elements of the strategy were:

- to realign relative prices to encourage production activities and exports, and strengthen economic activities;
- to shift away from direct control and intervention towards a greater reliance on market forces;
- to restore fiscal and monetary discipline;
- to rehabilitate economic and social infrastructure;
- to introduce structural and institutional reforms to improve efficiency and encourage private savings and investments.

Specific objective were laid down aimed at achieving these goals. These included the following:

- to arrest and reverse the decline in production, especially agricutural production;
- to control inflation;
- to stimulate exports and curb consumption of luxury imports;
- to restore the eroded overseas confidence in Ghana;
- to rehabilitate the highly deteriorating productive and social infrastructures;
- to mobilize domestic and foreign resources into restoring the living standards of Ghanaians;
- to ensure an economic growth of 1.5 percent;
- to stimulate substantial increases in the level of savings and investment;
- to improve the chronic balance of payments problem; and
- to improve public sector management (Government of Ghana, 1987, p. 3).

Explicit policy measures taken by the government to accomplish these objectives included the following:

- liberalization of the exchange rate system;
- introduction of measures to liberalize trade and encourage exports;
- introduction of reforms in the cocoa sector;
- introduction of stringent fiscal policy measures;
- introduction of tight monetary policy measures and other monetary reforms;
- rationalization of State Owned Enterprises (SOEs).
- liberalization of prices;
- measures to improve the climate for private investment;
- introduction of policies to reduce arrears; and
- introduction of a Program of Action to Mitigate the Social Cost of Adjustment (PAMSCAD).

The ERP led to a major turnaround in Ghana's overall economic and financial performance between 1983 and 1991; and even though the positive gains could not be sustained completely in 1992 and 1993, there were still some improvements in the Ghanaian economy. For example, between 1983 and 1991, the Ghanaian economy grew at an average rate of 5 percent per annum compared to an average growth rate of 2 percent for SSA countries, and 3 percent for LDCs (see Table 2). The growth was characterized by output expansion in the main sectors of the economy. Cocoa production increased by 3.4 percent between 1983 and 1990; agriculture and livestock by 2.8 percent; mining and quarrying by 8.2 percent and manufacturing by 9.5 percent. Annual rate of inflation decelerated from 123 percent in 1983 to about 18 percent in 1991, with an average annual rate of 38.8 percent. Ghana's external position also improved considerably. Both exports and imports increased by an average of 10 percent per annum between 1983 and 1990. Revenues and foreign grants increased steadily from 5.6 percent of GDP in 1983 to 16.3 percent of GDP in 1991. Narrow fiscal budget, which excludes capital outlays financed through external assistance, improved from a deficit of 2.7 percent of GDP in 1983 to a surplus of 0.2 percent of GDP in 1990. Broad fiscal budget, which includes capital outlays financed through external assistance, also improved slightly from a deficit of 2.7 percent of GDP in 1983 to a deficit of 2.4 percent of GDP in 1990 (see Table 2 and Figures 9 to 12).

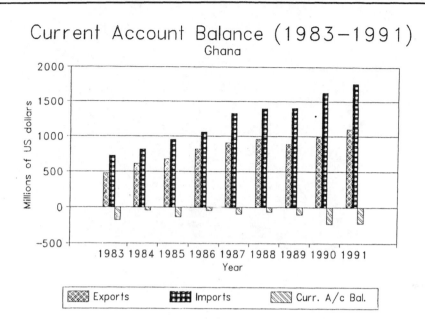

FIGURE 9

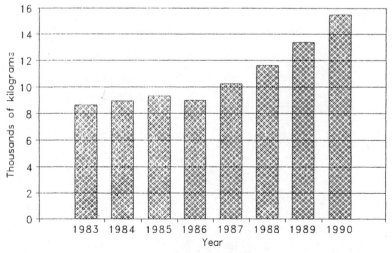

FIGURE 10

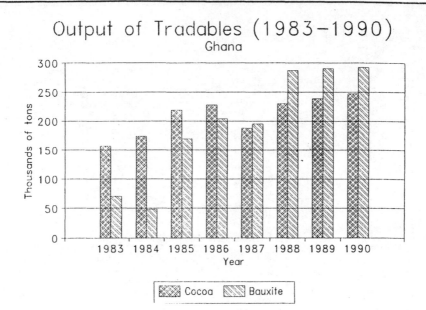

FIGURE 11

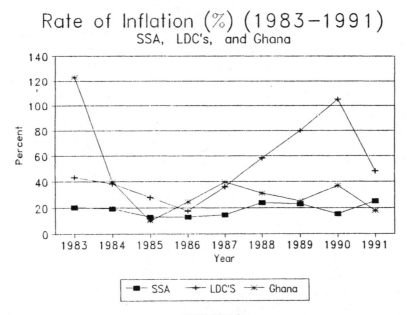

FIGURE 12

IV. PUBLIC FINANCE BEFORE AND AFTER
THE ERP AND THEIR IMPACTS

Fiscal policy reform aimed at reversing the economic conditions in the early 1980s, was an integral part of the ERP, and contributed to the success of the program. Policy measures focused on lowering the imbalances in the government finances, directing and fostering economic growth through the rehabilitation and expansion of the productive base of the economy, providing economic incentives through tax reforms, promoting a more equitable distribution of income and benefits of the ERP, and addressing social welfare issues. To put these policy measures in perspective, an analysis of Ghana's fiscal position prior to the launching of the ERP is given. This is followed by a review of fiscal policy measures implemented during the ERP and their evaluation.

A. GOVERNMENT REVENUES AND EXPENDITURES PRIOR
TO THE ERP AND THEIR IMPACTS

A major contributing factor to Ghana'a economic crisis in the early 1980s was the state of its public finances. At the beginning of the ERP in 1983, Ghana's tax system had virtually collapsed with the tax revenues declining from 13.9 percent of the GDP in 1975 to 4.6 percent of the GDP in 1983. Total revenues and grants declined from 15.4 percent of GDP in 1975 to 5.6 percent of GDP in 1983 (see Table 3). Several factors contributed to the decline of revenues. First, Ghana's narrow tax base was one such factor. Prior to 1975, taxes on international trade and transactions were the main source of government revenue. In 1975, 52.5 percent of the total tax revenues came from taxes on international transactions. Taxes on domestic goods and services accounted for 16.7 percent of total revenues and direct taxes were 20.6 percent of three revenues (see Table 3). The 60 percent decline in exports and the 43 percent in imports between 1980 and 1983 affected export and import duties and consequently government revenues.

The second contributing factor to declining revenues was the laxity in tax collection and the prevelance of tax evasion. Taxation of non-wage income earners, especially those involved in the trading and commercial sectors who were in the 32 and 50 percent brackets, was inadequate (Ewusi, 1987, p.86). In 1975, an analysis of income tax collection according to sources of income indicated that wages and salaries accounted for 84 percent of total income tax collected while the income of self-employed individuals contributed 16 percent of the same total (World Bank, 1983, p.24). The problem of low tax revenues was compounded by inadequate data sources, based on which decisions on tax liabilities were made, and the difficulty of tax collection.

A third contributing factor to declining revenues was the failure to allow market forces to determine the foreign exchange rate. An overvalued exchange rate, set artificially below market rates by the officials, caused the value of imported goods and hence the tax base to decline. The implementation of price controls at the wholesale level compounded the problem of tax base erosion. A final factor contributing to the declining tax revenues was the deterioration of tax administration prior to the ERP. Smuggling, unrecorded and underrecorded trade and other illegal transactions contributed to the low tax revenues as well.

The decline in tax revenues restrained government expenditures and led to its reduction from 21.7 percent of GDP in 1975 to 8.0 percent of GDP in 1983 (see Table 4). These reduced spendings led to major cuts in the development expenditures, declining from 4.5 percent of GDP in 1975 to 0.6 percent of GDP in 1983. Reduced capital formation in the public sector followed this sequence of events (see Table 4). The decline in capital formation is noteworthy given that the public sector provided the infrastructure and owned a large proportion of the assets in the agriculture, mining, and manufacturing industries. This slow down in capital formation in the public sector affected the critical sectors and the productive base of the economy.

The foregoing restraint also affected the functional distribution of total expenditures. The allocation for health was reduced from 8.3 percent of GDP in 1975 to 4.4 percent of GDP in 1983; allocation for social security and welfare was reduced from 11 percent of GDP in 1975 to 4.3 percent of GDP in 1983; allocation for other community and social services was reduced from 3.9 percent of GDP in 1975 to 1.8 percent of GDP in 1983; allocation for defense was reduced from 7.8 percent of GDP in 1975 to 4.6 percent of GDP in 1983; while allocation for the interest on public debt was increased from 6.5 percent of GDP in 1975 to 14.9 percent of GDP in 1983. Recognizing the importance of education and public services, 1983 expenditures in these areas were kept at their 1975 level (see Table 4). The reduction in the allocations to social security and welfare, and community and social services, coupled with the decline in the GDP meant that the expenditures were not sufficient in sustaining the basic community, social and economic services.

Table 2.

TREND OF SELECTED ECONOMIC INDICATORS (1983-1990)

Indicator	1983	1984	1985	1986	1987	1988	1989	1990
National Product								
Real GDP (mil. of 1975 cedis)	4747	5158	5420	5705	5876	6312	6634	6853
Growth in Real GDP (%)	-4.6	8.6	5.1	5.2	4.8	5.6	5.1	2.9
Real Per Capita GDP ('75 cedis)	389	419	430	439	449	464	475	478
Balance of Payments								
Value of Exports (mil of US$)	477.6	611.7	676.0	818.5	906.1	958.7	889.1	983.7
Value of Imports (mil. of US$)	724.1	812.8	952.3	1056.1	1327.8	1393.0	1410.0	1627.9
Curr. Account Bal. (mil. of US$)	-174.1	-38.8	-134.2	-43.0	-96.9	-65.8	-98.6	-228.3
Output of Major Commodities								
Cocoa ('000 tons)	157	174	219	228	188	230	239	247
Gold ('000 kgs)	8.6	8.92	9.31	8.95	10.23	11.63	13.38	15.52
Diamonds ('000 carats)	347	346	636	559	442	216	195	186.6
Bauxite ('000 tons)	70	49	169.5	204	195	287	290	292
Manganese ('000 tons)	190	287	316	259	254	231	220	208
Logs (mil. cub. metres)	0.6	0.6	0.6	0.9	0.95	0.97	0.98	1.0
Sawn Timber (mil. cub.metres)	0.2	0.2	0.22	0.23	0.28	0.29	0.30	0.31
Output of staple Food								
Maize ('000 tons)	172	574	411	559	553	600	620	637
Rice ('000 tons)	40	66	90	70	88	95	98	101
Cassava ('000 tons)	1721	4083	3076	3692	2943	3300	3392	3488
Yam ('000 tons)	866	1178	987	1048	1001	1200	1232	1263
Plantain ('000 tons)	342	1943	1629	1087	1005	1200	1234	1263
Central Gov't Finances								
Rev. and Grants (% of GDP)	5.56	8.4	11.7	14.4	14.9	14.6	15.1	14.1
Total Expend. (% of GDP)	8.0	9.8	13.3	13.8	13.7	13.7	13.9	13.5
Fiscal Deficit (% of GDP)	-2.44	-2.3	-3.0	-3.3	-2.40	-2.80	-2.1	-2.4
Recurrent Expend. (% of GDP)	7.4	8.6	11.2	11.90	10.8	10.6	10.5	10.5
Development Expend. (% of GDP)	0.6	1.2	2.1	1.90	2.50	2.8	2.7	2.5
Others								
Inflation (%)	123.3	39.7	10.3	24.6	39.8	31.4	25.2	37.2
Broad Money Supply (bil. of cedis)	20.95	36.05	57.5	88.37	135.2	193.3	245.3	289.5
Official Exch. Rate (cedis per US$)	20.5	36.48	54.4	89.2	162.6	203.45	270.0	326.33
Parallel Exch. Rate (cedis per US$)	120.0	200.0	250.0	300.0	320.0	340.0	350.0	360.0
Savings Ratio	0.03	0.07	0.08	0.08	0.07	0.08	0.08	0.06
Investment Ratio	0.04	0.07	0.10	0.10	0.13	0.14	0.15	0.16
Terms of Trade (1986=100)	48	93.8	88.5	100	91.2	83.2	68.1	69.0

Sources: Central Bureau of Statistics/Statistical Services: Quarterly Digest of Statistics (Various issues); Economic Survey. Bank of Ghana: Annual Reports, Quarterly Economic Bulletin.
Ghana Cocoa Marketing Board/Cocoa Board, Ministry of Agriculture, Ministry of Finance and Economic Planning. World Bank: World Tables (various issues).
IMF: *International Financial Statistics Yearbook* (various issues). May Ernesto, (1974), p. 127.

Table 3.

CENTRAL GOVERNMENT REVENUE AND GRANTS (1975-1991)

Classification	1975	1980	1983	1984	1985	1986	1987	1988	1989	1990	1991
					(In Percent of Total Revenue and Grants)						
Tax Revenue	**98.8**	**90.6**	**82.6**	**79.2**	**80.7**	**84.5**	**85.5**	**84.0**	**81.4**	**82.2**	**84.4**
Direct Taxes	20.6	26.1	18.0	18.2	19.1	19.2	21.8	26.3	21.3	20.6	17.0
Individual	8.5	11.8	8.6	7.3	7.6	7.2	7.4	7.2	5.7	6.5	5.2
Corporate	11.3	14.2	8.8	10.6	10.8	11.3	13.0	18.0	14.6	12.7	10.8
Other	0.8	0.1	0.6	0.3	0.7	0.7	1.4	1.1	1.0	1.4	1.0
Taxes on Domestic Goods											
and Services	**16.7**	**47.3**	**15.9**	**24.6**	**22.3**	**26.6**	**23.6**	**25.2**	**24.3**	**26.8**	**36.9**
General Sales	5.9	6.2	2.3	1.9	2.9	4.3	7.5	8.0	8.3	8.8	7.3
Excise Duties	10.8	41.1	13.6	22.7	17.9	13.3	11.5	9.7	8.9	8.6	7.9
Petroleum	-	-	-	-	1.5	9.0	4.6	7.5	7.1	9.4	21.7
Taxes on International											
Trade and Transactions	**52.5**	**17.1**	**48.7**	**36.4**	**39.3**	**38.7**	**40.2**	**32.5**	**35.7**	**34.7**	**30.6**
Import Duties	17.2	16.3	20.1	14.4	16.3	19.3	16.0	16.6	21.0	24.6	20.2
Export Duties	35.3	0.8	28.6	22.0	23.0	19.4	24.2	15.9	14.7	10.1	10.4
Non Tax Revenue	**10.1**	**8.0**	**16.9**	**16.8**	**15.3**	**10.3**	**9.1**	**8.5**	**8.7**	**7.4**	**6.8**

Table 3 (continued)

Grants	0.1	1.4	0.6	4.0	4.0	5.3	5.4	7.5	9.9	10.4	8.7
			(In Percent of Gross Domestic Product (GDP))								
Tax Revenue	**13.9**	**7.3**	**4.6**	**6.6**	**9.5**	**12.2**	**12.7**	**12.4**	**12.3**	**11.6**	**13.8**
Direct Taxes	3.2	2.1	1.0	1.5	2.3	2.8	3.2	3.9	3.2	2.9	2.8
Taxes on Domestic Goods and Services	2.6	3.8	0.9	2.1	2.6	3.8	3.5	3.7	3.7	3.8	6.0
Taxes on International Trade and Transactions	8.1	1.4	2.7	3.0	4.6	5.6	6.0	4.8	5.4	4.9	5.0
Non-Tax Revenue	**1.6**	**0.6**	**0.9**	**1.4**	**1.8**	**1.5**	**1.4**	**1.2**	**1.3**	**1.0**	**1.1**
Grants	-	0.1	-	0.3	0.5	0.8	0.8	1.1	1.5	1.5	1.4
Total Revenue and Grants	**15.4**	**8.1**	**5.6**	**8.4**	**11.7**	**14.4**	**14.9**	**14.6**	**15.1**	**14.1**	**16.3**

Sources: Central Bureau of Statistics/Statistical Services: Quarterly Digest of Statistics (Various issues), Kapur, et *al.*, 1991, p.30

Table 4.
Consolidated Government Revenue, all level[a]
(Billions of Dollars)

Type of Revenue	1978 Absolute	1983 Absolute	1983 % rate of Growth Since 1978	1988 Absolute	1988 % rate of Growth Since 1983	1991 Absolute	1991 % of Growth Since 1988
Personal Income Tax	25.02	48.10	92	77.84	62	100.41	29
Corporation Income Tax	8.80	10.28	17	18.02	75	18.30	2
Property and Related Taxes	8.10	14.04	73	19.48	39	23.05	18
General Sales Taxes	9.25	15.72	69	32.89	109	35.82	9
Fuel, Alcohol and Tobacco	4.10	7.03	71	12.15	73	12.10	-
Customs duties	2.75	3.38	23	4.68	38	4.15	-11
Health and Social Insurance Levies	8.77	17.93	104	27.73	55	22.07	-20
Total taxes[b]	69.54	122.26	76	200.00	63	228.90	14
Other sources of revenue (Total)	20.4	135.71	75	35.92	0.6	45.63	27
Total consolidated revenue[b]	89.94	158.17	76	235.91	49	274.54	16

Source: The National Finances (1993) Table 4.1
[a] Fiscal year ending nearest to December 31, 1978 to 1988
[b] May not add due to omission of minor revenue sources and rounding.

Since the rate of decline of revenues was larger than that of expenditures, budget deficits began to increase. These deficits were 6.3 percent of GDP in 1975 and rose to 11.5 percent of GDP in 1980 (see Tables 3 and 4).

B. FISCAL POLICY MEASURES DURING THE ERP

With the imbalances in the government finances, the slow down in capital formation in the public sector, and the deplorable state of the country's infrastructure in the early 1980s, the PNDC Government made appropriate fiscal policy an integral part of the ERP. Specific fiscal policy measures aimed at:

- revenue mobilization;
- restructuring recurrent expenditures;
- augmenting capital expenditures;
- improving income distribution and alleviating poverty;
- improving social welfare.

The policy measures in these areas are discussed below.

C. REVENUE MOBILIZATION MEASURES

With the decline in the tax revenues from 13.9 percent of GDP in 1975 to 4.6 percent of GDP in 1983, it was imperative that efforts to restore fiscal stability had to include revenue mobilization. The government therefore introduced measures to increase tax revenues. These measures focused on reforming the tax structure and improving tax collection, and began with various exercises by the government to ensure tax compliance among the self-employed. For example, a policy of tax clearance as a prerequisite for the renewal of business licences and registration of new businesses was instituted. Measures were also taken to educate the public on their tax obligations and to monitor corporate accounts more closely.

The tax reforms aimed at lowering the personal tax burden, improving tax incentives, rationalizing indirect taxes, and expanding the role of consumption taxes. For example, the standard tax exemption for single individuals was raised from 10,000 cedis per annum in 1987 to 24,000 cedis per annum in 1988; and further increased to 38,000 cedis per annum in 1989, and 60,000 cedis per annum in 1991 (Government of Ghana,

1989a, 1990, 1991). Similar increments were made for married couples from 15,000 cedis per annum in 1987 to 36,000 cedis per annum in 1988, 57,000 cedis per annum in 1989, and 91,000 cedis per annum in 1991.

In an attempt to reform the tax structure, the government changed the marginal tax rates. For instance, the marginal tax rate for singles in the income bracket 25,000-40,000 cedis was changed from 7.0-13.1 percent in 1985 to 2.8-3.5 percent in 1986. For a married couple in the same income bracket these rates were 6.0-12.0 percent in 1985. They were reduced to 1.8-2.9 percent in 1986. Similar adjustments were made in other income brackets.

Furthermore, the maximum taxable income was increased from incomes above 310,000 cedis per annum in 1987 to incomes above 984,000 cedis per annum in 1988, 1.2 million cedis per annum in 1989, and 2.1 million cedis per annum in 1991 (Government of Ghana, 1989a, 1990, 1991). The maximum tax rate was gradually lowered from 60 percent in 1985 to 30 percent in 1991 (Government of Ghana, 1991). In order to broaden the personal income tax base, all allowances paid to employees in both the public and private sectors were consolidated into the basic wage structure in July 1991 (Government of Ghana, 1991). These measures resulted in a decline in individual contribution to direct taxes from 8.6 percent of total revenues and grants in 1983 to 5.2 percent of total revenues and grants in 1991 (see Table 3).

The corporate tax rate for the manufacturing, farming, and export sectors was lowered from 55 percent to 45 percent in 1988 (Government of Ghana, 1989a). In 1989, a three-tier system was introduced; a 55 percent corporate tax rate for businesses in banking, insurance, and printing; a 45 percent corporate tax rate for firms in the manufacturing, farming, and export sectors; and a 50 percent corporate tax rate (down from 55 percent) for the remaining firms (Kapur, et al., 1991, p. 33). In 1991, the corporate tax rate for agriculture, manufacturing, real estate, construction, and services, was further reduced to 35 percent (Government of Ghana, 1991). Also, in the same year, capital allowances provided in the investment code were extended to all enterprises in the manufacturing sector, and the capital gains tax rate was reduced to 5 percent. Withholding tax on dividends was also reduced from 30 percent to 15 percent (Government of Ghana, 1991). The adjustments in the corporate tax structure together with an improvement in tax administration and tax collection resulted in an increase in the corporate contribution to direct taxes from 8.8 percent of total revenues and grants in 1983 to 10.8 percent of total revenues and grants in 1990 (see Table 3).

Export and import tax policies were also reformed. The reform included a gradual removal of import licensing requirements, changes in the duty rates, and an improved tax administration. The export and import tax reform resulted in an increase in import duties from 14 percent of total revenues and grants in 1984 to about 25 percent in 1990, and 20.2 percent in 1991. Export duties however declined from 28.6 percent of total revenues and grants in 1983, to 10.3 percent of total revenues in 1991 (see Table 3). An increase in the domestic value of imports due to the depreciation of the domestic currency, an increase in the volume of imports resulting from the import tax policy reform, and improved tax administration, all contributed to the increase in receipts from import duties. The decline in the share of export duties in total revenues was a reflection of the decline in world cocoa price from $2,394 7 per metric ton in 1984 to $1,274.4 per metric ton in 1990 (United Nations, 1991, p. 394), and a substantial increase in the share of world market price paid to cocoa farmers. The producer price of cocoa was increased steadily from 9 percent of the f.o.b. cocoa export price in 1984/85 to 47 percent of the f.o.b cocoa export price in 1990/91 (Kapur, et al., 1991, p.34).

Table 5A. Effective Income Tax Rates for 1984

Annual Income	Rate(%)
22,000 - 40,000	16 - 32
40,000 - 60,000	32 - 40
60,000 - 80,000	40 - 45
80,000 - 102,000	45 - 47
102,000 - 120,000	47 - 49

The system of indirect taxation was also reformed. In 1987, all excise duties on products other than petroleum, beverages, and tobacco were abolished. The revenue loss was compensated for by an increase in general sales tax rate from 10 percent to 20 percent and subsequently to 25 percent. The rate was however reduced to 22.5 percent in 1989, and further reduced to 17.5 percent in 1991 (Government of Ghana, 1989a, 1990, 1991, 1992, and 1993). Petroleum tax was increased as a means of raising revenue and bringing petroleum prices in line with those of neighboring countries. Consequently, the retail price of regular gasoline increased steadily from 180 cedis per gallon in 1987 to 230 cedis per gallon in 1988, 275 cedis per gallon in 1989 to 300 cedis per gallon in 1990, and to 1000 cedis per gallon in 1992 (World Bank, 1989, p.83; Government of Ghana, 1990, 1991, 1992, and 1993).

Table 5B. Effective Income Tax Rates (1985-1986)

Annual Income	1985 Rates(%)		1986 Rates(%)	
	Single	Married	Single	Married
25,000 - 40,000	7.0 - 13.1	6.0 - 12.0	2.8 - 3.5	1.8 - 2.9
40,000 - 60,000	13.1 - 21.4	12.0 - 20.2	3.5 - 5.8	2.1 - 4.5
60,000 - 80,000	21.4 - 28.6	20.2 - 27.6	5.8 - 7.9	4.5 - 6.9
80,000 - 100,000	28.6 - 34.1	27.6 - 33.2	7.9 - 11.1	6.9 - 9.8
100,000 - 120,000	34.1 - 37.9	33.2 - 37.2	11.1 - 13.8	9.8 - 12.4
120,000 - 150,000	37.9 - 41.7	37.2 - 41.1	13.8 - 18.6	12.4 - 17.1
150,000 - 180,000	41.7 - 44.7	41.1 - 43.8	18.6 - 22.6	17.1 - 21.3
180,000 - 210,000	44.7 - 46.1	43.8 - 45.7	22.6 - 25.9	21.7 - 24.6
210,000 - 240,000	46.1 - 47.5	45.7 - 47.1	25.9 - 29.2	24.6 - 28.1
Over 240,000	47.5 - 60.0	47.1 - 59.1	29.2 - 32.1	28.1 - 31.3

Source: Ewusi, 1987, p. 86-87

The fees on a wide range of licenses were increased, some more than ten-fold. For example, money lenders license fee was increased from 20 cedis to 200 cedis; registration and licensing fee in the area of trade, hotels, and entertainment was increased from a previous range of 250-3,000 cedis to 2,500-10,000 cedis (Ewusi, 1987, p. 85-86).

To improve the financial performance of the State Owned Enterprises (SOE), the government introduced and/or increased user fees for the use of public goods and services including electricity, water, telecommunication and postal services. Rates for water were raised between 150 percent and 1150 percent, electricity rates between 47 and 80 percent, telecommunications rate increased between 70 and 300 percent, and postal rates rose by 600 percent (World Bank, 1987, p.74).

The reform of indirect taxation resulted in an increase in the general sales tax rate from 1.9 percent of total revenues and grants in 1984 to 8.8 percent of total revenues and grants in 1990, and 7.3 percent in 1991. Petroleum tax rate increased from 1.5 percent of total revenues and grants in 1985 to 21.7 percent of total revenues and grants in 1991. Excise tax rates, however, declined from 22.7 percent of revenues and grants in 1984 to 7.9 percent of total revenues and grants in 1991 (see Table 3).

Altogether, the revenue mobilization measures resulted in a steady increase in tax revenues from 4.6 percent of GDP in 1983 to 13.8 percent of GDP in 1991 (see Table 3).

D.MEASURES TO RESTRUCTURE RECURRENT EXPENDITURES

The government restructured its recurrent expenditures with the objective of holding it within about 11 percent of GDP (World Bank, 1989, p. 63). The first step towards this goal was to improve the effectiveness of the civil service. A study by the Management Service Division of the Office of the Head of the Civil Service, with technical assistance from the Overseas Development Administration of the United Kingdom, identified that over 50 percent of the civil servants were unskilled workers at the junior level of the grade structure. Furthermore, while the higher levels of the grade structure in the civil service were understaffed, the junior levels were 20 to 40 percent overstaffed (World Bank, 1989, pp. 25-26). Accordingly the government introduced reforms in the civil service which aimed at reducing staffing in the junior levels, raising remuneration, and increasing salary differentials of different grade levels.

The government introduced a retrenchment program to remove redundancies in the civil service sector. Between 1987 and 1990, 50,000 mainly unskilled civil servants were redeployed and about 20,000 skilled staff hired, this net reduction of 30,000 was about 10 percent of the civil servants (Kapur, et al., 1991, p. 34). A further redeployment of about 5,000 workers was carried out in 1991. A "special efficiency" budget was established in 1987 to cover the costs of retraining and supporting redepolyed public sector employees. The efficiency budget accounted for between 2.0 and 4.7 percent of the total government expenditures between 1987 and 1991 (see Table 4). The estimated ratio of savings on the salary bill to compensation and training costs was about 1 to 3 (World Bank, 1989, p. 25). Staff recruitment in the higher level job categories was initiated to strengthen the capacity of the civil service for an effective implementation and monitoring of the adjustment program, while a freeze was placed on hiring in the lower job categories.

Prior to the adjustment period, salaries in the civil service were low and senior civil servants were grossly underpaid. For example, even after some adjustments in 1984 and 1985, the real salary of a Permanent Secretary[3] in 1986 was 10 percent of the 1977 level, while that of a messenger was 50 percent of the 1977 level (World Bank, 1987, p. 33). The government introduced measures to raise remuneration of civil servants. Expenditures on personnel were limited to about 5.5 percent of GDP (World Bank, 1987, p. 33). In January 1986, the government raised the salaries of the public service employees resulting in an increase in the minimum wage to 90.00 cedis per day and an 80 percent increase in the wage bill (World Bank, 1987, p. 10). Even with the adjustment, the real average wage rate was about 40 percent of the 1977 level for senior public servants and 65 percent for the junior civil servants (World Bank, 1987, p. 10). The salary adjustment improved the position of the civil service employees relative to the private sector. The government continued to raise wages and salaries in the public service sector causing the minimum wage to increase from 112 cedis per day in 1987 to 277 cedis per day in 1991. Apart from the across-the-board wage and salary increases, there was an additional of relative remuneration between the highest and lowest paid civil servants. This was done as a means of providing incentives to senior civil servants and improving morale and efficiency in the civil service. The salary ratio of the highest to lowest paid civil servants rose from 2.3 in 1986 to about 10.5 in 1991 (World Bank, 1987, p. 33; Kapur, et al., 1991, p. 34). The minimum wage of the civil servants served as a benchmark for the private sector. However, the matching of the public sector minimum wage by the private sector was qualified by an ability to pay clause and as a result many employers in the private sector could not keep up the wage adjustments. Because of these adjustments, expenditures on wages and salaries in the total government spending increased from 47.9 percent in 1983 to 54.2 percent in 1991 (see Table 4).

On educational expenditure reforms, a two phase program was introduced. The first phase had an overall objective of making education financially more efficient and ensuring that the total expenditure of the reformed education system was contained within the budget. The second phase focused on restructuring and expanding senior secondary schools and on cost saving through a tightened control on expenditure (IMF, 1991, p. 24). As one of the measures aimed at meeting this objective, the publicly financed boarding and lodging expense in tertiary educational institutions was replaced with a student loan scheme of 50,000 cedis per student per annum in 1989. A government scholarship and bursary scheme for outstanding students was introduced along with the student loan scheme. With these measures, education expenditures increased from 20.4

percent of total spending and net lending in 1983 to 25.5 percent of total expenditure and net lending in 1990 (see Table 4).

Efforts were made to streamline the activities of some public enterprise while others were liquidated or sold. By 1991, 50 public enterprises had been liquidated and 61 sold, out of a total of 329 (Leechor, 1994, p.164). These measures contributed significantly to the decline in government subsisdies and transfers from 27 percent of total expenditures and net lending in 1983 to 9.8 percent of total expenditures and net lending in 1991 (see Table 4).

Altogether, the reform of the recurrent expenditures resulted in a reduction in the level of these expenditures from 89.4 percent of the total spenging and net lending in 1983 to 74.7 percent of total expenditures in 1991 (see Table 3). Despite this decline, as a percentage of the GDP, recurrent expenditures increased from 7.4 percent in 1983 to 10.8 percent in 1991 (see Table 4).

E. MEASURES TO AUGMENT CAPITAL EXPENDITURES

At the peak of the economic crisis in 1983, capital expenditures by the government had declined to about 0.6 percent of GDP (see Table 4). Ghana's once well-developed infrastructure was in a state of disrepair. The government was quick in realizing that a well developed infrastructure was necessary for increasing productivity. Furthermore, the government observed that the reason many public projects were incomplete was because of the *ad hoc* procedure used for allocating public funds.

Consequently, in 1986, the government introduced the first Public Investment Program (PIP) as a major component of the ERP. The aim of the PIP was to improve the planning, implementation, monitoring, and evaluation of public investment in Ghana. Under the first PIP, (1986-88), the government planned public investment totalling 184.91 billion real cedis in 1986 prices (Government of Ghana, 1987c, p. 7). This planned investment was about 6 percent of GDP in 1986, and between 9 and 10 percent of GDP in 1987 and 1988 respectively (Loxley, 1991, p. 20). Seventy-five percent of the total planned investment for the first PIP was financed by foreign capital, mainly from aid, grants, and Overseas Development Assistance (ODA) sources; and 25 percent from domestic sources (Government of Ghana, 1987c, p. iii). A second PIP for the period 1990-1992 was introduced in 1990 with a total planned investment of 732.1 billion cedis (in constant 1990 prices), which represented about 10 percent of the GDP for the period (IMF, 1991, p. 15). For the second PIP, 62 percent of the total planned investment was financed by foreign capital, mainly concessionary ODA sources and commercial borrowing, and 38 percent from domestic sources (Government of Ghana, 1989b, p. 5).

The PIPs focused on the rehabilitation and expansion of basic economic infrastructure such as feeder roads, railroads, telecommunication and ports. The bulk of the planned investment, 72 percent in 1986-88 and 62 percent in 1990-92, was allocated to the development of economic infrastructure, mainly in the energy, and transportation sectors (Government of Ghana, 1987c, p. 8; Kapur, et al., 1991, p. 35). About 22 percent of the resources in both 1986-88 and 1990-92 was devoted to the productive sectors for the development of agricultural infrastructure, improvement in agricultural services, and for rehabilitating the industrial and mining sectors (Government of Ghana, 1987c, p. 8; Kapur, et al., 1991, p. 35). In the manufacturing sector, the emphasis was on rehabilitating selected units of the Ghana Industrial Holding Corporation (GIHOC) and operating the Tema Food Complex Limited. The government was counting on the private sector to invest in the manufacturing. Approximately, 8 percent of the resources in the 1986-88 PIP and 14 percent of the resources in the 1990-92 PIP went towards the expansion and/or an improvement in health and education services (Government of Ghana, 1987c, p. 9; Kapur, et al., 1991, p. 35).

The government also established criteria for selecting projects for the PIP. For projects with a total cost exceeding $5 million dollars, a minimum Economic Rate of Return (ERR) of 15 percent was required for selection into the "core" PIP (Government of Ghana, 1987c, p.9). In cases where the ERR critetion was not applicable, priority was given to:

- projects aimed at rehabilitating the infrastructure;
- projects that genearated additional revenues for the government;
- export oriented and efficient import substituting projects with relatively short gestation periods and quick returns;
- foreign funded projects or projects capable of attracting at least 60 percent foreign financing;
- ongoing projects;
- projects that had low minimal recurrent costs;
- projects that contributed to employment creation, poverty alleviation, and improved the quality of life in the rural areas.

With these measures, capital expenditure increased from 7.9 percent of total government spending in 1983 to 19.0 percent of the total government expenditures in 1991. These expenditures accounted for 0.6 percent of the GDP in 1983 and rose to 2.8 percent of the GDP in 1991 (see Table 4). This increased capital expenditures led to a rehabilitation of economic infrastructure in the country.

The increase in total government expenditures between 1983 and 1990 was relatively greater than the increase in government revenues, resulting in budget deficits in the period. Broad fiscal deficits fluctuated between 2.1 percent and 3.3 percent of GDP between 1983 and 1990 (see Table 2). These values were small relative to the average deficits of Sub-Saharan African countries which exceeded 6 percent of GDP within the same period. The revenue and expenditure policies enabled the government to increase its savings from -1.8 percent of GDP in 1983, to 2.9 percent of GDP in 1987, and 3.6 percent of GDP in 1991.

F. MEASURES ADDRESSING INCOME DISTRIBUTION AND POVERTY

An important aspect of a fiscal policy is the extent to which the policy aids the poorest members of the society and promotes an equitable distribution of the benefits of economic growth. Fiscal policy can improve the well-being of the poor either by using the public expenditures to provide services consumed by the poor or channelling goods and services to the poor segment of the society. Furthermore, through government transfer payments fiscal policy can be used to influence the distribution of income.

The changes in the tax structure discussed earlier affected both the level and distribution of taxation in Ghana. Even though it would be difficult to measure the impact of the changes on tax burden over time, some broad observations could be made about the impact of these changes. First, the level of individual direct taxation fell from 8.6 percent of the total tax revenues and grants in 1983 to 5.2 percent of the total tax revenues and grants in 1991 (see Table 3). In 1985, the mininum annual deductions for individuals was increased from 22,000 cedis to 25,000 cedis. The effective income tax rate for an annual income of 30,000 cedis was lowered from 24 percent in 1984 to 3.1 percent for singles and 2.5 percent for a married couple in 1986. The effective income tax rate was lowered for other income brackets as well (see Tables 5A and 5B). These changes resulted in a small increase in private savings from 5.4 percent of GDP in 1983 to 6.7 percent of GDP in 1990; and an increase in private investment from 2.9 percent of GDP in 1985 to 8.7 percent of GDP in 1990. These changes did not affect the poorest members of the society. They were too poor to pay taxes and were mostly involved in the informal sector or in subsistence agriculture.

Second, as mentioned earlier, there were considerable increases in petroleum taxes. The distributional impact of an increase in petroleum tax is very important because of the increased tax burden on consumers of petroleum and petroleum products, and the higher transportation costs. Even though the poor members of the Ghanaian society are not large consumers of petroleum and petroleum products, they do spend a considerable portion of their income on transportation, as well as on other fuels like kerosene. They are therefore affected by petroleum tax increases. Higher transportation costs lead to higher food prices especially in the urban areas and affect the urban poor considerably. Third, the increase in the general sales tax rates resulted in a higher tax burden for consumers. Fourth, the Government's policy to increase the producer price of cocoa effectively reduced cocoa taxes, and made cocoa farmers better off relative to other farmers. Finally, the changes in corporate tax policy which led to the increase in corporte tax revenues affected the distribution of the tax burden.

G. MEASURES ADDRESSING SOCIAL WELFARE ISSUES

Even though it is difficult to evaluate the impact of fiscal policy measures on social welfare to gauge the extent to which they address social welfare issues, one could speculate that the government of Ghana used its fiscal policy to aid the poorest segment of the society. Government expenditures on soical programs increased from 29.1 percent of total government expenditures in 1983 to 41.7 percent of total spending in 1989 (see Table 4); and from 2.3 percent GDP in 1983 to 5.8 percent of GDP in 1989. Furthermore, the government focused on primary education and primary health care to benefit the needy. For instance, the share of primary education in the recurrent expenditures of the Ministry of Education increased from 40 percent in 1987 to 43 percent in 1990. Using the combined expenditures on housing, community amenities, and services and expenditures on education, health, and social security and welfare, as a broad measure of social welfare spending, total spending in these areas increased from 32.5 percent of total government expenditures in 1983 to 51.2 percent of total expenditures in 1989. This reflects a rise in the share of expenditues on welfare from 2.6 percent of GDP in 1983 to 7.1 percent in 1989.

The special efficiency budget allocation set aside for retraining and supporting redeployed public sector employees was also a safety net addressing social welfare needs. Finally, the introduction of the Program of Action to Mitigate the Social Cost of Adjustment (PAMSCAD) with the objective of alleviating the social cost of the ERP for the vulnerable groups was well concieved. The slow implementation of the program due to the tardy process of actual disbursements had not made any noticeable impact by the end of 1990.

V. SUMMARY, CONCLUSION AND RECOMMENDATIONS

This chapter has shown that fiscal policy during the ERP in Ghana had a major impact on the financial performance of the government and on the overall performance of the Ghanaian economy. Fiscal deficit reduction was a goal of the government during this period. The reform of the tax structure shifted the heavy reliance on taxes on international trade to taxes on domestic goods and services. For example, cocoa export taxes declined while sales taxes and petroleum taxes increased. Corporate income tax increased while personal income tax declined. The share of capital expenditures in total government expenditures increased, allowing for the rehabilitation of the economic infrastructure. The government also made an effort to spread the benefits of the adjustment through increased expenditures on social welfare and the PAMSCAD. All these factors contributed to the remarkable success of the ERP.

This chapter has also illustrated that a fiscal reform aimed at lowering fiscal imbalances in public sector should be an integral part of any development program pursued by Sub-Saharan African countries faced with huge fiscal deficits. The reform should include the broadening of the tax base, a review of the income and corporate tax structures, and an improvement of tax administration. Governments need to consider the development of reliable sources of data on which tax decisions would be based. On the expenditure side, the restructuring of capital and recurrent expenditures is critical. Governments should structure budget allocations and capital expenditures so that they are tailored to the development and/or improvement of their infrastructure. When necessary, governments should ensure that the State-Owned Enterprises (SOEs) become efficient and contribute positively to public revenues. Political patronage, corruption, and favoritism in the SOEs should be eliminated, and the financial assistance to the SOEs curtailed or possibly eliminated. The size of the civil service and the SOEs should be examined and possibly reduced, with new hirings aimed at improving the efficiency and eliminating waste. Finally, the fiscal policy should make provisions for retraining and redeploying those who would be affected by the downsizing of the SOEs and the civil service, and initiate programs that would mitigate the social cost of the fiscal reform on the vulnerable groups of the society.

ENDNOTES

1. A brief discussion of the political and economic situations in Ghana and their impacts on the Ghanaian economy prior to 1983 is given under The Causes of the Economic Crisis.

2. Cedi is the domestic currency.

3. The highest position in the civil service.

REFERENCES

Abbey, J.L.S., (1990), "Ghana's Experience with Structural Adjustment: some Lessons", in James Picket and Hans Singer, eds, *Towards Economic Recovery in Sub-Saharan Africa*, London: Routledge.

Baffoe, J.K., (1989), *The Impact of Ghana's Structural Adjustment Programme on the Manufacturing and Small Scale Industrial Sectors*, Report Prepared for the Ghana Post of CIDA.

Baffoe, J.K., (1993), *A Structural Macroeconometric Model for Analysing Stabilization and Structural Adjustment in a Developing Country: The Case of the Economic Recovery Program in Ghana*, Unpublished Ph.D Thesis, University of Manitoba.

Chibber, A. and S. Fischer, (eds), (1992), *Economic Reform in Sub-Saharan Africa*, Proceedings from a World Bank Symposium, Washington D.C.

Ewusi, K., (1987), *Structural Adjustment and Stabilization Policies in Developing Countries: A Case Study of Ghana's Experience in 1983-1986*, Ghana: Ghana Publishing Corporation.

Fosu, A.K., (1992), "Political Instability and Economic Growth: Evidence from Sub-Saharan Africa", *Economic Development and Cultural Change*, Vol. 40, pp. 829-841.

Government of Ghana, (1984), *Economic Recovery Programme 1984-1986: Review of Progress in 1984 and Goals for 1985 and 1986*, Report Prepared for the Second Meeting of the Consultative Group for Ghana, Paris, Accra.

Government of Ghana, (1987a), *A Programme of Structural Adjustment*, Report Prepared for the Fourth Meeting of the Consultative Group for Ghana, Paris, Accra.

Government of Ghana, (1987b), *National Programme for Economic Development (Revised)*, Accra.

Government of Ghana, (1987c), *Public Investment Programme 1986-88*, Vol.1, Ministry of finance and Economic Planning, Accra.

Government of Ghana, (1989a), *Budget Statement*, Ministry of Finance and Economic Planning, Accra.

Government of Ghana, (1989b), *Public Investment Programme 1989-91*, Vol. 1, Ministry of Finance and Economic Planning, Accra.

Government of Ghana, (1990), *Budget Statement*, Ministry of Finance and Economic Plannning, Accra.

Government of Ghana, (1991), *Budget Statement*, Ministry of Finance and Economic Plannning, Accra.

Government of Ghana, (1992), *Budget Statement*, Ministry of Finance and Economic Plannning, Accra.

Government of Ghana, (1993), *Budget Statement*, Ministry of Finance and Economic Plannning, Accra.

International Monetary Fund (IMF), (1991), *Ghana: Enhanced Structural Adjustment Facility - Economic and Policy Framework Paper (1991 - 1993)*, IMF, Washington D.C.

Kapur, I., M.T. Hadjimichael, P. Hilbers, J. Schiff, and P. Szymczak, (1991), *Ghana: Adjustment and Growth, 1983-91*, International Monetary Fund, Occasional Paper No. 86, Washington D.C.

Leechor, C., (1994), "Ghana: Frontrunner in Adjustment" in eds., Ishrat Husain and Rashid Faruque, *Adjustment in Africa: Lessons from Country Case Studies*, The World Bank, Washington, D.C.

Loxley, J., (1991), *Ghana: The Long Road to Recovery 1983-90*, The North-South Institute, Ottawa.

May, E., (1987), *Exchange Controls and Parallel Market Economies in Sub-Saharan Africa: Focus on Ghana*, World Bank Staff Working Papers, N0. 711, World Bank, Washington D.C.

Ofosu-Appiah, L.H. (1974), *The Life and Times of Dr. J. B. Danquah*, Waterville Publishing House.

Ray, D.I., (1986), *Ghana: Politics, Economics and Society*, Lynn Rienner Publishers, Inc. Boulder.

Statistical Services, (1992), *Quarterly Digest of Statistics*, Vol. X, No.1, Accra, Ghana.

Statistical Services, (1992), *Ghana in Figures*, Accra.

Todaro, M.P. (1994), *Economic Development*, Fifth Edition, New York, Longman.

Toye, J., (1990), "Ghana's Economic Reforms 1983-1987: Origins, Achievements and Limitations", in eds., James Picket and Hans Singer, *Towards Economic Recovery in Sub-Saharan Africa*, London, Rutledge.

United Nations, (1991), *UNCTAD Commodity Yearbook*, New York.

World Bank, (1983), *Ghana: Policies and Programs for Adjustment*, Vols. I and II, World Bank, Washington D.C.

World Bank, (1986), *Ghana: Towards Structural Adjustment*, Vols. I and II, World Bank, Washington D.C.

World Bank, (1987), *Ghana: Policies and Issues of Structural Adjustment*, World Bank, Washington D.C.

World Bank, (1989), *Ghana: Structural Adjustment for Growth*, World Bank, Washington D.C.

World Bank, (1994), *Adjustment in Africa: Reforms, Results and the Road Ahead*, World Bank Policy Research Report, Oxford

SUBJECT INDEX

—D—

Goo, 183, 187
goods and services tax (GST), 128
government agency budgets, 46
government budget, 46, 147
government draft budget, 48
Government Employees' Retirement
Fund, 98
government expenditure ratio, 12,
18, 20, 69
government expenditures, 4, 5, 8, 9,
11, 12, 15, 16, 17, 18, 20, 26, 31, 38,
43, 57, 70, 73, 94, 96, 114, 127, 128,
129, 130, 131, 135, 136, 139, 140,
141, 143, 153, 157, 163, 165, 166,
169, 188, 193
Government of Ghana, 197, 209, 219,
220, 221, 225, 226, 230, 231
Government Sector, 23, 43
government spending, 8, 13, 14, 18,
69, 72, 73, 157, 163, 165, 166, 170,
176, 183, 186, 192, 224, 227
Government System, 45
Great Depression, 9, 79, 127
green return, 177
Gross debt, 74
gross domestic product (GDP), 43,
127
gross turnover taxes, 182
Growth, 22, 23, 24, 39, 41, 43, 51, 67,
68, 75, 79, 124, 125, 126, 140, 155,
166, 189, 190, 191, 192, 193, 200,
230, 231, 232
growth of the capital stock, 42
Gulf Crisis, 116
Gulf War, 62
Gultekin, 121

—H—

Hanyang, 159
Hartle, 153, 156
health, 10, 17, 36, 53, 58, 60, 61, 70,
71, 98, 99, 129, 136, 137, 140, 141,
142, 146, 148, 166, 167, 208, 214,
226, 228

Health and social services levies, 147
health care delivery system, 61
Health Insurance Societies, 60
Henning, J.A., 190
Herber (1983), 1, 194
Herber, B.P., 23, 190
Hershlag, 78, 106, 107, 118, 119, 120,
125
hidden debts, 72
hidden deficits, 67
high courts, 46
high-technology industries, 72
Hinrichs (1965), 32
Hinrichs (1966), 25, 26, 27, 28, 32
Hokkaido, 42, 46
Hong Kong, 42, 163
Honshu, 42
Hook (1962), 1
Hook, E., (1962), 23
Hoover, K.D. and S.M. Sheffrin, 39
horse race tax, 174
House of Councillors, 45
House of Representatives, 45
housing, 42, 47, 58, 59, 61, 68, 71, 81,
98, 112, 122, 166, 228
housing construction, 58, 59, 61
Housing Fund, 98
Housing Loan Corporation, 73
human capital, 166, 168, 171, 186

—I—

identification problem, 30
Ikeda government, 69
IMF, 23, 39, 86, 87, 97, 98, 113, 125,
126, 173, 192, 197, 201, 208, 224,
225, 231
import duties, 28, 31, 82, 213, 221
import prices, 70
import substituting projects, 226
import substitution strategy, 162,
198
imports, 18, 29, 32, 33, 35, 42, 68, 70,
80, 82, 113, 162, 163, 182, 199, 200,
206, 209, 210, 213, 221